# OPHELIA SPEAKS

HarperCollins books may be purchased for educational, business, or sales promotional use. For information please write: Special Markets Department, HarperCollins Publishers, Inc., 10 East 53rd Street, New York, NY 10022.

FIRST EDITION

*Designed by Nancy Singer Olaguera*

Library of Congress Cataloging-in-Publication Data

Shandler, Sara.
    Ophelia speaks : adolescent girls write about their search for self / Sara Shandler.
      p.  cm.
   ISBN 0-06-095297-0
   1. Teenage girls—United States—Psychology. 2. Teenage girls—United States—Physiology. 3. Self-esteem in adolescence—United States. 4. Body image in adolescence—United States. 5. Youths' writings, American. I. Title.
HQ798.S45  1999
305.235—dc21                              99-13534

99 00 01 02 03 ❖/RRD 10 9 8 7 6 5

# OPHELIA SPEAKS

### Adolescent Girls Write About Their Search for Self

## SARA SHANDLER

**HarperPerennial**
*A Division of HarperCollinsPublishers*

For Mom and Dad

*Thank you.*

# CONTENTS

# Part Three: The Best and the Worst of Friends

# Part Four: Touched by Desire

# Part Five: Overcoming Obstacles and Coming into Our Own

# ACKNOWLEDGMENTS

≈

I am grateful to the inspiring writers who contributed to *Ophelia Speaks*. I feel a special need to acknowledge talented contributors whose names or work do not appear in full elsewhere. Some of these girls wrote with compassionate unselfishness—they chose anonymity. Having stripped themselves of pretense, they could not bear to be exposed. Still, they wanted the truth of their stories to break though the isolation of other girls' adolescent pain. I admire their kindness. Others wrote pieces I chose for inclusion in *Ophelia Speaks*, yet their work was regrettably excluded. My original manuscript was 437 pages. Every page was worthy of publication, but *Ophelia Speaks* had to be shortened. Otherwise, it would have be an expensive book, beyond the reach of many girls.

In the editorial process, whole sections were cut and combined. Whenever possible, I quoted from girls' writing and incorporated their names in my commentary. Still, some contributions have been entirely omitted. I have apologized for decisions beyond my control. I know these girls are disappointed. They deserve to be honored: Alethea Beatrice Trottier Barbaro; Jasmine Evenstar Barclift; Elizabeth Bargar; Lorel Benningfield; Joy Boe; Larissa Chernock; Rachel Coker; Jessica Cunningham; Kit Dewy; Ericca Erikson; Karla L. Eilinsfeld; Jessica Eller; Mia Farhat; Caroline Fan; Jennifer Feinstein; Nicole Fonsh; Rachel Frazier; Rachel C. Furnari; Shachar Gillat; Joanna Elizabeth Grome; Marisa L. Hackett; Natasha Haley; Sierra Heck; Audra M. Hopf; Kelly Hogan; Peri Jacobson; Karen Elizabeth Jagiello;

Nikkita M. Kind; Bryn E. Keating; Jennifer Koob; Erin M. LeCorgne; Renee N. Lessard; Jessica Liberi; Kathryn Markovchick; Tracy Lee Martin; Sara McDermott; Amanda J. McLaughlin; Lynn M. Noesner; Lauren Alysia Norkus; Lenore Palladino; Terese Puma; Bethany Ann Reading; Christine Riley; Dana Schneider; Naomi Slipp; Jamie Smith; Melissa Smith; Megan R. Swoboda; J.L.T.; Eileen M. Talone; Amber Leigh Thompson; Jill Williams; Hillary Wright; Emily Zimmer.

Without exception, every submission I received while compiling *Ophelia Speaks* was moving and heartfelt. I wish I could thank each and every contributor by name—their keen insights, though they might not appear in print, gave me a greater perspective in selecting the pieces I did and played an invaluable role in shaping the message of the book.

None of voices in *Ophelia Speaks* would have appeared in print without the enthusiastic encouragement of my agent, editors, and publisher.

Agnes Birnbaum, my incredible agent at Bleeker Street Associates, greeted my idea with excitement. She nurtured my proposal and launched it into the publishing world. I am grateful for her sweetness, her ability to play hard-ball, and her thoughtfulness.

Laureen Rowland and Jodi Anderson, my editorial partners at HarperCollins, made the courageous decision to trust me, a seventeen-year-old they had never met. From our first telephone conversation, we have worked together to create this book. Together, they have been my valued advisers, unfailingly offering respect, patience, and support.

As with any major project, completing *Ophelia Speaks* required the effort of many individuals at HarperCollins Publishers. I am grateful to Susan Weinberg, Perennial's publishing director, for believing in this project, and putting her faith in me. Jen Hart, Rose Carrano, and Pam Pfeifer deserve my highest praise for their marketing and publicity efforts on behalf of *Ophelia Speaks*. Everyone I have worked with at HarperCollins has made publishing my first book a delightful experience.

The people in my day-to-day life have also helped me accomplish this task, a task that sometimes felt impossible. My dad used to say, "Sara, your eyes are bigger than your stomach." When I put *Ophelia Speaks* on my plate, I didn't realize how much I had bitten off. If I had not been surrounded by love and support, I'd still be chewing.

One of the blessings of becoming an adult is finally seeing my mom and dad as people, not just as parents. Even as they began a new chapter in their adult lives, they provided me with endless parental, and professional, support. Without their help this project probably wouldn't have made it off the ground; if by some miracle it had, it certainly would have fallen in midflight. I am more grateful to them than I can articulate. My older sister, Manju, put up with my sometimes obnoxious immaturity long enough to become my friend. I treasure our relationship. My grandma and grandpa, Mabel and Carl Silverberg, have taught me what it means to be kind and good, and to love others more than oneself. My grandma Fritzi Fuchs has shown me how to be generous—especially with love. My granddad Sonny Fuchs gave me my first real regret—I'm sorry I never knew him better. Margaret, Philip, Sathya, and Toon—the Gosselin family—not only gave me the security of good neighbors, but of real friends. Margaret, to me, will always epitomize life itself. I hold them all close to my heart.

Dedicated teachers have devotedly guided me toward my potential. Jan Saulsberry, a wonderful teacher and true friend, planted the seeds that made this book possible, and unknowingly made me learn to like myself again. John Warthen was the first person to tell me I wrote well, giving me confidence to develop my voice. Robert Kelly challenged me more than any other teacher while still giving me some of my only enjoyable high school classes. Phil Krafts, Jim Logan, Tiina Booth, and Dave Ranen made high school bearable, just by their presence. Bruce Penniman, though never my teacher, helped me to solicit contributions and offered support for *Ophelia Speaks* from the beginning. These teachers took a sincere interest in my life outside of my performance in the classroom. Together, they made my high school experience a positive one. I am sincerely grateful. In addition to my own teachers, I would like to thank Emily Farrell, an English teacher in Wallingford, Pennsylvania, who carefully mentored her students and sent me some of the most extraordinary writing in *Ophelia Speaks*.

Many of my classroom teachers enriched my life—through our daily contact they offered me learning as a tool and supported my intellectual growth. Some of my other teachers have no idea I exist, but they unknowingly offered me knowledge and supported me through difficult times: I am grateful to Maya Angelou and Alice Walker for offering me wisdom on the written page, and to Oprah Winfrey and Rosie O'Donnell for giving me such positive role models to view when I turn on the TV. I am hopeful that other adolescent girls, who haven't already, might come away from *Ophelia Speaks* and move toward these women. At least for me, they are great sources of inspiration.

Finally, to my friends, from different places and times, who always made me feel loved. Toon (Gabrielle) Gosselin, Emily Zimmer, Trina Heinisch: You have taught me so much about what it means to love. Tamar Barnoon, Nyla Rosen, Shira Kafer: As friends I grew closest to as I got older, you showed me that time is not a prerequisite for love. Larissa Chernock, Jessica Bulman, Nikki Fonsh, Naomi Cairns: You grew up with me, giving me some of my warmest memories. Lindsay Slan, Karina Nunez, Shakira Villanueva, Joshua Sparber, Rachel Coker: You are summer friends who became so much more. Gavin Harrison: You are the only friend I have to share with my parents, but you always make me feel special. You have offered me so much wisdom and support. Drew (Richard) Stoddard: I had so much fun. Daniel Souweine: A lot has changed; I'm glad we're still friends. Nolan Zeide: I will always remember you. Allison Odato: You are a wonderful roommate, but mostly you are a wonderful friend. Rothschild, Leeatt, and Caroline Winters: You bring me happiness even in Mocon. WestCo Up Two: Thank you for being funny.

# Introduction:
# THE VIEW FROM WITHIN
# THE WHIRLWIND

"It's just a little coke, Sa. It's not like I'm smuggling kilos over the border or anything," Jade's eyes searched for my approval, "Just don't worry, okay?"

My shoulders hunched around my emptied lungs. I forced the single word from the bottom of my stomach, "Okay."

Jade pulled the screen door shut behind her. I stood, forehead against the thin wire mesh, and watched J.'s headlights run away. I breathed in the last of summer's warm nights and reviewed my day: Rachel ate only rice for lunch, Alexis took an HIV test, Jade bought cocaine. Today's events were not unusual. Today, as a whole, was not even disturbing. Deadly diseases, hard drugs, and eating disorders should rattle me. Instead, these issues seemed alarmingly commonplace.

In my room, I glanced toward my desk. The shelf leaned against it like a heavy drunk, sagging under the weight of its contents. My rows of journals reminded me of my own struggles gone by. There was junior high: drinking in the baby-blue book, rumors of too many boyfriends on the yellow Mead perforated pages. Tenth grade: My pleas with God to figure out why I slept so much and cried so much in the small wirebound book. Now, I can place my struggles into neat categories—subtitles to journals that are far removed from where I am now. But, I watch my friends continue to struggle. Sometimes I still struggle with them.

It is not for lack of understanding or intelligence that my circle of friends is plagued by drug abuse, eating disorders, and depression. We have all been told to love ourselves. We are all intelligent. We are all aware that we have been raised in culture that cradles double standards, impossible ideals of beauty, and asks us to listen. But we are caught in the crossfire between where we have been told we should be and where we really are. Self-directed girls are sometimes lost. A friend summed up her struggle in one phrase, "I'm afraid of the sound of my own voice." Even assertive and independent girls are troubled by their own ideas and assertions. Academic overachievers are silent in the classroom. Extroverts are frightened to read poetry out loud or dance in public. So-called perfect girls feel trapped by others' expectations.

In *Reviving Ophelia*, Mary Pipher calls upon a Shakespearean metaphor, linking Hamlet's lover, Ophelia, to the adolescent female experience. In *Hamlet* the men are the protagonists of the play, while also dominating Ophelia's life. Young Ophelia concentrates only on fulfilling the expectations of others. Trying to be good and righteous, she loses her father's love, her lover's respect, and her own dignity. Ophelia is drowned by the weight of her clothing.

As I finished Pipher's introduction, I felt her describing me—an adolescent girl caught in the Ophelia syndrome. Her case studies looked behind the facade, describing the whirlwind of adolescence. She wrote about our teenage experience with clarity and sensitivity. However, Pipher viewed the whirlwind from the outside. Her portrayal of young females was accurate, but her representation was limited by her role as a psychologist, a parent, and most importantly, as an adult. Given these limitations, Pipher's book is truly exceptional. *Reviving Ophelia* was an incredible gift to me and, I believe, to other adolescent girls.

Pipher not only spoke about me; she spoke to me, offering honesty, acceptance, and hope.

Yet, by book's end, I was left unsettled. In fact, I felt Pipher was speaking for me, and I wanted to speak for myself. As I shared my thoughts with my friends, we all agreed—*Reviving Ophelia* had been a gift to us, but it had also sold us short. If Ophelia is to be revived then it must be done by the collective voice and actions of Ophelias everywhere.

As I described this frustrated desire to speak for myself and to hear the voices other girls, my dad half-supportively, half-jokingly retorted, "Sara, you should write a book called *Ophelia Speaks*." The next morning, I announced my plan, "I'm going to write that book."

From the beginning, my intention was to enable girls to tell their own stories and to hear the stories of other girls. I hoped to take the adult intermediary out from between us. I wanted us to see one another's intelligence and experience, pain and power directly, free from adult interpretation.

I began collecting sample contributions from friends and acquaintances I had known in different places and at different times—summer programs, youth organizations, and school. I wrote a letter explaining my intention to write *Ophelia Speaks*, asking them to write about their adolescent female experiences.

My friends were excited. Ms. Salisbury, my Women in Literature teacher, was proud. My parents were supportive.

I was appalled.

Before I began this project I had limited my perceptions to what I wanted to see; I saw my friends as others saw them—the high-functioning, popular, National Honor Society crowd about to enter the halls of the Ivy League. Sure we had problems, but we were basically healthy girls. That falsified vision was shattered by their contributions. With tear-filled eyes, I saw through the facade.

With each essay my friends and acquaintances gave me, I became more shocked by the wide gap between what we have been told to think, what we say we think, and what we truly think. We regurgitate false pride on a whim, masking the reality of what we do to ourselves. I cried the day Jade gave me her contribution and told me I couldn't talk to her about it. The harsh reality of being young and female gnawed at me.

Creating the proposal for *Ophelia Speaks* made the idea of our collective voice begin to take a form of its own. It explored the struggles of adolescent girls and represented our reality to publishing houses. But not until after I obtained a publishing contract with HarperCollins Publishers did I begin my serious research into the lives of adolescent girls. I sent *Ophelia Speaks* packets to 6,750 professionals who work with teenagers. The packets included a cover letter describing *Ophelia Speaks*. It described my aim of representing a collective female adolescent voice, and asked for their help in allowing girls' voices to be heard (Appendix A). The packet also contained a "Message to Adolescent Girls," a letter I wrote directly to other adolescent girls inviting contributions to *Ophelia Speaks* (Appendix B); a letter from my editor, Laureen Rowland, at HarperCollins, verifying the validity of the project; and a few black and white posters with basic information about *Ophelia Speaks* and guidelines for contributions. I asked for "personally self-disclosing contributions." I suggested a number of possible topics, ranging from eating disorders to family to relationships to religion. I also wrote that girls should not feel confined to these topics, and that any other personally important experience was perfectly welcome.

These packets were mailed to 5,500 secondary public-school principals, 600 public-school psychologists, 50 clergy members, 600 public-school English teachers, and 100 private-school English teachers. The National Association of Secondary School Principals and the National Association of School Psychologists supplied a representative sample of their members in urban, suburban, small town, and rural environments. The National Council of Churches provided names of Regional and National Youth Ministers. The National Council for English Teachers posted a notice to their members (roughly 600) on the Internet and published my "Message to Adolescent Girls" in their monthly newsletter. Private-school English department heads were notified through a published directory. Many of these adults wrote, e-mailed, and called me offering their support. Some teachers even assigned pertinent personal essays as class assignments or for extra credit.

Packets were sent out over the span of two weeks in April 1998, with a deadline date of June 1, 1998. In the end, I received 815 contributions from adolescent girls from different religious, racial, and economic backgrounds, from small towns to large cities, in every major geographical area of the United States.

Invited to speak honestly, girls told treasured and hidden stories. They wrote to communicate, to heal themselves, and to help other girls. With intelligence, they reflected on the most important experiences in their lives. Sometimes, their stories made me laugh. More often, they made me cry.

I am aware that some critics may challenge my sample, arguing that the suggested categories may have elicited only "heavier" contributions or that more so-called "troubled" girls were contacted rather than "normal" girls. I would like to dispel some of this doubt about the representativeness of the contributions. Of the more than eight-hundred contributions I received, about one-hundred fell outside of categories I had envisioned. In fact, I had not anticipated several of the chapters in *Ophelia Speaks* before I received girls' personal essays, stories, poems, and journal entries. Girls' contributions were truly the impetus behind the construction of *Ophelia Speaks*; this book was compiled with their words and experiences in the forefront of my mind.

I am not saying that all adolescent girls, or even most, are overwhelmed by emotions or circumstances. But girls are incredibly complicated. I am a generally happy and healthy adolescent girl, but I was very depressed at one point in my life. I still smiled a lot, did better in school than I ever had, worked out, and ate well. But, inside, I felt like I was dying. Even now, despite my general happiness and healthfulness, I have moments of intense insecurity and self-deprecation. I was most compelled to write when I was living in darker times or in more difficult moments.

The disturbing contributions to *Ophelia Speaks* are not written by uniformly self-loathing or victimized girls. We are not dyed in just one color. Rather, we are made from a complex pattern, intertwining weakness and strength, sadness and joy, pleasure and pain. Still, given this opportunity, invited to write what we are encouraged to hide, most girls, but certainly not all, opened the door on dark and disturbing times. Still others allowed light, instead of darkness, to glitter in their contributions.

In creating *Ophelia Speaks*, I feel a tremendous responsibility to not only the contributors, but to all adolescent girls. But I am fearful that I will be perceived as attempting to represent all adolescent girls. No one individual can speak for all of us. Rather, I am hopeful this book will provide an audience for the many voices included in these pages, and that together we may represent the inherent complexity of our common voice. A number of these contributions come straight from our journals. Many are the result of further deliberation. All are incredibly self-reflective and startlingly honest.

I believe girls wrote to me with such frankness because, when I elicited their writing, I was a seventeen-year-old girl. With *Ophelia Speaks*, I provided the ear of a peer, not the watchful eye of an adult. There is a capacity for openness among adolescents; adults are rarely entrusted with our emotional reality. Even so, I had to compile this book in order to truly understand my friends' struggles. The candor of *Ophelia Speaks* is exceptionally self-disclosing, even for adolescent girls.

I am hopeful that this book will help adults understand us, but mostly I am hopeful that other adolescent girls will hear their own voices in these pages. Numerous submissions arrived at my mailbox with cover letters that read like this one: "At the time I wrote this, I felt very alone. I want you to know that even if this isn't published it was really therapeutic for me to write it. If I am published, though, I would like to remain anonymous—I only want other girls to know they are not alone."

Many of the contributions I received were written from a lonely place, where girls unself-consciously admitted to self-loathing or disappointment. However, I am hopeful that the readers of *Ophelia Speaks* will see not only the despondency of our contributions, but also the inherent strength in our ability to articulate our experiences. Many contributors did not write with a heavy message; many contributions are light-hearted, loving, or playful. But I want to emphasize that *all* of the contributors to this book are very strong young women. Although I expect most readers will be interested in glimpsing our afflictions, I am hopeful that readers will also listen to the strength of our collective voice, our ability to articulate our ideas and experiences, and ultimately, our hope for our future. This is not a disheartening book. We are troubled, but we have hope and tremendous promise.

In the coming pages, we write about the view from inside the whirlwind. Like the startling images captured by tornado chasers, such is the writing from today's teenage girls. We do not need an expert intermediary filtering our experience through interpretation. We can tell the world who we are directly and with an intimacy and accuracy inaccessible to those outside our generation. In this collection of personal essays, stories, and poems, we open a door, inviting adults intent on understanding us, and other adolescents eager to hear their own voices, to enter our reality. We show how our world looks and feels from the inside.

In these pages, *Ophelia Speaks*.

# PART ONE

## THE BODY UNDER ASSAULT

# Media-Fed Images

≋

I was a media-fed child. I can't remember a time when the television wasn't my favorite baby-sitter, my most reliable companion, my preferred role model. *The Cosby Show, Growing Pains, Head of the Class, Different Strokes,* and *Fame* jumped out of the fluorescent tube and planted expectations in my preadolescent mind. Every Thursday, in health class, the *After-School Special* offered a "realistic" view of years to come. For years I wished my name was Sam because I positively idolized Samantha Miscelli on *Who's the Boss.* Then, after years of preparation, of longing to talk on the phone, go out with my friends, and wear mascara, I finally became a teenager.

Adolescence is not what I thought it would be. Happy endings aren't inserted conveniently before the last commercial break. The peer pressure isn't unrelenting, the wild parties aren't dangerously tempting, the first loves aren't thrillingly perfect. But, more unsettling than the unforeseen tedium, my face isn't blemish-proof and my stomach isn't immune to bloating. I was fed a cookie-cutter standard of beauty, and I do not invariably meet the media's image of perfect. As a media baby, I'm a disappointment.

I do not have a cute nose, perfect skin, long legs, a flat stomach, or long eyelashes. My awareness of these facts makes my body a backdrop for my everyday life. My stomach, back, skin, knees, hair are always in my peripheral vision. Never my sole focus (I'm too healthy for that!), but always just tickling at my consciousness. I sometimes catch myself comparing my body to those of actresses, models, women walking down the street. Then I remind myself: Healthy, happy, normal girls don't notice, don't envy, other women's small frames or sunken cheeks. They don't find pride in the comment, "Wow. Your collar bones really stick out." They don't feel guilty for not being as thin, or as muscular, as the star in the magazine clipping. Oh, they don't, do they? My mail tells a different story.

Judging from the writing of adolescent girls that I received, I'm not alone. When I sent out my invitation for contributions to *Ophelia Speaks,* I never suggested "The Media" as a topic. Yet, nearly twenty girls sent me essays specifically blaming the media for their poor body image. Countless others mentioned its negative effects on their self-confidence. One girl described cutting out the body parts of models from magazines and piecing together her "goal" body. In self-asserting anger, Elizabeth Fales wrote, "Someone making millions of dollars has decided to play on every adolescent girl's feeling of inadequacy. Insecurity is 'in,' confidence is 'out.' In American culture, there's always room for improvement. The blond-haired, blue-eyed size four, as-close-to-Heather-Locklear-as-possible look is the social norm, and the people who fail to qualify don't even get a consolation prize in the game of adolescence." With a courageous admission of a media-fueled anxiety attack, a teenager who calls herself Laverne Difazio wrote, "All of a sudden I'm insecurity-laden, nervous, and dedicated to becoming Miss Skin 'n' Bones Teen USA."

I wish I couldn't relate to letters I received—to standing in front of the mirror poking, squeezing, and sucking in. I know I don't work out just because it makes me feel healthier. In tenth grade, I pulled away when my then-boyfriend touched my stomach. Shocked, he shook his head in disbelief, and asked, "Do you know practically every woman in the country would kill for your body?" Now, some three years later, I do not remember the words he used to describe my intelligence, to encourage my artistic talent, to support my ambitions—but I do recall that one compliment, word-for-word.

These confessions will come as a surprise to many who know

me—most of the time I walk around with a genuine air of confidence. Just as often, I'm glad braces made my teeth straight, platform shoes make my legs look longer, and makeup covers my blemishes. I owe my confidence in my physical appearance to what the media-inspired world offers me to achieve the "look" I desire. I owe that "look"—long-legged, clear-skinned, bright-eyed—to the same media that inspired my self-destructive desire to achieve it.

The three contributions to this chapter honestly and insightfully reflect the feelings and thoughts of so many girls. The first short piece, *Catalogues*, poignantly articulates our frustrated desire to possess the media's "ideal" body. The second, *Looking Through a Magnifying Glass*, personalizes how the media leaves its impression on our body image. The last, *Mirrors*, is a startlingly honest portrait that looks past the facade, revealing how the media hurls us into self-loathing. In *Mirrors*, one of the most astute pieces of writing I have ever read, Charlotte Cooper speaks with such emotional nakedness that she exposes the truth for many of us. When I shared Charlotte's poem with friends, all were stunned by its accuracy. Her image of us standing before our mirrors sets the stage for the next chapter, Eating Disorders.

## CATALOGUES
*By Jessica Bulman, 17, from a small town in the Northeast*

Searching through catalogues
you wish you could order
the bodies not the clothes.

## LOOKING THROUGH A MAGNIFYING GLASS
*By Olga Levinson, 15, from a suburb in the Midwest*

"Isn't she soooo pretty?" Tamara would ask, pointing at a stick-thin model with a Barbie-doll body, in *dELiA*s* catalog. "I'd love to look like her. She's so skinny." She'd say and continue flipping through the magazine. We had been down this road many times before.

"You already do!" Lindy and I would say in unison. And she did. At five foot six, she had a small body frame, small arms and thighs, small hips, narrow waist, and a flat stomach. She had the athletic body figure all the models seemed to have—the type of body millions of girls only dream of.

"Why do you say that? For once, why can't you just tell me the truth?" She'd stand in front of her full-length mirror, lift up her shirt, and frown at the invisible fat nobody seemed to see, but her. She'd then pinch together some of her skin. "See this! This is definitely fat!" Tamara would insist, falling dejectedly on the bed, and then continuing to look through the magazine. It was always the same thing. In the bathing suits, all of the models looked alike. You always saw pearly white smiles, tan skin, and long legs. And if you looked close enough, you usually saw ribs. Most of the time, they protruded so much, you could actually count them.

"Ugh. She's so *fat*! Why did they put her in this magazine?" Tamara would exclaim and point. We'd look, of course. There we saw another gorgeous model, with the same long, silky hair, bright smile, tan legs. Only this one didn't look anorexic.

"Yeah, what about her?" Lindy would ask, beginning to get a little annoyed. But we had been through this before.

"Well look at her. She's got such a big stomach. At least I don't look like *her*. Why is she even in here?"

"Personally, I would love to look like her." I'd say. And I would.

"No you wouldn't. You are *so* much skinnier than her. Look at her. She looks like a cow!"

"If she's a cow, then I must be a whale."

"Whatever. You don't need to lose any weight. You're fine. I, on the other hand, need to lose about ten pounds before the summer. I'm not putting on a bathing suit until I do. I don't feel like being depressed yet." Tamara declared this new mission and then proceeded to explain her plan about how to lose weight.

Something about keeping a daily journal of what she ate, never consuming more than 1,000 calories. Meanwhile, Lindy just sat there silently, staring at Tamara. I looked at her too, and sighed. It's not that I was fat either, but I had excess fat on my stomach and I had big arms. Even my mother said so.

"You know what, I need to lose some weight too." I said all of a sudden. After all, if Tamara had the right to dislike *her* body, I *definitely* had something to complain about.

## MIRRORS
*By Charlotte Cooper, 18, from a suburb in the West*

I often hear,
Mostly from psychologists on talk shows,
How teenagers see distorted images in our full-length mirrors.
The ones that set decorators in movies and on television
Border with Prom pictures, snapshots and
Cute boys: Ben Affleck, Matt Damon, David Duchovny, David
    Boreanaz.
In my room, Ben and Matt and both Davids are next to my bed.
They are on the wall across from the mirror.
On my desk.
On my ceiling.
But not around my mirror.
Around my mirror are women: Nadia Anerman, Kate Moss,
    Amber Valletta, Shalom Harlow.
I get to see them as I look at myself
They are my goals. They are my aspirations.
And then I wonder why I hate myself.
When I am alone in my room, I look at myself
And I am disgusted.
After seeing what I should look like around the mirror,
I hate my body and self.
I truly believe that I should look that way,

Because no matter what I say in class about images,
I truly believe that it is my own fault that I don't look like a
  model.
I feel that I don't deserve anything when I look in the mirror.
And the reflective image shocks me,
Because in my mind, I have a very different self-image.
I'm not skinny-skinny in it, but trim and fit.
Then I catch sight of myself; and I think,
"What everyone must think of me!"
It is *always* about what everyone else thinks.

I know I'm going to slap my mother one of these days
For telling me to eat less,
And giving me the look.
I know she is ashamed that I'm not as thin as she was in high
  school.
I can't wear her vintage cardigans,
I can't even fit into her wedding shift.
She says it's about health . . . maybe it is.
But when her eyes are sorrowful as I walk into the kitchen,
Maybe not even eating,
And the corners of her lips curl inward in implication,
I scream at her, shout, "Leave me the fuck alone!"
And she just looks at me like she always does,
And that just makes me want to stuff myself.
If my own mother can't accept me with my body,
Who am I to love myself?
Mother knows best.
I'm letting her down.
I know if I were my mother I'd be ashamed of me,
Ashamed to take me shopping
And ask the sales ladies if we can order a bigger size.

I can't torture myself physically
I'm not dedicated enough to be
Bulimic

Anorexic
Exercising all day
Starving myself
I read all the stories.
And I know, while saying out loud,
"How could anyone do this to herself?"
That I still wish to be like them.
I like me too much to mutilate,
But not enough to accept.
I am jealous of anorexic women
I know,
*know*
That anorexia and bulimia are diseases.
I know they are destructive.
I know they are deadly.
But I want to join.
Where do I sign up?
If risking my mind, my sanity, the body I hate to inhabit,
Is the price for thinness, I am willing to pay.
I laugh, because even as I am willing to pay,
I can't.
I lack commitment.

So on go the long, silent talks with the mirror image
The image I dread to look at but
From which I can't tear my gaze away.
Purple lines mark my body, battle scars?
No, scars of cowardice.
I wouldn't have these brandings if only I had some control, I
    berate myself.
And I stare, as if looking will make them go away.
I stare at car accidents, too.

As a woman who loves herself in the mind
I know I deserve everything
And I should get it.

As a girl who hates herself in the body
I know I deserve nothing
And I should get it.
It froths.
I feel my blood hurtling.
But I can't stop looking at myself.
And I can't stop hating myself
Sometimes I just cry.

# Eating Disorders

≋

A few months had passed since the three of us had sprawled about together. In August, when camp ended, we vowed to see each other again soon. I knew it would be different to hang out in houses instead of cabins, but I didn't anticipate other changes. The last time I saw Rachel she was a size four, maybe even a six. Now, she's a size one. At the Gap, maybe even a zero.

But, it was great to see each other. We talked and laughed and bonded. Rachel went to bed first—as always, she had a lot of work to do tomorrow. Allysa and I sat on the couch watching her go upstairs, hearing her close the door. Then we spoke more honestly than we ever had. We laughed about how we can speak objectively about anything, so long as we don't have to attach a first-person pronoun to the discussion. Even then, with all our light-hearted criticism of our mutual aversion to the word "I", we didn't disclose much about ourselves in the next few hours. Instead, we talked about Rachel.

Last Friday afternoon at the train station: Allysa and I saw Rachel climb out of the train. Her tight black bootleg-cut pants were pulled taut. Her legs looked like a wishbone—stick thin and bowed outward—an upside-down U where she once had thighs. The top of her legs looked identical to the circumference of her knees.

Sitting on my floral couch, Allysa explained. She had always been closer to Rachel than I was. "Right after camp ended Rachel and I decided we would do this low-carbo diet together. I never really did it, but she *really* did."

Allysa paused, momentarily. "I talked to Rachel about all the weight she lost—told her I was worried. She cried and told me she wasn't anorexic."

She took a another breath before continuing. "Rachel asked me why I couldn't just be happy for her. She says she's happy with her body for the first time in her life."

Listening to Allysa, I heard the unvoiced accusation in Rachel's question—You're jealous because I'm thin. Maybe Rachel was right. Maybe she is simply, perfectly thin. Maybe we did envy as much as we worried. In the world of adolescent girls, thinness—sometimes at whatever cost—evokes profound jealousy. We lust for the perfect body. We crave control over our lives. Even when we publicly condemn those who "control" their food intake, many of us privately admire their "willpower."

Allysa confessed, "The first time I saw Rachel post–weight loss, I was disgusted with myself. I was worried about Rachel, but I was really jealous, too."

In the quiet, after-midnight hours, Allysa and I had allowed ourselves to be hauntingly honest about our mutual insecurities and envy.

My size-four body has walked with a warm cup in hand, feeling suddenly anxious, cold, concerned, confused. Then with guilt—judging my own lack of discipline—my mind turns to self-accusation: I should have gotten a skim-milk mocha. I can't believe I didn't work out last night. What did I have for lunch?

Still, I never starved or purged myself. I wanted to believe the same of my friends—when Allysa assured me Rachel had "just dieted," I didn't want to figure out the logistical odds against her losing so much weight, so quickly, without damaging her health. I just told myself: She's so determined. If anyone could stick to a healthy diet, it's Rachel. I couldn't believe one of my friends— one I most admired—could be afflicted with a self-destructive disease.

I read more than eight-hundred contributions in the process of compiling *Ophelia Speaks*. The single most written-about subject was eating disorders. Nearly fifty girls wrote pieces specifically focused on their self-destructive relationship with food. One girl, while wishing to remain anonymous, explained her reason for writing:

> I wrote this for anyone, boy or girl, who has had to see that pained look in their mother's eyes as she begs in vain for them to "take just one more bite" or whose mother leaves the unfinished half of chicken breast on your plate hoping that you will "pick at it." This is for anyone who ever wished that they could just enjoy one meal without feeling as if they have failed themselves. For anyone who stands in front of the mirror, pinching and poking at hated curves and bumps. For anyone who wishes fervently that all traces of fat would just disappear, leaving you thin. I want you to know you are not alone.

In proportion to the importance of this theme, you will find more contributions in this chapter than in any other. Choosing fewer would have painted a dishonest picture of girls' adolescence. The following personal essays and poems present the full range of our food-focused discontent.

In *Food Is Not My Enemy*, Elizabeth Fales views the devastation wrought by eating disorders. In a covert war, where society is the aggressor and our bodies the victims, Elizabeth calls us to a new feminism. In the old feminism, our mothers fought for the right to choose an abortion. In our generation, we must fight for the right to eat.

In the second contribution, E.G.K.Z. speaks from another reality, from a vulnerable place where thoughts and emotions battle over the fate of our bodies. The chapter moves from E.G.K.Z.'s startlingly honest internal reflection to *I Am Scared*. An anonymous poet brings us to what she most fears: a room with a mirror. Here she discloses her disgust with herself. She can no longer see "every bone and organ visible"—she's determined to once again achieve the ideal body of an anoretic.

In *Me, I See Me*, Lorel looks in the mirror and confronts a different reality. Seeking self-punishment for a guilt-ridden day, her bulimic mentality nearly deposits her on death's door. In the end, she sees herself clearly and finds herself comforted by a loving God.

In *I Never Thought*, Jennifer K. Lavoie speaks for girls whose eating disorders have robbed them of both their normal bodies and their normal lives. She describes the shattering of her dreams—the loss of health, friendship, and family.

This chapter ends with a brilliant poem, *Lighter Than Air*. We accompany its author, Christi Marie O'Donnell, to the funeral of a friend who achieved her ultimate goal. She became, literally, lighter than air.

In all these contributions, girls have courageously stripped away all pretense. They have let us into their minds to view their bodies—to see and feel as they do. Their words shatter the facade of the "beautiful" body.

Still, I dismiss hints: I want to believe this disease lives somewhere else. I half-calculated my defense of Rachel, refusing to imagine she had starved herself. I try not to count how many times Allysa said, "Well, you know my deal with food," and I let the comment go with an easy, "Yeah." I've nearly forgotten Rachel's self-isolated end-of-lunch trips to the bathroom. I hardly notice. It's just so much easier to look the other way.

## FOOD IS NOT MY ENEMY
*By Elizabeth Fales, 18, from a small town in the Northeast*

"Food is not my enemy; control is not my friend." Why can I learn to befriend food and banish control while they can't? How did every girl I grew up with learn to measure their merit by the size of their skirt? Why does the Gap make size zero? How can their mothers look into the pale, sunken eye sockets and see daughters, instead of dying victims? Where are their parents during dinnertime? Why does the lunchroom monitor pass over them, shudder, and move quickly on? Why is it wrong to tell them they have a disease? The ultimate question: Who designed Barbie? I am furious with the world today.

Everyday at lunch, the girls at the table next to me split a plate of salad—six ways. The girl beside me only has yogurt (fat-free, sugar-free) and water, tricking her stomach into fullness, the same way famine victims do to defy death. How did eating become a plague in the land of plenty? Why do I let myself feel guilty in the face of their empty plates? Why? The other girls, right across from me, eye the grinder line, each one mentally willing another to go, to be brave; it is war. Surrendering to their fear of food, they sit, amusing each other with gossip so the thundering of their bellies will be silenced. Some of them, the old pros, need only to tell their stomachs to be quiet. The new ones, so recently won over by pop culture standards, have to speak loudly so no one hears what their bodies tell them. They are hungry—for more than food.

Who told them that skin and bones are beautiful? They have lost their membership cards to womanhood—their hips, breasts, periods, every biological feature that makes woman distinctly different from children. They become children again, mentally, physically, hormonally, intellectually. They lose the body structure, the energy, the hormonal processes, and the mental capabilities that make them women.

I find it so easy to make this a war—a war of society versus women, or America versus fat. I call this disease a war and I can keep it impersonal—so far away and so untouchable. My country has the best defense in the world. I can pretend I don't know the soldiers. But I do.

Everyone knows someone. Right now, I can think of ten people who are definitely anorexic and three who are bulimic. And everyone is yelling, "Look the other way, *look the other way!*" We justify averting our eyes with lame excuses: "We've all dieted." No need to see the disease now. Sure, it could qualify as an epidemic by the way it spreads in my school. Sure, it's killing sisters, daughters, mothers, best friends, girlfriends, nieces, cousins, team members, classmates, teachers, students, and selves.

No one important, right? Be a world enslaved by superficiality and shallowness and "just look the other way."

Every day books and essays are written and published, enlightening and awakening books. But the general public continues to fumble in the darkness. The light can be blinding. Letting in the truth takes some getting used to. Then all of a sudden, you can see so much clearer. And there is no need for stumbling in the darkness.

For years people just have taken whatever the world dumps on them. Even the freedom fighters of my mother's generation didn't fight this battle. They fought for the right to abort a baby, while sporting platforms and hot pants, but they failed to fight for the right to eat, to live, to survive. Survival of the slimmest is the newest Darwinian-based theory.

> Consummation at last. To every woman a happy ending.
> —*Marge Piercy*

## My Hand Holds the Taco
*By E.G.K.Z., 17, from a small town in the Northeast*

my hand holds the taco
against the will of my anorexic mind.
but most days i'm strong
the self i know as my Flesh
is the winner.
it fights my other self,
the irrational self that is my Thoughts,
that tells me not to consume,
that tells me that food is evil.
so i eat . . . and to shove the fact that i'm eating
in the face of my Mind
i binge
—all the things that i don't want to eat (dairy, chocolate)
the things that give me comfort

and separate me from my starving friends.
until my stomach is so full
i can feel it stretching
. . . and i know that this is a feeling that i don't want,
disgusting and bloated
and now i have disappointed *both* selves
—the self that wanted to starve
and
—the self that simply wanted nourishment
i neither have the self control to starve
nor the normalcy to simply eat
and so the battle continues . . . i listen to Mind
and i walk inconspicuously into the rest room and plead
with God
to let me be able to throw up—
(i know i'd feel much better)
and i push on my abdomen, stick a finger down
my throat and gag . . .
and nothing.
i can't do it. i want to, like nothing else, but
no one ever taught me how to make myself throw up.
i wish that i was in the movie *Heathers* where my best friend
would do it for me—
stick her fingers down my throat . . .
but my best friend will never know about this . . . ('cause i don't
    have a problem)
how can i justify being upset
over a nonexistent
problem
when all of my friends have *real* problems?
they *really* don't eat. they have *real* eating problems.
they are the ones that i have to pretend to not approve of
when really
deep down
i am dying of jealousy.
they are so lucky.

and of course my conscious observing self
knows that this is
*Sick*
and i let the *hate* for Myself
simply grow inside me
while none of my friends suspect a thing.
*I am alone* in this.
and that is how i want it.


## I AM SCARED

*By Anonymous, 14, from a suburb in the Northeast*

I am scared as I walk into this dreadful room
Unwilling to accept what is soon to come.
I gaze deeply in through the blurred reflection
And stare hard into my eyes, searching.
There is this saddened look on this girl's face—like she is in
    pain.
I feel ashamed at what I look at
I am disgusted with this worthless girl—this failure.
Tears of fear slowly start to creep up into her eyes
But she has to hold back—has to stay strong.
I am hoping to see a figure which is perfect and beautiful,
With every single bone and organ visible
Protruding sharply through a pale paper-thin layer
But come to find a different girl
Now with all this excess flesh
That which suffocates this poor girl
I am disgusted and feel empty inside.
I am weak and have failed—for once I have lost
My precious battle in which I had so greatly mastered.
I want to go back—I am lost and alone.
I wish to step into the mirror
And fall back and become that girl I long to be
That of whom I was . . . and will be once more.

# Me, I See Me
*By Lorel, 16, from a suburb in the South*

Me, I see me, my disgustingly fat body blown out of proportion. The shower is running, the mirror is foggy, I am on my knees and my hair is back. I bend over the toilet, cold, white, unyielding. It is strong, my stability into which everything falls. My nails are chipped and peeling in places. I notice their imperfect polish as I see the rim around the edge of the bowl. Over I bend and shove my fingers back. Finding the ticklish place at the end of my throat, I can feel the nastiness inside me. It's warm, and bad, and not yet digested. Up it comes in bits and pieces in a clear, pinkish liquid. Chunks of the food I've consumed throughout the evening come up my throat, into my mouth, flowing over my fingers, into my refuge, on my fingers as I pull them out of my mouth. I'd rinse them off, but I know they work better if I don't. All of my rage, my depression comes up with the nastiness. I can feel the evil being purged from inside me. I must continue on until there's nothing left.

I pause when I retch too loudly. My body is just resisting what it knows is inevitable, trying to hold what little bit of substance it can inside. I can't allow it. I rinse my hands and listen. *Good, my parents are still talking.* Once again, I lower myself back down on my knees. This time I move harder. I have to be clean, closer to perfection, and I can't be, not with this inside me. *Who will see me tomorrow? Everyone.* They all will look at me and see how far from perfection I really am. So up it must come. It almost tastes good, close to eating it all over again, but with a bitter aftertaste.

Only clear bile comes up now. I feel wasted now, but pure. The water running in the shower is cold. I took too long. The coldness feels refreshing on my burning face and hand. I see the remnants of my purge washing down the drain.

Five minutes later, I am clean. On shaky knees, I go to my bed. I lie there reviewing the day's escapades. I had coffee this morning which kept me going all day, along with two energy pills

I stole from 7-Eleven. After school walking over the bridge, a friend gave me one SweetTart rabbit. I carefully studied it and let my eyes play with its beauty, pink and perfect with tiny little ears. *How it would taste slowly dissolving in my mouth?* I could take it no longer and hurriedly slipped it between my lips, letting it rest on my tongue. The sweetness, the tartness, was an evil luring me to ruin the entire day's perfection. This was a sin. I quickly took one last suck and spit it into my awaiting hand. *She didn't see, did she?* I saw it falling, falling as I tossed it off the bridge. Closer to its impending death beneath the truck's tires below. I imagined the pink pieces in between the traction being carried to a better, happier place. All of this drifts through my mind as I drift off to sleep, but suddenly I feel a shock of terror spring through my body.

I know I will get no sleep tonight. There might still be food inside me. My stomach gets heavy as I think of how much I purged. *The toilet bowl looked full, but how much did I eat? Three plates of spaghetti, and two garlic breads. What if the toilet bowl was not full, what if everything was just floating on the water, giving the impression that it was full? Some might still be left inside me. I can't throw up, it's too late for that, it's probably already been digested.* The only way to cure this dilemma is to exercise the rest of it off. Thirty minutes of jumping jacks, forty minutes of sit-ups. I start to loose my pace, but I must push on. On and on and on. I'm exhausted. I feel dizzy as I stand up. The world spins for a second and then stands still. I crash into bed, where I hope this hell will end.

Tomorrow comes too soon, as it always does. I struggle to drag myself out of the warmth and comfort of my bed. *It's a cloudy day. Again.* I lumber into the kitchen where Mom sits eating cereal. I see her look at me, those suspicious eyes drifting over my face. I know what will come next. She wants me to eat breakfast, but I know this is not possible. Eating this early will upset my balance. When she leaves, the Toaster Strudel goes into the trash can under a wad of paper. *What a waste.* I really am hungry, but, no, I can't. A dab of icing smeared onto a plate goes into the sink as I drink my morning coffee.

The school day wears on. It is lunch again. Someone offers to buy me lunch, I look too thin they say. Of course that is a lie. *Just look at me and you can tell how fat I really am. They're just being sarcastic.* I see the sparkle in their eyes, evil and mocking. I'll buy my own lunch. Thank you very much. So I eat a burrito and drink a Coke. I eat the whole greasy, flaky disgusting thing. I feel the fat from it go straight to my hips. I feel them expanding by the second. *As soon as I can get away I'll rid myself of this.* As soon as the coast is clear I run into the rest room. After the first retch someone comes in. *I've failed miserably once again, this time a whole three weeks is ruined. I have no self control.* After dinner, I lay in bed hating myself. I didn't throw up dinner either. *What would be the point? I've already ruined today anyway. When everyone else is in bed I'll go into the kitchen and get a knife. I must punish myself for all the wrong I've done.*

"Something in the Way" by Nirvana is playing softly. I feel the words, I breathe them, I live them, I am them. The knife traces across my wrist, barely touching the skin, in a graceful horizontal motion. I push slightly harder, it's almost breaking through now, but not quite. I can feel each pinpoint of texture of the knife on my skin. It is rough and not very sharp. *That's all right. I'll feel more pain.* I consider all of the mistakes I've made today. Each and every foolish word and action. *How can I ever forgive myself? How can God? I should not even be allowed to live my idiotic existence.* My life is a tunnel. A spiral of darkness, depression, and death. My descent down is eternal. I almost feel claws around my wrists and ankles pulling me down deeper. They are burning my flesh. The light at the top is fading along with the image of Jesus above. I try to stretch my fingertips upward, begging, pleading for him to see me and rescue me. Evidently I am not screaming loud enough, because he never does answer my prayers.

*Just by being alive I am hurting everyone I love and care about. I should just end it all now. And this hell called life will be over.* The strokes with the knife get stronger, cutting the skin now, tearing it. I feel the pain, relishing it, knowing I must compensate for every wrong I've done. I feel a warm thick liquid oozing down my arm. *What am I doing?* The knife is sticky with its warm wetness. I run across the room to turn on the light. My entire arm and pillowcase are red. *Is this blood? Have I done this to myself?* I seem to have awakened from some sort of dream, still dazed and uncomprehending. *I must change the sheets and rinse myself off.* The cuts really are deep. One more cut, slightly deeper, and I would've severed an artery. I can see it pulsing through an open wound. *Has it really come to this?*

I've cut myself many times before, but never this severe. Usually just scratches, just enough to feel the pain. It has always felt sweet and helped me to think more clearly. Out with the blood has flowed the evil.

But now I wonder, *How much evil resides in me? Is this the extent of my insanity?* I am looking at myself in the bathroom mirror. For a moment I can almost see myself as everyone else sees me. Sunken eyes and cheeks jutting from hollows below. I see the scratches and the scars on my soul. The tears begin to drip down my hollowed face. Sobbing, I lower myself to my knees. *Will God ever forgive me for all of the wrong I've committed? Am I worth saving?* In my eyes, I am worth nothing, but maybe in His I am worth salvaging, if only for tonight. I beg, I plead, and I pray. I feel His strong arms encircle me and lift me up. I no longer feel as if I am falling, but instead beginning on a upward journey. In this time of weakness, I know He is there.

## I Never Thought . . .

*By Jennifer K. Lavoie, 17, from a small town in the South*

I never thought my life would ever be the way it is today. When I was in kindergarten I imagined my life as a teenager. I imagined how much fun I would have with freedom to make more choices and do more things. I couldn't wait until the day I would turn sixteen. I thought for sure there would be a car in the driveway with a big red bow and a card. The card would read:

Dearest Jenny,

Congratulations! We really hope you will enjoy your new car. Have a Happy Sweet Sixteen! We love you!

Love,
Mom and Dad

I dreamed of going to high school, having lots of friends, dating a guy, falling in love, going to parties, driving my car, dancing at my prom, having a job, and feeling happy.

Unfortunately, my life has not gone as planned. I thought I would be in control, but the control I once had, years ago, has been lost. Instead of me controlling my life, I was being controlled by depression, anorexia, anger, and fear. They locked my mind and heart in a prison—a cold, concrete room, damp from the tears I cried. I was in solitary confinement—alone with no one to talk to or be with. Obsessions, fears, and images of how to attempt suicide visited my mind.

I had no place to go. I rode my bike miles, fantasizing what it would be like to be someone else, pedaling past houses, imagining happy, loving families inside. After miles and miles, I became tired and weak. It became harder and harder to pedal. The smell of ammonia filled the air. It was real strange. The smell was so strong, it gave me a headache. My stomach growled and cramped. Hunger pain strongly struck. Logically, I knew I needed food. I needed to eat. I tried to sort out the reason for my weird exhaustion: The diet coke and piece of bubble gum I had consumed that day must not have been enough. But why not? Who really knew if the liquid in the Diet Coke was calorie free? And, what about the bubble gum? It contained sugar. Sugar contains calories! As I looked down at my legs, all I could see was fat. So I continued pedaling. Now I had to burn the fat off my legs.

Finally no matter how hard I tried, I couldn't keep pedaling. I felt hopeless and began to cry.

Once I started, I couldn't stop. I cried for so many reasons. The pain that ached so much my body hurt. The pain that ached so much my heart hurt. I felt scared, sad, helpless, angry, and weak. For what seemed like the hundredth time that week, I wanted to disappear. I no longer wanted to live. I couldn't understand the pain I felt inside. I wanted to get rid of that agony. I thought dying was the only way to lose the pain.

After my tearful attempt to run away failed I attempted suicide many times. The slashing of my wrists, opening of the car door on the highway, holding my breath, knocking my head against the floor or wall, all gave me exactly what I did not want—help. After months of suicide attempts, arguments, isolation, crying spells, and a more than forty-pound weight loss, I was admitted to a psychiatric hospital about forty miles from home. The other patients were alcoholics, drug addicts, and schizophrenics. I tried to fight my way out the doors.

Then, I broke down and gave in. I didn't care what happened to me anymore. I didn't even feel alive. I was no longer living. I was only existing. Everything I did was mechanical. I couldn't feel any feelings.

After two months I returned home. I was just under five feet, six inches and weighed 76 pounds. My hair was falling out and my skin was dry and flaky. People stared at me. Some said I looked like a victim of a concentration camp. I took these comments as compliments. I thought these people were jealous of my body, envied me for how much weight I had lost. Their comments reassured me—confirmed that I was doing a good job restricting my calories. I was successful.

Not long after, I was admitted to a medical hospital. My heart rate went down to 28 beats per minute. My body was constantly shivering from being cold. I had calories pumping into me twenty-four hours a day through a tube that went up my nose, down my throat, and into my stomach. I felt controlled—controlled by people I did not know. They strapped me to the bed and inserted the tubes. These strangers forced my greatest fear upon me. They forced me to gain weight.

A little over two months after I was admitted, I was discharged. I planned never to be admitted again. But I was.

Another four times I found myself lying in a bed with tubes pumping nutrition into me. I was also admitted to several other psychiatric hospitals. When I wasn't hospitalized, I was placed in foster homes.

It's been a few years since I lived at home. At this time, I am living in a hospital for women who suffer from eating disorders and survival issues. I look at life differently now. I am able to have goals and I strive to reach my goals. Yes. I still have struggles. I have difficulty facing the fact that I actually eat more than three meals a day. I have to sacrifice things I want—things like living with my family—in order to recover from my anorexia and depression. Recovery is the hardest challenge I've ever had—the hardest thing I've ever had to do. Recovery is a choice. This choice is hard, but I don't want to exist in hell, like I did before. I want to live.

## LIGHTER THAN AIR
*By Christi Marie O'Donnell, 16, from a small town in the Northeast*

I wander,
Bewildered,
Through this maze of flesh and tears
And wonder why they cry
At your happiness.
You deserve better.
A party
(no cake or ice cream)
In your honor.
We should celebrate!
Your battles won.
March 20, 1980–
November 10, 1997
17 years old
Where are the real numbers?
124

118
113
107
103
98
They should be there, too.
After all, those were your life.
I look at myself,
Seething with envy at
Your achievement,
Gliding on your golden wings,
You're finally lighter than air.

# Self-Inflicted Wounds

≋

As I did everyday for three months, I came home from high school and headed for my mailbox, hoping to collect more contributions to *Ophelia Speaks*. One day I retrieved a particularly thick envelope, packed with poems. Settling in to read Joisyphene Poe's work, I came to these sentences:

> Geez, I was skinny. I hid it well though,
> didn't I? No one knew.
> Band-Aids are made flesh tone. How
> convenient!
> I had a hollow teddy bear, full of
> bandages and razors and pills, hid well . . .

I exhaled until my chest was concave. Her words frightened me. They paralyzed me, throwing me into confusion. I, too, still sleep with my teddy bear. But Joisyphene's reality was one I had never envisioned. How can I possibly speak about self-mutilation? I can't pretend to comprehend. But these girls certainly don't need an interpreter.

I received fewer than ten contributions to *Ophelia Speaks* admitting to self-mutilation. But all had a common characteristic: They were vividly and captivatingly written by intelligent, self-reflective girls. Their thoughtfulness and insight made each piece even more disturbing.

In the first, *On Edge*, Sarah tells her darkest, most hidden secret—her frightening fascination with the act of taking a razor-sharp blade to own body. She fights the forbidden attraction, knowing consummating the act can only lead to self-destruction. In a cover letter to me, she confessed that she had never shared this awful moment of unwanted insight with anyone.

In *A Question for Peter*, the anonymous writer reacts to a friend's scars. But she has her own self-inflicted lacerations and her own story. With transparently poetic words, she describes her motivation to wound herself—the loathing of her body, the rebellion against social expectation, the power of physical control.

In the next poem, *Suicide*, Joisyphene Poe opens the way to a more vulnerable and repentant place. She brings us behind the closed door of her shower, exposing how her depressed mind once straddled the space between self-mutilation and suicide. In an accompanying note, she wrote: "I never could figure out why I started cutting myself, but the experience became quite addictive. I swear it's worse than nicotine. . . . Though I am, fortunately, healed now, the memories will never be forgotten and the scars will never disappear."

Joisyphene shared much in common with the author of the next poem, *Insomnia*. Both saw their wounds as evidence of self-destructive despair. Both wished to warn others against physical self-destruction. For *Insomnia's* writer, the decision to have her work included in *Ophelia Speaks* was burdensome. Her contribution also came with a letter:

Dear Sara,

I just want you to know how hard it is for me to write this. I am such a private person that this feels like nudity, you know. But I want other girls to know they aren't alone. I'd like to help others if I can.

I realize that some of my language may be strong, and my writing rather juvenile. However, this diary entry is preserved exactly as it appeared in my journal two years ago. It was written right after the first time I'd gotten caught with self-inflicted wounds. I was almost locked away. Things like that just didn't happen in my affluent, pretty little town. It was all very hush-hush. And that secrecy made me worse, like a skeleton in the family closet.

I regret the actions. But the terrible mistakes I've made have helped shape me into who I am today. I am strong with goals and a future. And I want so many things from life, a life that I almost, very foolishly, threw away.

I know my story will help someone someday . . .

• • •

I'm sure it will.

## ON THE EDGE
*By Sarah, 15, from a city in the West*

I want to. I know it. It glistens. The blade sharp as a razor. I feel it in my mind. I know without question that I want to. This desire simultaneously thrills and horrifies me. *What am I thinking? Am I crazy?* I can see the blood flow in my mind. I can see where the incisions would go. *If I do it there, no one will be able to see. It will be my secret.* So tempting. Just cut. Not deep. Not fatal. Just enough to leave a straight, perfect, purple scar.

That day will haunt me for the rest of my life. I had read a story, incredulous that someone could actually cut their own flesh and enjoy it. It horrified me, it turned my stomach. Then came the thought that froze the very marrow in my bones. *It sounded good. Just a little cut. So easy, so simple.* I didn't know exactly why I felt that way, or what could be so wrong with me.

I realized quickly I could not tell anyone. What would they do? What would they say? I'm not that kind of girl. I'm the cheerful one, the happy one, the talented one with everything going for her. So I lock this secret inside my heart, and try to forget it in the black velvet folds of memory.

But it does not work. I must constantly fight the battle. Every time the urge comes back, I am tormented. I know that if I do it once, just once, I may never be able to stop. I pray to God to make me strong, to fight the knife. To fight myself.

"Lindy was sent to the hospital today. You'll never believe it. They say she's been cutting herself with an X-acto knife, apparently for years. All that time, and we never knew. She was generally so happy—a little moody, pensive, but not depressed. We were living under the same roof and we never noticed. I can't believe it."

I can.

# A QUESTION FOR PETER
*By Anonymous, 16, from a small town in the Northeast*

Peter said:
Here are my scars,
not to impress but these pinkish folds of flesh
are not merely desecration of the body,
they are more.
He said: Here is my poetry,
may it trigger you to deal with your own scars.
So I, who suffers from wounds long neglected
and never taken seriously,
gaze at them with a derision
I save for my own foolish theatrics.
Bitter beads of blood
nestle in the shallow white valleys
created by deliberate slashes.
A thin razor ripped from its blue plastic casing
so that I might draw forth this blood
that washes my legs, cleansing them

of the dirt encrusted under my skin.
"Poetry?" What is more poetic
than pain? And after pain:
Desire, Blood, and Shame.
These rivulets of red are my poems.
They slide across my thighs
each a thought expressed in the only way
left to me, now that the words are gone.
There is no better way to say this.
These actions are my excuses.
I am unable to be perfection (thin, intellectual, sexy)
but this—
to slice, cut, mutilate, and hurt—
this is easy.
I said:
These are my scars Peter,
must you subject them to the
brutal scrutiny of words,
or shall you be content in knowing
of their origin?
I am not content.
The tightened lines
crisscross my skin, a raw web of arcane symbols
layered one upon the next—
a mystical bind.
They pull at the smoothness
of youthful skin, marring the soft surface.
I have control of my body.
The seduction of the razor is my only frailty,
the pain of the cut the only passion unsuppressed.
The blade bites deep and hard, readily accepting the shrine
I have offered it without reservation.
They said: Sick.
Such behavior will not be condoned
nor will it be understood.
Would they still speak in such tones

if they knew the power this brings me?
The stinging is no more than
physical weakness
overcome it, you are free.
I learned my lessons well.
I ate from the dishes they placed in front of me.
I listened to the wisdom they had passed
from generation to generation.
I trusted.
They sent me to my slaughter,
to die and be punished
by the only person who really could—
Myself
They knew better than I did.
I could not foresee the endless nights alone
languishing in pity and self-inflicted misery.
My actions are motivated by fear,
like the young girl who lies unmoving
on the bed, paralyzed by the knowledge
there might be worse things than what has already taken place.
Her heart beating so quickly
a tiny hummingbird locked inside her chest,
unable to pause.
How do my scars compare with yours Peter?
Am I dealing with them?
Don't come near me,
Don't try to heal me,
I am all I can be.
These are my scars
Peter.
I am not proud of them,
I do not tell tales to impress,
these are not myths of battles passed,
I have no enemies but myself.
These words are written in blood—
*Do you understand that?*

I will pay a dear price
For their honesty and truth,
So don't begrudge me my moment
of melodramatic freedom.


# SUICIDE
*By Joisyphene Poe, 15, from a small town in the West*

Schick: Silk Effects
Good job. You smiled today!
The day is over for now
School was hell, as usual.
So glad to be home
and awaiting a bath.
I never know just when the timing
will be right.
I'm putting the stopwatch
in someone else's hands.
I'm tired
tired of life.
I pull back the curtain,
step aside, then enter my shrine,
set the temperature too hot,
so hot, it burns my flesh but will
cleanse my soul.
It's looking at me with a smirk.
Argh! I can't say no.
I swear I'm addicted to it (ha ha ha.)
I reach for it then think,
Why? How? Why, why, why?
and then why?
And then come the unwelcome, of course,
the thoughts . . .
the echo of words
that never go away

no matter how hard I wish
"Fuck up . . . I was wrong about you . . ."
Disgrace, disappointment.
"What a screw up you are.
I'm sick of you.
Look what you've done.
See what you've done!
Huh?! *Answer me!*"
And then I'm crying
and I can't stop now.
Too late now.
Then I fall, slip to the tile
and big black spots
block my vision
I feel so sick, so so sick.
I lean forward and throw up
and in a while I get up and think,
That damn timer!
When is it ever going to go off!?
Loud pounding . . .
God, that's loud!
My heart?
Oh, it's the door too.
Someone's pounding for me to get out.
But I'm rocking
I gotta stop,
but I can't.
Red is everywhere.
That's all from me?
What will Mom think?
I better start cleaning up.
Doesn't Dad always say
to do chores right when I get home?!
He'd be proud
actually no, I take that back,
he wouldn't.

I fumble for Band-Aids.
I hope no one sees my eyes.
Well, chores done.
Tomorrow is another day,
another day in hell
another
fake . . .
cheap . . .
smile for tomorrow.


# INSOMNIA—A JOURNAL ENTRY
*By Anonymous, 15, from a suburb in the Northeast*

Staring at the seeping blood I become transfixed.
The flash of silver back and forth is hypnotizing.
It becomes the center of my consciousness, my soul.
And it makes me ashamed—
I don't know why I do it,
Embrace the pain, but I do know, on a different level.
It doesn't hurt like my head, my heart,
But it is an outlet—
Expression
It's so hard to hide
I do it to parts of me that no one sees, but run out of space.
It's almost summer, you see.
Right now all I want is to tear my flesh.
Purge, for a while, overwhelming feelings.
The need to talk is so fucking *strong*,
But there is no one left to listen.
No one who knows and shares.
I thought I was okay again, but
What do the doctors know?
The diagnosis of a goddamn textbook.
It doesn't help that I won't talk to him, but
He is an asshole.

Cardboard, fake plastic smile and nod.
I take pleasure in confusing him.
I can just feel it now, sliding back, into
familiar waters, sliding back, into
hated and loved territory.
Deeper and deeper.
I feel like shit, but it is so familiar.
It's almost like it's all I ever knew anyway.
No one will look for me, they all just
Disappear
I am so bottled up I feel as if to
Explode
would be disappointing.
And escape holes are so hard to
Make.
I don't want to die.
I want to purge.
I want to sleep at night, where nightmares
can be woken from.
I am not crazy.

# Intoxication

≋

In eighth grade Brooke, Matt, and I sat knee to knee in a circle. Brooke's overgrown backyard surrounded us. Matt pulled out a joint from his Marlboro box. Around the same time, Brooke and I bonded with another pair of best friends. We started swindling sips of wine from opened bottles in our parents' fridges. Not long after we graduated to stealing bottles of cognac and wine from Brooke's cellar. Our weekend sleep-overs became dowsed in alcohol. Our parents never guessed our little group was cemented with clandestine drinking. After all, we were the good kids—smart girls with the good grades and sweet smiles.

"Partying," with alcohol and marijuana, often feels like an adolescent rite of acceptance. Lauren Alysia Norkus wrote about initiating younger girls into the partying culture during an intoxicated birthday celebration.

"Where's your sister? I want her to smoke pot with me." Sarah laughed and pointed down the hallway. I invited her to join me, but she told me she needed to supervise the keg set-up. Wandering down the hall, humming Led Zeppelin, I stopped in Sarah's room to get the bowl Luke gave to me as an early birthday present. Taking it out of the tattered newspaper, I was reminded of summer. "Crazy good time." I said to myself out loud, as I continued down the hall. I opened the door to a thick cloud of smoke and found thirteen-year-old Carrie and two of her friends scattered around the room, looking shy. "Hey guys, mind puffing down with one of the birthday girls?" They simultaneously shook their heads and I began to recognize the influence and power of being an older kid.

Like these girls, my own experimentation started early, but was soon tainted.

New year's eve in ninth grade: Amid the smell of ten girls' sloppy drunkenness, Maya's pale blue face, purple lips, glazed eyes, shivering body, rested on my lap. I whispered into her ear to keep her awake. Her slurred words quietly asked me for two things: not to tell her parents, and not to let her die. With all our friends looking silently on, I prayed for her breath to remain steady. I stayed up all night watching her chest rhythmically rise and fall. The next day she thanked me for saving her life. "Don't be silly," I told her. My dismissive words didn't mask what we both knew: Under different circumstances, alcohol poisoning may have killed her.

Inexperienced girls, innocently looking for a "good time" can unexpectedly find themselves in danger. Errica Erikson wrote from a small town in the Northwest. Gathered with friends around a campfire, she reluctantly began drinking:

We drank one beer, then a few more, soon I was stumbling around looking for Jessica.

"What time is it?" I asked her when I saw her getting warm by the fire.

"Eleven-fifty, why?" she said in a slurred voice.

"We have to be home by twelve!" I cried with wide eyes.

The two of us then stumbled toward her car and drove away from the music and noise.

"Be careful, but try to hurry!" I said.

The road had a lot of turns and corners on it. As soon as it became straight, the car began to pick up speed. I closed my eyes because everything was becoming blurry and hard to see.

All of a sudden I felt myself flying through the air. Jessica screamed and my eyes shot open. We were in the air, then the car rolled, stopping only because it hit a fence post. Our heads hit the windshield so hard, we were knocked out.

I sat there in the dark, blood running down my face. I reached over and shook Jessica.

"Jessica wake up!" I cried. "Wake up! Please, Jessica!" I shook her so hard, yet she made no response. "Jessica!" I cried again in desperation. Moments passed, then she groaned.

Errica vowed to stay away from alcohol.

My friends reacted differently. None of us forgot the night Maya poisoned herself, but none of us sobered up entirely. Gaining respect for the destructive power of alcohol didn't destroy our desire to party. Intoxication and friends were too inextricably linked. With our entrance into high school, we also entered the world of casual partying, casual drinking, casual drug use. We were typical: We drank at parties, smoked pot on weekends. Sometimes other drugs got mixed up in our lives. I tripped on LSD the night after I saw *Romeo and Juliet* . One of my best friends fell in love with Ecstasy our senior year. I do not glorify the drugs that we did; our experiences were mixed. Intoxication was sometimes fun, sometimes awful, often more dangerous than we understood.

But I never did cocaine or heroin. When I was in junior high school, the brother of a classmate died from a heroin overdose. In that same year, one of my sister's friends died after snorting heroin. The autopsy showed it was alcohol, not heroin that killed him. Regardless, white powders scared me. Besides, those drugs never became an emblem of admission to my social group. Some acquaintances did do coke at their graduation party, but it wasn't for me.

The three contributions to this chapter do not focus on simplistic or moralistic attitudes. These three exceptionally talented writers bring us into their substance-induced realities and reflect on the reverberations in their lives. The first contribution, *Simple*, is a poetically written timeline of drug-saturated experiences. Margaret L. Roberts freeze-frames a succession of moments, capturing ecstatic, nightmarish, frightening, dangerous, and peaceful scenes. In this piece, reality and imagination merge. All sense of solid footing melts. Next, in *Spun Like a Turntable*, Liz Fullerton-Dummit transports us to Mexico where the allure of friends and drugs ruptures her already frayed ties to her mother.

Finally, in her piece *Aan Het Einde Gevangenis: For Myself,* Corrie Zweedyk chooses each word with artful deliberation. Translated from Dutch, the title means *Desperate Prison.* When I first read Corrie's work, I felt I had been given the privilege of introducing the world to a rare talent. In scene after scene, Corrie transports the reader into the world she occupied before the birth of her baby. Her life consisted of an unhealthy party—drugs, alcohol, sex, and abuse. She demonstrates how her son has changed her; how giving birth has given her a future. Corrie's experience may look and feel unusual, but it's not. I received other contributions from girls who left behind substance abuse when they became young mothers.

My selections in this chapter represent a truthful perspective. Here, the voices of adolescent experiences speak without the deterrent of disappointed adults.

## SIMPLE
*By Margaret L. Roberts, 17, from a small town in the Northeast*

I sit back and let the rolled paper touch my moistened lips. I inhale and pull away. The gently rolling clouds seem as real as they are. The colors are bleeding into each other as I sit in the car, which is parked on a hill in a graveyard somewhere that I forgot how to get to. The feelings are swarming and surrounding me.

I step out onto the porch and look at the leaves. Millions of them, all stemming from the same seed. The clouds are still there, like running ink they drip into one another.

I sit down and look into the mirror. I stare at the white powder that controls my every move. Inhale and then the numbness. I lay down on the bed to enjoy the tingle, and then the taste comes.

A flash, millions of people drinking the white man's poison, dancing around a handmade fire. The blood, and then the rush of the police. Up it goes, then me out the window. We run. Moments later, I'm leaning over a fence, my insides pouring out through my mouth. As I lay completely immobile, except for the convulsions, death rushes in front of my eyes.

As we drive I exhale and the smoke rings float away. I close my eyes and the music plays. The desert and the sage. The absolute insanity is accepted and seems perfectly normal. And I wonder . . . why?

I watch the man die of an incurable disease, and then the casket that slowly rolls down the aisle. I listen to the words spoken and the guns that ring cut into the night. What's it like? Curiosity kills.

The feeling of being dirty overwhelms me as I lie here. I wonder exactly what lays behind the eyes of this stranger lying next to me. All that is left is regret.

In my dream, I'm alone. All by myself in a dark room with white walls. There's a screen and on that screen a road, my road. A road of choices, that lead to a bell which rings of freedom.

I sit in the sun, sitting on water. I sit on a dock which floats in the water. The moon's reflection lights up my face and once again I bring the rolled paper to my moistened lips. And I run, I run like the rivers, run like the oceans, and like my blood, I run. From what, I do not know, but I do know that I'm scared. Scared of something so big that I only quiver in it's shadow.

I let myself sink and the calm is soothing. Peacefully, my spirit comes to life. I live in the mountains, up in the forest, alone. Here I was born and here I die. Do not take me for I am pure and that belongs to me. As the sun sets on my page, it rises upon another. Crazy Horse, dancing.

Winter. I walk through the accumulation of snow, and just

keep walking. I find myself standing in an intersection, light's blinking. It's too white.

I sit in the bathroom, alone. People drift in and out. The walls melt and so does my reflection. The flame grows small and the candle burns out. Someone gets shot and just the night before I was with them. Who was watching me? Thanks.

I scream and I cry. He threatens me. "Yes, I'm fucking insane, you made me this way!" Why? I got a phone call and before I even got on the line I knew that it was bad. Grampa's dead.

I turn around and see her running right at me. Quick finger, the flash of a blade and her bloody hair left hanging in my hand. Then me, walking carefully through the shadows.

We're parked in a car that's filled with smoke. The smoke that makes us laugh. Then we open the window and it's gone . . . just like everything else, it's gone. I sit in the park and take off my clothes. I walk around in the grass and it feels good to my naked body.

I climb and I climb. The adventure is a rush. Then we stop, and no one wants to go any higher. I go up, alone. The fire shoots into the sky and babies fall to the ground. I see my reflection in the shop windows as I walk by.

I put the paper on my tongue. The darkness sets in. I watch the lights go zooming by as I stand on the double yellow line. I sit with a stranger playing cards in the middle of the road.

He runs through the fire, poisoned by legal death. I sense danger and so I jump. I do not stop, but when I do I'm pressing up against a tree. I look up just to see someone else jumping.

We drive and I feel like a goddess of the night. There's such class. Remembering that everything I do becomes a memory. Moments of relaxing, sitting in the grass, under the big sky. Sometimes the sun and other times the moon. I look up in the starry sky and see happiness.

The wind whispers a sweet song. The petals fall from the eternal flower and the clouds still drift by. We drive. The sun is out and we are happy. The music describes our journey and this is a good part of my dream.

The independence of the day, beginning to love myself. Being alone is good sometimes, getting lost in a thought or a dream. I look into the flame and in my glare it flicker's. I see men dancing, dancing for joy, for pain, for the loss of love. Dancing for life.

## SPUN LIKE A TURNTABLE
*By Liz Fullerton-Dummit, 16, from a city in the South*

I was restless, annoyed with myself, and bored with what life had to offer. Nestled back into Mexico's crowded streets, I was drawn to the smell of forgotten pieces of food, still smoking on the grill. Then it hit. This was the smell of my childhood. I walked through the market, distracted by the genuine laughter and smiling faces of the plump vending ladies. I caught myself giggling with them. Underneath their laughter, they hid the fear of disappointing their families, arriving home with only the change in their pockets to offer. I was hiding a similar fear of disappointing my family. Only I went home completely empty-handed. My craving for the smells of my childhood diminished. My hunger for freedom was eating at my soul.

My freelancing friend was in town again. When I saw her I held her in my arms like a mother held her newborn. Gently I lightened my grip to look at the woman she had become. Her hair, in tangles, spun themselves into a cocoon around fragments of sand, sand still clinging from her peyote trip in the desert. After she arrived, I spent less time caged in my home and more time wasted with her. We sat on her roof. After I took that first hit, the sun crept behind the shelter of the mountains, being tugged toward the night, and the whole world lightened up just a bit.

The mentality of my parents disgusted me. They were too conventional—the restrictions and the rules, the requirements, the expectations. They didn't understand me. They expected me to finish school, write an epic poem, be the first female president, instigate world peace, cure AIDS, and, at the same time, do my daily chores, smile, and live like a child. Fuck that. In my silent rage, I detached my heart from my parents, and opened my mind to a utopian world, the world of drugs.

Rolled up in its little paper blanket, the joint pressed between my lips and smoked my cares away. It was a gradual progression. At first, only on special occasions. Just when I was celebrating something. Ironically, life became a celebration, twenty-four hours a day, eight days a week. Still, I was adamant that I would only indulge in what nature had to offer—no chemicals.

My boredom became a half-dreamed idea, and my parents were drowning in oblivion. My mother became the enemy. With drugs, I had an escape from her. She was jealous of my confidence and happiness. She was now a child's forgotten favorite toy, and I was the new item on the market.

The clause about nature's gifts? Forgotten. I softly closed the bathroom door and let the shower run to eliminate my mother's suspicion. My eyes skimmed the shelves. My fingers stumbled across a familiar bottle. I slipped it into my pocket. I laid the pill of Valium gently on my tongue, like I was trying not to disturb its slumber, and waited. I was floating. I was mellow. The world was hilarious.

Eventually I started rolling acid, an incredible high. Music had a shape. Everything spiraled for my amusement. I was losing weight, five pounds a week. And sleep didn't fit into my schedule. My mother noticed my mood changes. But she was unaware that my mood corresponded to the drug of choice for that day. My affection for her became a vague, a half-forgotten childhood memory— this my mother knew. The concern in her eyes was genuine, but painful. The concern wasn't for me. It was for the facade she had created in her mind, the kid she yearned for me to be.

My mom resorted to the last sane idea she had about how to save my life. She put me on plane and shipped me to my father. I let my body sink into the seat. Every pore absorbed the pain, until it flooded my soul. My mother had rejected me. My envy for people's freedom had turned into enmity for my mother. The plane's feet scampered down the runway, finally getting the lever-age it needed to step off Mexico's back. And I lost my smile.

The streets in America were cold and sterile compared to the warmth of Mexico's. Every tree was strategically placed. Every sidewalk free of loitering people. Every corner lacking lingering smells. For a week my feet unwillingly walked me up and down the streets of America. Everything was so separate. Not one arm brushed mine with understanding. Not one laugh invited me to sing along.

Finally my mother came to revel in my despair. She trapped her burdens and the world's burdens in her palms and set them on my shoulders. My mother said, "You are worthless, ungrateful, selfish—a bitch. Everything I never wanted in a child. You will never get back to Mexico."

My heart withdrew. My knees pressed themselves against my chest, doing everything they could to protect my heart. My arms wrapped themselves around my knees, in a last attempt to blockade myself. Not a tear welled up in my eyes. My body shook and trem-bled. Screams and wails of sorrow climbed up my neck and choked me at the throat, trying to get out. I never let my mother know, never gave her the satisfaction. Yet, every night I crawled into my bed, cried my eyes to a desperate close, and slid into the comforting and cradling arms of Morpheus. When I caught Dawn rising to her throne, my only wish was to wake up dead in my coffin. I had noth-ing remaining in my left hand, and the right was empty. All around me, my dreams and hopes were desiccating.

It has been two and a half years since I have smelled my child-hood, since I have been swept up into a crowd that stands as close as spoons, since I have found myself giggling with strangers. That was the most devastating summer of my life and the most enlightening. I was repeating my mother's own childhood—turn-ing to drugs for help, for courage, for confidence, for answers, and for the amusement. Not a day goes by that I don't long for Mexico, and try to unravel my parents' disappointment in me. So today, like yesterday, I will wait for my parents to be proud of me.

Every time the phone rings, I hope it's her calling with my invitation home. I depend on the sun to give me my smile, the moon and her shadows to make me mellow, and the stars to get me high. So when I do go back, it will be a trip in itself.

## *Aan Het Einde Gevangenis:* For Myself
*By Corrie Zweedyk, 18, from a suburb in the Midwest*

Two months passed like two years. Time seemed to stand still. Maybe it was the drugs that made it last forever. Maybe my perception was altered by all my emotions. It was winter in my trailer park, but we acted like it was summer. Most people stay inside during the cold winter, but we didn't. The cold made the nights last longer. It wasn't a mild winter; the streets were paved with ice and the lawns were made of snow. We wore shorts and leather jackets. We were high at least five days out of the week.

There was always a party happening somewhere. I was never actually invited, but I always seemed to end up there. If it wasn't at Terry's, it was at mine. If it wasn't mine, it was at some unknown place with people I'd never met before.

*People who I don't know surround me, their muffled voices and the loud music crowd the walls of my head. Their images blur and twist as they dance in front of me. I close my eyes. The constant flash from the strobe light almost causes me to collapse. I lean against the counter and open my eyes.*

Drunken couples maul each other on beer-soaked furniture. Others dance wildly. They jump and slam into each other while swearing and puking. I shake my head and continue to walk through the house.

I step over bodies sprawled across the floor, drowning in their own vomit. As I walk toward the bedroom, the sweet mixture of incense and pot smoke drags me into the cloudy room. I join the circle.

*Hours later, I wake in a large, strange bed with only half my clothes on and a strange guy who smells like beer lying on top of me, while two other couples lie on the floor. In the distance, I hear a clock chime eight o'clock.*

I shove the stranger off me, he crashes to the floor with a loud thud that wakes the couples on the floor.

I attempt to find my clothes. I only find my jeans and one of my shoes. Angrily, I kick the guy for losing my clothes, but he doesn't wake up.

I walk into the bathroom; a boy about my age is asleep with his head in the toilet. I pick him up and lean him over the bathtub where a half-naked girl is sleeping.

I look in the mirror, my eyes are bloodshot and the little makeup still on my face is smeared. Most of my hair has fallen out of its ponytail. I search for a brush to pull it back again. With no luck, I pull the rest out and throw the alcohol-soaked scrunchie away. I look in the mirror again. Dark hickeys cover my neck and shoulders. I turn on the faucet and splash my face with warm water, I feel more human. I sigh and walk out.

Topless, I search the living room for a shirt. Beer and puke stain the white carpet. The stench of the room almost causes me to fall over. I walk over to the window and open it, the light and fresh air disturbs the sleepers.

"Turn off the light, man," someone mumbles, his voice trailing off as I pull on a torn Metallica shirt and stumble out the door.

I walk down the litter-covered streets of my trailer park. On the corner stands a group of twelve-year-olds smoking cigarettes and "talkin' about bangin' and gettin' high." It feels like forever since I last had a bath. I think I took one yesterday, but this dirty feeling covers my body and soul. I want to scrub off my skin—anything to get the dirt off. Reaching my location, I walk toward my friend's house. I knock on the door and Jack answers it. He has a blanket wrapped around him and a girl clings to his arm. He looks me over and invites me in.

"Can I crash here today?"

"Sure. . . . Rough night?" He replies.

I nod and walk toward the back of the trailer, and turn into the bathroom. My face's still dingy from the night before. I look in the mirror. I touch my face. It seems so old. I'm only fourteen. I leave the bathroom and curl up against the refrigerator in the kitchen. I feel sick. Tony hands me a 40-ounce and I drink myself into blackness.

There was time before my partying. A time I never have been able to talk about openly. Nightmares, visions, and memories wouldn't allow me to think back with a clear conscience. I always felt guilty for what happened. I knew in my head I wasn't to blame, but in my heart, I felt differently. Society says I should hate my dad for what he has done to me. I should blame all my problems on what happened. I should be a miserable man-hating wreck. I should be a drug addict and an alcoholic. I should want to end my life. I was all of those things at one time. I blamed him; I hated him, and because of him, I drank heavily and got high. I was suicidal.

I was thirteen when my adoptive dad sexually abused me. I've never been able to call it rape or incest, because it never seemed that way to me. I wasn't like all the other stories of incest I've ever heard. It wasn't like Uncle Jon touching little Sarah where he shouldn't, or putting himself where he shouldn't. It wasn't like that. For me, it was more like the slutty little daughter stole the innocent mother's man. Even though I didn't try to steal him, and I didn't even want it to happen, that's the way I felt. I felt like I was betraying my mother. He wasn't biologically my dad, just legally.

They got married when I was six. As soon as he moved in, he changed all the rules. I could no longer do anything I wanted. My mother was controlled. She went along with anything he said. I wasn't allowed to have friends over after school. I had to go to my grandmother's day care during summer vacation. I couldn't stay home like normal kids. I had to be watched at all times. I wasn't a bad kid. I hardly got in trouble in school before fourth grade. I rebelled heavily against the iron fist of my father. Something inside awakened when he moved in.

By the end of fourth grade, I had stolen my classmates' book fair money, stole several tapes from my best friend, lied, cussed out the teacher, got into several fights, and wrote over one thousand sentences in the office.

My mother sent me to a psychiatric ward in the local hospital for suicidal/homicidal teens. I was barely eight when I went in. Everyone one else was at least fourteen. They asked me why I was committed. I never could tell them why. I didn't even know. During an EEG, they found three "blips" in my brain waves while I was sleeping. They put me on drugs for it. I bounced on and off antidepressants and antianxiety drugs. They controlled my behavior. If I seemed rebellious again, my mom and dad hauled me back into the office and declared the drugs weren't working. I remember being on Lithium once. But there were so many different drugs.

During my "drug-treatment" my dad began touching me. I was about twelve. I don't remember much during that time. I just know that's when it started.

When I was thirteen, in seventh grade, I got my first boyfriend. I was still bouncing on and off pills. The ones I took then made me sensitive to the sun, so I couldn't go out much during the day. I loved him and I wanted to show him how much I loved him. The only problem was I didn't know how. During one of our many talks, I told this to my dad. He said he would allow me to go into my room with Terry with the door closed, if I did him a favor. I knew what that meant. In fact, I eventually started to use it for my benefit. If I wanted a friend over, I did him a favor. If I wanted a CD, I did him a favor. If I wanted something all I had to do was tell him. "I'll do a favor, for a favor."

All those favors ended one day, when I went to my drug doctor. That day my mom's friend drove me, because my mom was working and dad had another appointment. After the meeting with the drug doctor, I broke down in the car and told my mom's friend. She and I set it up so I could tell mom. I thought my mom would yell at me and kick me out. I thought she'd think it was my fault. Like I said, I always thought I was betraying her trust.

The next morning my mom's friend called the cops and I wasn't supposed to be around my dad. I had to move out, into my grandparents' house for several months. I started using caffeine pills and smoking cigarettes.

After he went to prison the thought that I betrayed my mother's trust continued. I turned to drugs and alcohol to protect myself from my memories and the truth. I couldn't take caffeine pills because of an accidental overdose that left my stomach in ruins. At the end of eighth grade, I started using speed and rolling powdered drugs in cigarettes. By ninth grade, I was using pot and drinking alcohol. Once in awhile I got pot laced with something, but for the most part my experimenting stopped there. I continued to use pot and drink, increasing the doses. I hung out constantly with a group of friends who always seemed to have some form of drug on them. There were nine of us, but only two of them knew what really happened between me and my dad.

It was winter in my trailer park. The cold rattled throughout the old trailers. The warmer, newer ones seemed so friendly. Loving families dwelled inside. The love inside radiated to the outside. The old trailers stood drunkenly on the street; they swayed with the wind, and creaked and moaned. Most of us were only freshmen; the rest of us had dropped out.

February passed very slowly. The winter seemed to drag on and on. I enjoyed the late night parties and drug hunts. I loved to be with my friends. I loved the feeling of being high.

My twenty-one-year-old boyfriend, Tom, would stay overnight at my house and we would sleep in the same bed like we were married. I cooked for him, I washed his clothes, and I had sex with him anytime he asked. I loved being with him because he made me feel special. He told me he loved me; he hardly acted like it. At times he disappeared for weeks at a time, worrying me to death, but he would always come back. One of the times he was gone, I cheated on him with two different guys because I was told he had broken up with me and he was cheating on me. I loved him, but there was no trust. I had sex more times than I could count; all of it unprotected. When I missed a period, I knew. I didn't need a test to tell me. Abortion wasn't an option and neither was adoption. I would keep the baby.

I found out I was pregnant around the end of March, two days after Tom and I broke up. My mother cried in the doctor's room as the pregnancy test showed a plus sign. I was unsure of whose baby I was carrying. I had slept with the two other guys and Tom during the time the doctors figured the baby was conceived. When I told Tom, he proposed to me in front of my mother. After he left that night, I didn't see him for days. No one knew where he was.

About a week later there was a knock at my door. I opened the door and there stood Tom and his friend, Richard. They pushed their way into my house. Tom smelled of beer and Vodka. He had a weird look in his eye. He told Richard to sit down, he'd only be a minute. Then he pushed me into my bedroom, and onto the bed, while Richard sat out on the couch in the living room. He forced my hands back and unbuttoned my jeans. I told him no, but he acted as if he didn't hear me and continued to strip my pants off. I lay still (I didn't want anything to happen to my baby) and let him. . . .

He left right after he was done. I closed the door and locked it, then ran to my bed and cried. I cried for about a half-hour and then took a shower before my mom came home from work. I felt dirty.

I told my mom a week later. She pressed charges.

The cops finally caught Tom three months later and put him in the county jail. After they had picked up Tom and taken him to jail, a large woman, who claimed to be his fiancée, a large black man, and another large woman knocked at my door. When I opened it they told me the cops had come to get Tom. They wanted to know why. I blew them off and shut the door. Then rumors about Tom sending someone to kill my mother and me flooded the trailer park. From then on, I feared for my mother's and my life. I wouldn't leave the house without my mother. I hated to be home alone, out of fear one of Tom's buds would come over and try to hurt me. I lived in fear. My sleep was filled with nightmares of my death. During the day, I watched my back and carried a knife.

When my pregnancy finally fully sunk in, I stopped drinking and using. Stopping was very hard at first. Many times I failed and took a hit off a joint. But after the fifth month, I was clean and sober. All my friends seemed to disappear one by one. They stopped coming around my house, and eventually stopped talking to me. Since I no longer partied, they no longer needed me.

In December my son, Matthew, was born. I knew he was Tom's child. Matthew has Tom's eyes. Matthew is tall and skinny just like Tom. There is no doubt in my mind, Tom is the father. I never put Tom's name on the birth certificate. I didn't want him to see my baby. I was afraid he or his parents would try to take Matthew from me. I was always afraid my using would have hurt him or caused him to be handicapped in some way, but Matthew is a very smart and athletic child.

Days after Matthew was born, Tom was sentenced and sent to prison. Still, the rumors about hostilities flew around the park. I was no longer as afraid of death, but more afraid one of Tom's friends would come and steal my son. I boarded up his bedroom window and put bars in mine. I always kept the door locked and lived in constant fear of someday finding Matthew gone.

I am eighteen now. In a week I will graduate high school. I have a part-time job and I just finished a college English class to start off my college education. Matthew is two and a half. He has never met his dad, but he has talked to him on the phone twice. Tom receives every picture I have ever taken of Matthew. He can see what his son looks like. Tom's name is still not on the birth certificate. I don't know if it ever will be. I suppose if Tom fights to get it on, it will.

I have fully forgiven my dad for what he has done. I visit him on a regular basis. He went before the parole board and we are waiting for the decision. If he is paroled I will have to move out of my mother's house because my dad is not allowed to live with a minor. I am happy to move and start my new life. I know it won't be easy, but I know I'll have help from my mom and dad.

Despite all that has happened to me, I have hope for my future. I don't blame my problems on what happened. I take responsibility for my actions. I look forward to having my own place. I look forward to the beginning of my adult life. I know it's hard for most girls to deal with a situation like this, but, for sanity, for a chance at life, it has to be dealt with.

# Rape and Sexual Abuse

As I neared the end of editing *Ophelia Speaks*, I entered college. During freshman orientation I was asked, "Would you use the escort service on campus?"

I looked at my feet, then again at my questioner. I knew the right answer, but instead I was honest, "Probably not."

I watched her smother disgust at my reply, as she retorted, "Give me one good reason why not."

I sighed, "I don't want to recognize the possibility of my being raped at my new home. If I call the escort service, I'm admitting to myself I can't be safe here walking alone. I shouldn't have to think, 'I'm not safe.' Maybe it's stupid, but I don't want to think that."

A week later there was an attempted gang-rape outside my dorm.

I shouldn't have to fear shadows. Now, I do.

I have never been raped or sexually abused. Yet, the mere existence of sexual violence shapes me. I am one of the lucky ones. I have only had to fear shadows. Other girls, some who wrote to me, have suffered real sexual violence and vicious assaults. I'm hopeful my fear of what could be in no way belittles the actual experiences of survivors of sexual abuse and rape. I know I do not, cannot, represent their reality. But, I am fortunate to be allowed to bring their truth to you—to break down the loneliness of other girls who share their experience, and to increase the understanding of those of us who haven't.

This dark chapter begins with *Dolls Fell*, the story of how an ordinary sleep-over turned into a disturbing look at incest. In this true story–like piece, the anonymous writer shows us that the separation between those who live in innocence and those who live in perversion is a thin, transparent veil.

In the second contribution, a fourteen-year-old remembers how her virginity was stripped from her. This anonymous writer faces her pain, questions herself, and wishes, above all else, to turn back time. In a letter she told me: "I didn't write *If I Could Turn Back Time* for anything specific, but to get it on paper, instead of always in my head. . . . It's hard to forget about it, because it's something I thought would never happen to me."

Next, you will read the heart-wrenchingly graphic description of a rape. Naomi, the fifteen-year-old victim, made the pain of being crushed under the abusive weight of unsuspecting attraction more real to me. She has changed my gut-understanding of date-rape forever.

The final two pieces bring you to the site of most rapes—the family. For every submission I received about sexual violence outside the family, I received five describing sexual abuse inside the home. Girls wrote about being abused by their fathers, step-fathers, older brothers, uncles, and family friends. They described assaults and threats and bribes beginning in childhood. For some, the abusers had come and gone without reprimand or punishment. Others had brought the perpetrators to justice. All wrote as a path to healing themselves. They talked about seeing the reality of their past and walking on with strength. Perhaps above all, most wanted to reach out to other victims with stories that pierce through the loneliness of incest. In *Dark Corners* and *A Childhood Lost* you will hear the voices of so many more. These brave and compassionate girls thanked me for listening, for providing an opportunity for them to voice their trauma of betrayal. I thank them for their honesty, openness, and above all, their courage.

# FALLING DOLLS
*By Anonymous, 16, from a rural area in the Midwest*

Dolls fell from the closet. Out in the open, she admitted to playing with dolls. She didn't giggle in embarrassment or seem aware. No one in our class at school played with dolls. She set up a beauty parlor and lovingly smoothed yesterday's tangles.

"Stand here." She ran from the hall. Only a box hung on the white walls. I felt naked standing in the draft of open doors. Bells played up and down in a strange melody. She had rung the doorbell.

Staying up past midnight, we wiggled under the covers, protected by a unicorn overhead. Rolling on her side, hot breath in my face. "Have you ever had sex?"

"*No.*" I was only twelve.

"I have. But we can't talk about it. You wouldn't understand what happens deep, deep inside."

"Liar."

"No, see I can talk about it with Prudence. We both had sex."

"She did not."

"She even got pregnant, but she didn't know until she went to the bathroom. She thought she pooped, but it was a funny wrinkled-up half baby."

Horrid drowned things swirled in my mind with the sound of flushing toilets. Her story went on. I felt as if I were being smothered.

"My brother, we did it together. He put in a tape and we did what they did. That's all I can tell you. You wouldn't understand the rest—what happens deep, deep inside."

She rolled over. I lay there gasping, sucking in the new air that came down.

She handed me the two ugliest dolls, since I had laughed at them.

# If Only I Could Turn Back Time
*By Anonymous, 14, from a rural town in the South*

Trying to scream or hit, knowing you can't because he is stronger. But still you struggle. Crying inside and out because he's hurting you, and he's taking something away from you that can only be taken once! Deciding whether or not to tell anyone, because you feel as if it's all your fault. Asking yourself, Did I give him all the wrong impressions? You know if somebody finds out about it, you'll feel embarrassed and ashamed. Sometimes you cry yourself to sleep, because all you can see is his face. You feel weighed down, because his heavy body is on top of yours. In the end, you try to forget about it. But then, you remember that you're all by yourself, and no one can help you but you. You think to yourself, Is he doing this to someone else? Is someone going through the same pain and suffering that you are? Then you blame yourself again, because you could have done something about it. You know you have to face this pain, because no one else can do it for you, and you know you'll carry this memory with you forever. Thinking, If only I could turn back time.

# Crushed Under His Weight
*By Naomi, 15, from a small town in the Northeast*

Crushed under his heavy weight, my neck arched, my face suffocating. I feel him drive into me. The car is too warm. I feel like I am vulnerable and alone. He drives himself into me, thrusting into a person he doesn't know, doesn't care to know. I feel like dying in his numb arms. His mind cannot say my name. I am a body, a vehicle for his sick pleasure. I push and plead, begging him to stop his invasion. Pushing, I extricate myself from his folds and crevices with pain. He grabs for my naked body as I pull on his unbuttoned shirt and curl up in the front seat. The windows are filled with the expulsions of my silently screaming breath. He sits up, gets dressed, and we drive. The quiet and rural darkness surrounds my pounding head and makes me feel a little more safe. He never says a word, just looks ahead with silent anger. The blackened forest, hidden behind my sullen heart, shelters me from his piercing gaze. I want to scream out, I'm sorry, I'm sorry, but I am afraid. His silence is plain and seething with disgust. His quietness hurts me and smashes the picture perfect image I built of him, like a shrine inside my mind. God, I hate my sweet surrenders, my silent accepting ways. I am the stupidest person I know. I close my eyes, press my sweating forehead against the cool, windswept pane of glass and pretend that I can sleep.

## DARK CORNERS
*By Anonymous, 16, from a suburb in the Midwest*

The black corners of my bedroom meant fear to me when I was
    a girl lying in my bed
I never knew what could be there
I ought to have been more concerned with the dark corners of
    my mind
where I did not want to venture for fear of what lurked in the
    shadows
In my room I would have found a mere pile of clothes stacked
    after laundry
In my mind I would have felt the shadows touch over my body,
his hands rubbing back and forth on my stomach
while I lay pretending to sleep and that nothing was there
while he slipped into my panties and made me forever a child
    lost,
a girl stolen,
body numb with unforgiveness and shame
Waking to fingers groping this strange and new me with curves
    and small breasts
I would have felt the darkness leap onto me with a deafening
    silence

He coveted me but I was silent.
I made a resolution to forget because I felt helpless
like a hollow empty shell
After tears in a pillow not mine I wanted to die
and melt into the water to be clean
make new dreams
If I had looked into the corners of my mind,
memory would have realized that he was as real as
the man posing as the clean and dirty clothes stacked together
forcing me into tight breathing
Always a man
and always will I be a little girl
But the darkness frightened me for years and I still sleep with a
     light on for comfort
I am afraid of the sinister silhouettes that cause me to be
     reminded
Because I know them they have taken part of me
by pouring over my body in the night
I have known them all my life
and now I will always wonder what lurks
I will never lock things back in the corners in the shadows
fearing the danger of memory.

## A Childhood Lost
*By Beth Anthany, 17, from a small town in the Midwest*

Sometimes I wonder why some people have it better than I do.
But then again you never really know someone. You look at me
and see a happy, energetic seventeen year old. But behind my
mask reveals my secret scars.

Many people who have divorced parents have a hard time
coping with it, as I did. I just happened to choose the wrong
paths. Or the wrong paths were chosen for me.

Since I was about seven years old, I have been forced against
my will to have sex three times, and made to do other unwanted

sexual acts upon older men. Most of them I thought I knew. Since it had been happening for most of my life, I thought it was right and was supposed to happen. So I stopped fighting and told no one of my secrets.

I don't remember much about the first two rapes. I don't remember pain. I don't remember the sound, and I don't remember the voices. I can only close my eyes now and see their faces towering above mine. Those memories are something I can never erase. One of the rapists, I have only seen once since the incident; I remember the smile he gave me when he was through. The other, I see all the time. He's my brother.

It used to be hard to admit to people about the incest that took place so long ago, but I was only seven, and he was twelve. After eight years we got together and talked about the situation. He apologizes profusely for his actions, but like I said—I don't remember much. Sometimes I try not to think of him as one of my rapists. All I have are small memories, and he is my brother. You only see those kind of things on soap operas.

Through the years, the abuse continued on and off. On many occasions, I went to my own little world in the back of my head, convinced that the pain I was feeling and what was happening was right. After the pain and remorse built up, I stopped fighting. Then my parents divorced and I was alone. I had no one.

Now that my dad was gone, I would see my mother crying a lot. Sometimes looking over old pictures. Sometimes listening to a sad song. I remember on one occasion, my mother coming upstairs to my bedroom. She was crying pretty hard. She began to spank us telling us we needed to get the pain out; that we needed to cry. I cried for the simple fact that my mother was scaring me. I didn't feel the spanking, only the fear.

Years moved on and I grew older. Then one cold winter day, it happened again . . . and I remember everything. I closed my eyes so tight trying to ignore the excruciating pain. And those cold, cold eyes that burned into mine so deeply with anger and power. Sometimes I can be sitting in school, or in a public place, and I will smell something, or see someone, and it will all come back to me. The pain, the voice, the words he said to me when he was through: "Don't tell anyone about this because I could get into big trouble."

I was eleven by then. I never thought about the chances of getting pregnant or transmitting a disease. I was placed in foster care months after the incident. When the time came, I was called to testify against him and the others. I was deathly afraid. God was on my side though, and I did not have to be present in the courtroom. It was hard to go back and recall all the information for the paperwork. To remember all the details, all the words said. It made me realize what was really done to me. It was not my fault; it was forced upon me. Now I can truly say I was abused, and not feel responsible.

I have seen at least three of my abusers since the incidents. Some intimidate me and scare me, but others I have the will to stand up to. I've worked through everything for a few years, attempting to put it all in my past. There is always a time you will remember. Or, you will fear it all at a certain moment. But you have to learn to fight it. Otherwise you let yourself lose and they will know that they won.

# PART
## TWO

# FAMILY

# MATTERS

≋

# Mothers

New England humidity can be unbearable sometimes. That August afternoon it flooded through the open windows in my mom's car. The heat brought out the smell of her car—a combination of a broken bottle of sesame seed oil and the warm scent of her moisturizers. I leaned sideways against the door of the car, my elbow poking out the window, and looked toward the train platform.

My mom put her hands under her Capri-panted legs. "You don't have to sit here with me, Sweetie. You can wait for the train by yourself. I know you're all grown up," she told me.

I smiled. Mom's small frame and self-conscious words were very cute. Instead of rejecting her company, I asked hopefully, "Will you come wait with me?"

"You want *me* to come wait for the train with you?" She seemed confused by my request. "But, people might see us out there," she said, pointing toward the train platform, in direct view of nearby Main Street.

"Mommmmm," I exclaimed, varying my intonation to depict my intent. "You think I'm still in sixth grade. I'm not afraid to be seen with my mother anymore." I laughed. "I got over that when I was like twelve."

"I know. I just forget sometimes," she sighed. "You have to bear with your forgetful mother."

I put my hand on the car door handle, remembering how I had made her so insecure. One night in seventh grade, she whisper-yelled at me, "Why do you act so mean to me? Is it just to impress your friends?" I had squirmed, tightening every muscle in my body. Offended by her accusation, I had vehemently denied acting like a brat to seem cool. For a few years, we had a lot of similar arguments. I'm still not a perfect daughter, but our relationship has improved immensely—being in public with Mom is no longer painful.

So, I pushed open the door, unpeeled my legs from the plastic seats, and gathered my things. I walked to the train station with Mom's arm affectionately encircling my hip. My platform sandals made me four inches taller than her. She looked up at me and said, "I love you, Sweetheart."

"I love you, too, Mama."

Looking down at her made her appear even smaller than usual. It was strange to see my mom that way. In my mind's eye, she still towers over me.

I've looked up to my mom, unbeknownst to her, for years. My mom is my first and most important female role model. That fact compounds the complexity of our relationship immensely. Most of her quirks—the ones I roll my eyes at—are the very things I don't like in myself or fear I will develop. Sometimes she knows me too well. Sometimes she doesn't understand me at all. She always loves me unconditionally.

My mail reflected this complexity. Negative submissions about mothers outnumbered positive contributions four to one.

Still, four girls wrote glowing accounts describing their love and respect for their mother. Three of these girls admired how courageously and caringly their mother faced the emotional and financial hardships of single parenting. Fifteen-year-old Emma Kelle Martinez described a memorable Christmas from when she was younger:

A couple of days before Christmas, my mom called me upstairs. I walked into the room and laid down beside her on the bed. She had my Christmas list in her hand and a tear in her eye. She began to tell me that Christmas this year wasn't going to be the same. By now she was crying and I was trying to comfort her. She then proceeded to tell me that Santa Claus wasn't real and that I wouldn't see as many presents under the tree, because we didn't have nearly as much money as we used to have. My mom wanted to reassure me that receiving fewer gifts didn't mean I was a bad girl. She was crying heavily and we sat for awhile hugging each other.

Now I can completely understand her feelings. . . . It broke my mother's heart to tell me, a little third grader (who had a pretty good idea Santa Claus wasn't real anyway), that even though I would have less presents to open I was still a good girl. . . . That Christmas is one of many memories that I have looked back on and thought to myself, Wow. How can one person be so giving, so strong, so special?

The contributions contained in this chapter represent more complicated emotions, more perplexing mother/daughter relationships.

In the first, a speech-like piece titled *A Message to Mother*, Carly Sanko tells her mother what she needs from her. Confronting her mother with her conflicting desires for nurturing and for independence, she verbalizes the feelings of many adolescent girls.

In the second contribution, *Leaving Mom*, another fifteen year old, who wished to maintain her anonymity, describes the friction erupting between mothers and daughters born to different ideals.

Finally, in *Overcoming Life's Obstacles*, Melissa Laliberte tells of a childhood wrought with neglect. She forgives her troubled mother, and feels grateful to her uncle and his companion. Melissa's recognition of her mother's loving intention is a true testament to the bond between mother and daughter.

Reading this chapter, I hope both mothers and daughters will put their often-stressed relationships in perspective. In the end, growing up doesn't have to mean growing apart. We can begin respecting each other as individual women, apart from the shadow of sometimes stifling family ties.

## A Message to Mother
*By Carly Sanko, 15, from a suburb in the Midwest*

I am a teenager now. You look at me and see a sassy, smart-mouthed, obnoxious, insolent little girl. I'm crying out to you, to everyone, with all my heart. I beg you to understand me, understand how I feel, share with me what is going on in my mind, my body, my life.

But most of all, Mother, I want to know you love me. I know you've had a hard day at work. I don't want to bother you, but will you spend some time with me? Please, Mother, I need someone there for me when friends are just not enough. I need someone to talk to, to trust with my deepest secrets, someone to share in the pain of my losses and join in my laughter of happiness. Friends may come and go, Mother, but you will always be here. Please, be there for me to share my life with now, while I need you most.

The "sassiness" you see is what I've seen from you. Don't they say, Imitation is the highest form of flattery? And, haven't I always strove to be like you? Is it not your speech, your ways, that I have learned from?

Or, does it hurt you more that I'm doing things differently from you? My aloof attitude and smart mouth are the result of pride. Yes, I have some pride left after all you've stripped from me for yourself. My pride is the base of my self-confidence. As you've tried all these years to tell me how stupid I sound when I say this or that, I've put up my guard. The barrier between you and me is getting taller. Give me freedom to be my own person, have my own ideas, my own way of doing things.

My "insolence" is my escape. You hold me so close mother, not to your heart, but to your breast in a selfish grip. I'm suffocating here, Mother. I need some way out or I will wither like flowers in late fall.

Please try to understand me. Try to compromise. Let go a little, but still bide your time. For once, Mother, step aside. Look from afar and be my friend. Let me fly from the nest now. Give me a taste of the world, and I will come back. Hold me here in my suffering and loneliness, and I may not be here tomorrow.

## Leaving Mom
*By Anonymous, 15, from a city in the Northeast*

The moment I decided I had to kill my mother was when I was discussing feasible future jobs for myself. I was sitting in the car with my mom, on my way home from another day at the small, elitist private school which I attend—a sanctimonious pit full of empty ideals and hypodermic needles—with a prestigious name. The father of a boy I love is a political science professor at an Ivy League University—again unnamed, another bastion of the good old ideals mixed with abortions and a distinguished name. If you didn't already know, they're sister schools.

Anyway, I'm coming home from school, sitting next to her, and I say, "Hey, whaddya think of me becoming a professor at Ivy U? You know I hear they don't make all that bad money. And, I'd be doing something I really like, you know, teaching my passion or whatever. Of course, I'd have to decide which passion of mine I'd want to teach, but I guess that'll all get figured out later." I was in one of those moments of pure *My So-Called Life*, like there was a camera or some crap in the car next to me taping this reaction, like it would mean something what my mom said in response. She breathed in real deep and exhaled, like she was so exasperated with my naiveté or something and said, "There are certain things that women can't do and that only men should be left to do." And she left it at that. I am totally honest here. She actually said that. Of course, I, the liberated female in the car, tried to set her straight, but it was no use. She just pursed her lips after my tirade and didn't say anything else the rest of the way home.

Now, I don't mean to insinuate that my mother is an evil relic of the '50s. She is a '90s gal in her own right, a career mom who raised two kids pretty much single-handedly while Daddy built up his business after moving to the East, where he went to graduate school. And she is willing to fight tooth and claw for my only sibling, John, and I. She has never pushed me into anything, she was always willing to let me quit something if I decided I didn't like it after a while. That's what happened with me and ice skating. After eight years of it—*eight years!*—I finally grew up and knew I wasn't going anywhere, so I quit. But it was like mom had been deluded all this time, and now that I'd popped her little bubble, she had to rationalize all those thousands of dollars she had spent on my lessons, costumes skates, and what have you. She would always say, "You know, you always were the best skater out there." Or, "People always used to come up to me and tell me how graceful you were out there." Almost like she was trying to cajole me back into it. It's like she feeds off my triumphs, because she doesn't have any of her own.

There's this one thing she said to me that really sticks in my mind. She was sitting on the couch in our living room. It's a really big couch, I think it's called a sectional or something. It's a light pink color and is stained from the early days of my childhood with ice cream and lollipops and soda. It was nighttime, and the large, open room had gaunt shadows thrown into the corners from a small reading lamp positioned near the end of the couch, where my mother was sitting. She had been reading, or perhaps just flipping through, one of those women's magazines, you know, like *Seventeen*, but for fifty-year-old women. I think it was called *Ladies' Home Journal*, or something like that, really cliché and stereotypical. She was sitting there after a long day's work teaching a bunch of Hispanic first graders in the only real inner city around here. She breathed tiredness and exhaustion in every wrinkle, and was falling asleep. Her chin-length brown hair was in curlers, though they serve no purpose other than to make her think her hair is curly, I guess. Her legs were up on the couch, sprawled next to her, and her varicose veins were plainly visible. I was walking down the hall, coming from my bedroom, where I'd just been listening to my CDs, mostly all stuff I don't like at all. I was in my nightgown, a really huge T-shirt with a picture of a bunny in a bed on it, that reads "Do Not Disturb." It's a deep blue. I walked over to the couch and stopped about two feet from her, and I just watched her ancient chest that had been through so much pain rise and fall, and rise again. I was mesmerized by it. I couldn't stop looking at it, like if I did look away, it'd stop and the rhythm would be broken.

I touched her shoulder, clad in a shirt with a small floral print all over it that faintly clashed with her puke-colored pants. She smelled like menstrual fluid, and her pudgy shoulder felt very matronly to me. She jolted awake and looked at me. She stumbled over incoherent words that she'd brought with her from her sleep. I looked at her, smiling, and said, "Could you get me up early tomorrow? I want to make sure I e-mail Fred about sleeping over Friday night."

The whole room had this dreamlike glow to it, and a hazy taste. But suddenly, she was fully awake. "Fred?" she said, sitting as upright as her body would allow. "You can't sleep over his house Friday," she said, shaking her head, her mouth agape as if she were astounded at the idea of it. I *had* slept there twice before.

"Oh no," I said, my body shaking slightly as if in preparation for the battle about to come. "Oh no. Not this. I don't want to fight mom, just say yes." I was babbling, and clearly upset, ready to cry if the occasion called for it.

"Oh no, you don't. I don't want you sleeping over someone's house. I want you staying right here." She defended her indefensible decision with indignation, as if she were unused to being challenged, even though we went through this every freakin' time I have ever been in slight proximity of a friend, or trying to get there. "You'll stay *here* Friday night. And that's it, because I'm your mother."

I was furious, seething mad, my face turning red, my jaw grinding down dangerously on my bottom teeth. I was ready to fight. "Why," I said declaratively. At this point it didn't matter what she said in response. I would just shoot it down and disregard it, no matter how valid. She gave me her reason, "Because my leg hurts and I don't want you somewhere else Friday night, that's all." And she said this so plaintively, as if it were obviously excellent reasoning and I was badgering her and being demanding, even though this was not really why she opposed me being with a friend.

"Mom! What the hell does your leg have to do with me going to a friend's house! I can get a ride!" I was flailing my arms dangerously close to her head at this point, shouting.

"It just does! Leave me alone. I'm tired!" She whined in that annoying, high-pitched voice of hers.

She tried to turn back to her magazine, but I wouldn't let her. "*Why!*" I screamed at her. I was crying full force now. "Why can't I see my friends!" I moaned out.

"Because we want you here Friday night. That's all." She said pleadingly. Her brow knit up, her eyes asked for me to capitulate.

But I would not be silenced so easily. "Don't you understand!" I screamed. "I don't want to be here! I hate this house! I hate this family! We aren't even a family! Dad is working constantly, and he is never home! We have the most dysfunctional family I know! We can't even be in public together because we end up screaming at each other! The neighbors called the freakin' police because they thought someone was being murdered during one of our screaming fights! *Wake up!* This family is destroying both of us, and I need to get away! Why won't you let me go! I hate this place, and I hate you for not letting me escape!" I was flailing, crying, screaming, yelling, and saying everything that I've said three thousand times before. And finally I collapsed on the other end of the couch, about ten feet away from her.

And she said, "I just want to make you happy, okay? I just want you to be happy. I've had such a bad life. I'm just trying to make sure yours is better. Leave me alone, I do everything for you. Don't you understand?"

She looked over at me, her face twisted as if she had asked a question and was waiting for the answer. It was as if the truth were incomprehensible to her, as though her lie of the happy family was the actual reality. Really, that's the only way it ever could be for her. I don't think she would be able to handle the truth, if you want to know.

I said, "No. I'm sorry mom, but I'm already gone. I might still be here, but I left you a long time ago." She was just peering at me through her thick glasses, and a piece of straight hair fell from the curlers, almost looking pretty. She just sat there, small and old and weak and near the brink of wherever it is you are just before you crack, and almost . . . sad. I bit my lip to see it, it hurt me that much.

But I had left that stage of feeling sad for her long ago. Now, it was just pathetic. And I turned my back to her, and walked off to my room.

## OVERCOMING LIFE'S OBSTACLES
*By Melissa G. Laliberte 15, from a small town in the Northeast*

Today is a very important day for me. It marks an anniversary of a day that would change my life forever. It has been exactly five years since I began living with my uncle and his companion. It has been five years since I was forced to leave my mother and start a new life. As I look back, I find myself feeling very grateful for the way things have turned out.

The first thing that comes to mind is the way my mother and I always seemed to be running, running from our problems, that is. I can remember moving three times in five years. We moved from our first apartment to the Projects when I was only six years old. This is when I remember things starting to get bad. My mother was on welfare and spent most of her money on drinking, parties, and hanging out with these scary motorcycle people who wore lots of leather. There was never enough money to stock the refrigerator with food or even fill it with essential items like milk, orange juice, eggs, butter, bread, or fruits and vegetables. The only food in the house was junk food. I ended up eating lots of sweets and junk that was not good for me.

Sometimes when I would leave for school, my mother would

still be asleep and I would have to get dressed by myself. She would leave out the clothes she expected me to wear. One morning I didn't like what she had selected, so I decided to choose my own outfit. When my mother discovered this, she came down to my school and took me out of class. In the hallway, she started yelling at me for not wearing the clothes she had left out. She wasn't making much sense, but I listened anyway. From that day, I knew that something was wrong with my mom, but I didn't want to believe it.

We ended up moving a year and a half later to a big green apartment on Kinsman Street. Things were okay at first. I went to school and saw my friends, but I was never able to do my homework. I needed help, but there was never anyone around who could help me. Before long, things had gotten worse. Our apartment became trashed with dirty laundry, garbage, and cigarette butts. My mother refused to take out the trash. She stopped allowing me to see my friends. She grounded me for no reason. I didn't want to upset my mother in any way. I tried to do what she said. I refused to tell her about how I was wetting the bed almost every night and then sleeping in it. I was afraid she'd yell at me, or put me back in diapers, like she had threatened.

My mother began to cry a lot. She continued to smoke cigarettes. They were the only constant thing in her life. She never worked. She sat on the couch all day. When I needed food, I would ask for some money, but she usually refused to give me any. She would say there wasn't any, so I would have to steal it. It got to the point where our neighbors started to complain. One night a woman from down the street saw me outside at eleven o'clock at night. She must have called the police on my mother, because from that day forward the police would stop by my house at least once a month. They would ask me lots of questions about how things were going. I always tried to make it sound better than it was. I would watch as they examined the holes in the wall. One time, they found broken glass on the floor, which was a result of my mother's hallucinations the night before. She thought she was fighting off evil demons, but it was all in her imagination.

The last day of living with my mother is traced vividly in my mind. I had gone to the store to purchase some more junk food. Before I left I put my hair up in rubber twists so it would curl. When I came back home, there were two cars parked out front. One was a police car and the other belonged to my uncle. I entered the house through the back way to find my mother crying in the corner. Standing in silence were my uncle, two police officers, and a lady who I later found out was a social worker. No one even had to confirm it, I knew I was leaving. I didn't know how long I would be leaving for, but I knew it wasn't going to be overnight.

My uncle helped me pack my things. He placed all of my clothes into one bag. Most of them were dirty and urine stained. My mom said good-bye and told me that she loved me very much. As I got into my uncle's car, I ripped the curlers from my hair and started to cry. The social worker told me that I might never see my mother again. She said that my home would now be with my uncle.

It took me awhile to adjust to living with my uncle and his companion. They did their best to make me feel at home. They provided me with a warm home, clean clothes, lots of love, and a good education. My mother continued to struggle with her mental illness, but finally agreed to seek help for it. I was able to visit her, but not very often.

It has been five years since I stopped living with my mother. It has been five years since I returned from the store to find my life changed forever. I look back on those days and I am not bitter. I have gained the strength and knowledge that is often needed to survive in this world. It took me a while to realize that everything happens for a reason. If anyone had told me five years ago that being taken away from my mother was an actual blessing, I would never have believed it. Today, I know differently. I am now able to appreciate the wonderful angel who came into my life five years ago and rescued me. I love you, Uncle Paul.

I would like to dedicate this to Uncle Paul, Vernon, my mom, and the people who love me the most.

# Fathers

≈

"Capital O, o, b, l, u, m, capital G, o, o, b, l, u, e—Ooblum Gooblue." I recited one letter at a time, telling my dad how I spell one of his father-given pet names for me. He smiled at me, pleased, I think. We had just made a nice connection. These days, it's easier to float by each other than to really make those connections. Now, I value those special moments, no matter how seemingly insignificant.

Our relationship, like mine with my mother, is complicated. When I was little, we bonded over cars and sports. He liked that I preferred trucks to baby dolls, and taught me to identify the makes and models of cars. He also liked that I was good at sports and didn't really mind that I hated the competition.

But, by junior high I had invested myself almost solely in my peer friendships; he felt ignored. In high school, I think he felt replaced by my boyfriends. As the years went by we seemed to have less and less in common.

Then I turned sixteen. He was excited to teach me to drive. It would be like when I was little—I would be the coordinated daughter, and he would be proud. "You'll be a natural," he told me. Anticipating renewed father/daughter bonding, he drove me the Registry of Motor Vehicles. He waited and watched while I aced my written Learner's Permit test and had my picture taken. Once I actually sat behind the wheel, however, the eagerly awaited moment turned to frustration. His prized Acura Legend jolted and bucked as I tried to learn the meaning of the phrase "gentle on the clutch." My first driving lesson was as hard on our relationship as it was on his beloved, aging luxury-liner. Disappointed, as much by his own unexpectedly jangled nerves as by my slower-than-expected learning curve, he relinquished the role of driving instructor.

Now, I've mastered driving a stick shift, and returned to my childhood infatuation with cars. He likes my obsession with motorized transportation, but my admiration of sports utility vehicles strikes him as "terribly impractical." And I guess he finds my admiration of him somewhat implausible too.

I recently adopted one of his favorite questions, "I love you, you know?" When he used to ask me, I habitually replied: "I know. I love you, too." Now he usually replies: "You do?"

Perhaps he doubts my fondness of him because, like my mother, like everyone I care about, he grates on my nerves sometimes. Perhaps it is because I, often unfairly, let my eyes roll more easily when he's around. Perhaps he thinks I don't realize I still need him. I know I do, usually more than I let on. I am balancing in the precarious position between adulthood and childhood. In the struggle to spread my wings I think I sometimes flap them too wildly. I'm still learning how they work.

All the contributions to this section divulge our need for our father. The often mixed emotions and loyalties of adolescence do not shake our desire for a loving relationship with our dad. But reality does not always bring the fulfillment of that desire. Growing up sometimes forces us to confront the distance between our childhood hope and the truth. As in the mother section, submissions describing negative relationships with fathers outnumbered positive descriptions four to one. Repeatedly, girls wished for simple appreciation and recognition from their too often too-distant fathers. Fifteen-year-old Kristina Westmore wrote:

> I got to the point where I wanted a relationship with my
> dad so bad I was willing to stick my neck out on the line,

and just go for it. For the first time, I was really going to actually try to talk to my dad. I began to tell him what was going on in my life. Things at school and things at work, McDonald's. While I was in the middle of telling him a story, the dryer buzzed, signaling that my laundry was finished. I said, "I'll finish the story in a minute Dad. I just have to get my laundry." He replied, "To tell the truth. I don't really care." Those words hurt me more than anything he ever said. At that moment, I realized there was nothing I could do but pray.

The first contribution to this section, *Hoisted Upon My Father's Shoulders*, further demonstrates this longing for an unmarred father/daughter bond. Erika Waeckel allows us to feel the lonely melancholy that entered her life when her parents separated, shattering her paternal connection.

The next author, Ixchel Lechuga, gives us a journal entry, written while her dad lay in a hospital bed. Her fear of losing her dad compels her to acknowledge her devotion to him. Like Ixchel, tragedy induces the next author's true appreciation for her father. In *Missing: My Father*, Sandra Hidalgo longs for a dad who has been abducted—stolen from his family because of his political ideals. While Sandra's frightening and beautifully told story falls outside the experience of many girls, many of us can identify with her veneration for his accomplishments, her steadfast loyalty to his memory, and her undying hope for his return.

I hope hearing the voices of girls who ask for nothing more than their father's caring attention will break through the isolation suffered by girls with a similar longing. I also expect these stories will engender an appreciation for fathers who do their best to maintain a connection with us as we deal with the demands of adolescence. And, finally I hope fathers will read these contributions and recognize the message carried within: Girls need their dads.

# HOISTED UPON MY FATHER'S SHOULDERS
*By Erika Waeckel, 17, from a suburb in the Northeast*

Hoisted upon my father's shoulders, six foot two inches above the faded brown carpet, I reached hesitantly toward the top of our Christmas tree with an angel in my hand. My head grazed the top of the ceiling. Flashes of crashing into the ornately decorated Douglas fir raced through my mind. But with Daddy's hands holding me steady, I knew I would not fall. Nor would I flop to the hard ground when he taught me how to ride my bike. Or fall when he showed me how to hold a bat and throw a ball, demonstrating with his hands where mine should go. Strength, stability, determination, and direction are characteristics of what makes a father a dad. So what if Dad's version of "Goldilocks and the Three Bears" conflicted with Mom's? The three bears bought Goldilocks a convertible and they all drove to the beach together for the weekend? Who cares if Dad's idea of dinner was a bowl of Cocoa Puffs? He was everything to me.

We did special things. For instance: Everyday when he came home from work, I ran to his favorite brown chair and waited for him to sit on me. He pretended not to know I was there and said, "Where's Erika?" Then, a five-minute tickle game followed. He even had nicknames for me, beginning with Bonkers to Eeka B. My father showered me with gifts. Anything I desired was mine at the drop of a dime. I was Daddy's little girl.

When I was ten, my view of my father changed. To this day, I do not know exactly what he had done. I awoke in the middle of the night to hear the hushed voices of my parents in the next room. The secretive tone of my mother was accusative. I soon drifted back into sleep to awake to hear my father's hand smashing through the bathroom door. Immediately, I realized this was not the usual argument. My parents had decided to get a divorce.

Divorce, legal dissolution of a marriage; to me it meant I would never see my father again. Who would lift me up now to place the angel on the tree? Who would play baseball with me?

Who would sit on me? Who would greet my first date? Feelings of hate toward my father flowed through my veins. How could he do this to his only daughter, his Weezie?

Now, I am seventeen years old. My parents are still separated. Everyday my father drives from his house to our house and stays until around nine-thirty at night. We pretend to be a family for those three hours. I probably see my father more than my friends see their dads, and their parents are together. However, when I do see my dad we do not talk much. He asks how school is going and I question how work is for him. Every night he kisses me on my head and says. "Love ya. See ya tomorrow after work." I love my father, yet I feel numb and awkward around him.

A couple of weeks ago, my father hugged me for the first time in years. And, as I buried my head into his chest, a wave of relief swept over me. I felt like crying and allowing seven years of grudges, hatred, and uncried tears to dampen his shirt, but I did not. Instead, I reserved them for a depressing movie. The hug meant so much to me, bringing back memories of when we flew kites on the beach, had hose fights while we watered the flowers, and especially the times we played Jaws, when he attacked me from behind in our pool, then swooped me into his arms, and tossed me into the air to splash back into the cool, crystal water.

When he released me from his warm embrace, the numbness returned. I used to wish my stuffed animals could come alive and play tea party with me; now, I wish my father could be my Dad again.

## My Father: Mr. Pride
## A Journal Entry

*By Ixchel Lechuga, 15, from a suburb on the West Coast*

My dad's in the hospital. A "work-a-holic." I didn't think that was a real thing. I always thought it was an exaggeration. People always know when to stop. Why didn't he know when to stop? I never realized how important he is to me until I saw him raise his hand to his chest. I was terrified.

*No. This isn't a heart attack. What am I going to do? It's just me and my dad driving home.*

Why did that trip seem to take hours when it was only five minutes? I could only think of how much I still need him.

*There's so much we haven't* done! *I haven't made you proud of me yet! No! We have so much to talk about. You have to teach me how to write. You have to tell me your secrets. We're going to be wizards. Remember?*

My father, Mr. Pride, never let me know when he had a cold. Yet here he was, clutching his chest and telling me he wanted my sister to take him to the hospital. He didn't tell anyone that he had stopped taking his diabetic pills, that he had forgotten to eat for three days, that he hadn't slept in two days. All because he had "work to get done."

Maybe I don't see him everyday. Maybe, sometimes, he's too busy to pick me up from dance. Maybe I don't always agree with his extreme opinions. But sitting there for an eternity in the hospital waiting room, I forgot it all. He's my dad. He's not always there physically, but he'd do anything for me—not because he spoils me, but because he depends on me.

Sometimes, I think I'm the only person who makes him happy. He laughs and smiles when he's around me. Real smiles. I know he's high strung. That's why I'm always there. He needs me. I'm his chirping little parakeet. But I need him too. I like his wry jokes and occasionally evil laugh.

*Oh God, don't die! Remember when we used to go looking for rocks for our Japanese garden? Remember when we did archery and I got fourth place? Or, do you remember when we would go exploring in the truck? The truck—all smashed up. Now you have a sweet little sedan. You go to the mall. You have six pairs of Ray Bans and regular appointments with Steve, your expensive hairstylist. But you are still you. Right?*

My dad told me it was a muscle spasm. I don't think he knows I know. I was there. I called my sister. I waited in that sterile hospital green waiting room, pretending to watch *M.A.S.H.* until four in the morning. I was crying for him. I was dying for him. His fiancée went back to sleep after we called her. Later I helped him to pick out the engagement ring. I will never tell him how I hurt. I love him too much. Besides, it's easier to forget the pain.

Maybe he'll go on vacation now. He really likes New Mexico. He says it's very sleepy there—no speed, no sound, just silence.

## MISSING: MY FATHER
*By Sandra Hidalgo, 17, from the West Coast and El Salvador*

Anyone would say that I am crazy if I told them: I dream of him every night. For me it is like he is here with me. I feel like he never left me at all. Every single day, I pray to God to bring him back. I also wait every day for him. I know that he will come back.

Maybe not today or tomorrow or the day after tomorrow, but someday he will come back.

I just know it.

My father disappeared when my second birthday had just passed. He disappeared in July 1982. I don't know the exact date. All I know is that my whole life changed because of this.

I don't have any memories about my father. All I know about him is what I had heard from my mom, and my brother, and other people. My father was a lawyer. He was twenty-seven years old, one meter, eighty-three centimeters tall, and very thin. His eyes were green as his mother's. He had dark blond hair and he seems pretty handsome in pictures.

He didn't like the kind of government that we had in El Salvador so he decided to join the FMLN (*Frente Farabundo Marti para la Libercion Nacional*), which means the Front of Farabundo Marti for the National Liberation. They held secret meetings in different houses, sometimes in our home.

We had to move from one part of the city to another. We

were like the referee in a soccer game. We had to run to where the ball goes. My mom feared that the police would kill him, or worse—that they would kill everybody in our house.

There were two groups during 1982–1986 that were killing people for not liking our kind of government. One was called the *Black Hand.* This group killed people in cars with black windows so nobody could see into the car. They dressed all in black and wore black masks. The other one was called *Escuadron de la muerte,* the troop of death. This group went to people's houses after midnight. They took the people out of their homes and their family never saw them again. People couldn't go to the police because this group would come back and kill the whole family. A lot of people were found dead days later, after being taken by this group. Many people say these groups were a part of the police.

My father knew things would get worse. He told my mom we were going to leave the country for Mexico or Canada. My mom and dad started to prepare all our documents. Soon, my father began traveling to different countries—Mexico, Canada, Cuba, Costa Rica, Panama, and some other countries. Sometimes these trips were for the university. Sometimes, these trips had to do with politics.

He received money in the United States. The people who sent money were rich and supported *El Frente* in our country. He had to take this money in cash, so he could give it to the people who lived in the mountains. This money was used to buy food and other supplies for the people who were fighting in the war. They hid the money in different places in their houses because they couldn't put it in the bank. A guy whose name is Leo knew my father had received money. Leo may have turned in my father. My mom says if he did she doesn't blame him. Every one was terrified during that time.

The day my father disappeared he went to work and never came back. My mom said it was almost 11:00 P.M. He wasn't home. She started to worry, but she couldn't do anything. I imagine her with a cup of tea in her hand looking at the window and the door, listening for every car outside, thinking each one was my father, walking up and down through the house, checking the time that was going by too slowly.

Later in the morning around 3:00 or 4:00 A.M., six to seven guys entered our house with guns, asking for the money. They weren't wearing masks, so she could see their faces. One of them hit my mom and covered her eyes with a piece of clothing to make certain she couldn't see them. Still, my mom said, she recognized a guy with dark skin and dark eyes. He was the one who hit her.

Two of the guys went upstairs to take care of my brother and me, who were sleeping with our baby-sitter. My mom says she was really scared. She imagined all of us getting killed by the men. She imagined my father coming back and feeling sorry for what had happened. She remembers they mentioned someone had told them about the money. They looked everywhere. They found the money on top of the closet. They left after finding the money and told my mom not to tell anyone about this night. They left like pigs after eating the corn.

She looked for my father the next day, but he didn't appear. She got consumed by the time, crying and not knowing what to do. She started to look for him in the newspapers, radios, TV stations and other places—the police, Red Cross, and hospitals. She had no results at all. She even wrote to the government of the city. This search went on for days, weeks, and months. Soon, we had to move to another house.

My uncle, my aunt, and my father's adoptive mother thought they owned everything that was my father's. They burned books and papers, even poems my father had written. I can't believe they were burning the only things we had left from my father. They said the police would find these things and kill them. The fires were like hell, burning my father's images and our right to keep his knowledge.

When I was thirteen years old, I went to visit my Uncle Jose. Playing with my brother and cousins, we found my father's diplomas from 1979 and from a first prize in poetry. We took the diplomas and asked my uncle if we could take it home. "No! Those are mine and I will keep them. You are just little children and wouldn't know how to value them," he said. I got really mad, like when someone gets hit in the face.

We got home and told my grandma what had happened. Then, but only then, she opened an old closet. She showed us all my father's clothes. She gave my brother a necklace that belonged to my father. She gave us some books of poetry and stories. We read the poems again and again and again until we memorized them.

The next day my grandma went with us to Uncle Jose's house. My brother went into the room where we found the diploma. He was as white as the diplomas in his hands.

"Don't you touch that!" my uncle said while raising his hand to hit my brother. My grandma got in the middle and took my brother's hand.

My grandma said, "We are leaving right now and we are taking these diplomas." My uncle's face was red but he didn't say anything. These diplomas are our treasures, like the documents of the house you own.

I have missed my father since the day he left. My father is not dead. I feel it, and I know that somewhere he is alive.

Is he alive? Maybe that is just an illusion, like when the sun rises up in the morning. Like that, every day my illusion is born. That's why I know he is alive. I don't care what other people say. I wait for him every day. It doesn't matter for how long, but I am going to keep waiting until the day I pass away.

# Sisters and Brothers

≋

When I was little I used to sneak into my sister's bedroom and steal things. When my mother wasn't looking, I'd hit my sister, then cry and say she'd hit me. When our relatives sent her better presents, I'd throw fits. I drove her crazy. We always fought. We were often banished to the tiny quarters of one of our rooms for a "double-time-out," forbidden to exit until we had "worked it out." We drove our parents crazy. Then something incredible happened: Manju left for college.

I was only in sixth grade, but already we were beginning to bridge our seven-year age gap. With each progressive year, the age difference has become less significant, and our relationship has become closer. I no longer steal things from her, except for the occasional unmentioned "borrowed" shirt. I no longer hit her and say she did it, I just occasionally enjoy my ability to playfully squash her sub-five-foot body under my superior five-foot-three frame. With these changes, I have gained a new appreciation for the intrinsic weight of our relationship. For the first time, she is not only my sister, but my friend. She is my only friend who understands our family without any explanation. She is my only friend who will unquestionably be part of my adult life.

As my relationship with my parents gained new complexity in adolescence, my relationship with my sister gained new dimension. Loving her is no longer a chore, but a choice I would make regardless of our genetic similarities. I thought, until recently, that Manju's and my relationship was unique. After spending time with other adolescent and young-adult siblings, I realized how typically we play out big-sister/little-sister roles. Disappointed as I was by recognizing that our relationship is not so rare, I still felt comforted by seeing the relatively universal affection among brothers and sisters.

When girls wrote about their sisters and brothers, this steadfast attachment permeated nearly every contribution. At times this connection was expressed as sibling rivalry; at times as sisterly devotion. In her contribution, *Acid Torches of Doom*, Emily Carmichael captures the battle of wills and desire for dominance mobilized by a competitive brother. In the next contribution, *I Hear Her Laughter*, Chelsea Duffin's writing glows with the easygoing affection and happiness only a sister can evoke. Chelsea, Emily, and I echo the sentiments of girls who are sometimes crazy about, and sometimes driven crazy by, their siblings. Together, our writing represents the lighter side of sibling love and rivalry.

Other girls wrote from a heart-wrenching side of sibling devotion. An anonymous eleven-year-old girl described her brother's suicide attempt:

> Mike was lying on the floor hidden behind some boxes. All around him was a pool of blood. I will never forget that sight. The sickly smell of blood seems to stay with me forever. My arms felt numb and strangely cold. A lot of what happened next was a blur. . . . My mom called a friend to take me to her house. She knew I was really getting upset by then. As we drove away, I kept seeing the scene in the basement over and over. I cried and cried. I felt like it was all my fault. If I hadn't gotten so mad at Mike, maybe he wouldn't have done this to himself. I was sure Mike had already died. It felt like everything wasn't real. I remember rocking back and forth saying that it was only a dream. I slapped my face several times trying to wake myself up from the nightmare.

This young girl was not alone in her agony. Others wrote about siblings who committed suicide, became irresponsibly pregnant, lied compulsively, or suffered from developmental disabilities.

The next contribution demonstrates the concern and pain we feel when our brothers and sisters struggle. In *A Sister's Tragedy*, another anonymous contributor teaches empathy for the seldom-acknowledged anguish felt by sisters of girls plagued with eating disorders.

Whether writing from the light or dark side, girls unerringly professed a permanent attachment to their brothers and sisters in their contributions—a connection founded in common biology and cemented by shared pain and joy.

## ACID TORCHES OF DOOM
*By Emily Carmichael, 13, from a city in the Northeast*

"All right, all right. Gimme someone good to play."

"Be Eiji. He can throw Acid Torches of Doom."

Somehow, my brother James has convinced me to play *It*. It is the latest: Thousands of hours and hundreds of dollars of kilobytes of RAM invested in making you *feel* like you're kicking some guy's ass. So mindlessly violent. So typically male. Ah, rejoice for being the mature sex.

"I wanna be a girl. Aren't there any girls?"

This male-characters-dominate phenomena is a trend in video games, and clearly part of a subversive government effort aimed at the self-image of young girls. If a woman cannot fight, she can't fight back.

"Be Mondo, then. His special move is a flaming karate somersault back-breaker."

"There are never any girls. Okay, one. Two, tops. But they always suck."

"Fine, you little zealot. Be Ellis. I'm Rungo. Prepare to die."

So the match begins. James' character is a poster boy for anabolic steroids. He has a granite club the size of several Buicks and an aircraft base. I am a twelve-year-old girl wielding toothpicks. I wonder how this happened.

Soon I am familiar with our special moves, his where he

swings his boulder-on-a-stick and levels anything in his path, and mine where I jump in the air and sparkle a lot. I learn to use Ellis' strengths and formulate a trademark attack sequence, that's somewhat free-form and involves pressing a lot of buttons, *without knowing what the buttons do.* Channeling my speed and agility, I nimbly dart around the oafish Rungo, applying a slice here, a jab there. He flattens me with his two-ton rock. The match goes fast.[1]

"Come on, I thought you'd be good at this!" He complains, as if society hasn't taught me from a tender age that I am inadequate at all forms of aggression.

"It's not my fault. The only girl uses cocktail forks! Tell me someone *good* to be this time. It had better be a girl!"

So now I am Sofia, the second of two females, which is like, how unfair, considering there are eight males. Sofia has a whip and leather knee-high boots. Her costume is two strategically placed shoelaces. I want to throw up.

I notice Sofia makes orgasmic noises whenever she is hit. I have no opportunity to hear her attack. Round two ends fast.

"Look, do you want to play Elli or do you want to lose again?"

"This is chauvinist propaganda and I can't take it."

"It's not the programmers fault you can't play!"

"Another victory for male supremacy. The system wins again. I give up. Why don't I just go inhale some Windex?"

"Do you want to play Eiji? Eiji has red sneakers." My brother is baiting me.

"He'll get a painless death when the revolution comes."

"He has spiky hair. You know, that kind of Animae hair that sticks up really far?"

"So maybe I'll keep him as a pet."

"He has a samurai sword. And red sneakers."

So now I am Eiji, and almost winning. He's not so bad, I

---

[1]Author's note: This story is only a story. I can beat my brother in real life.

guess. It's not his fault he's stuck with a Y chromosome. Besides, he can throw Acid Torches of Doom.

## I HEAR HER LAUGHTER
*By Chelsea Duffin, 18, from the Northwest*

I hear her laughter, loud and full, through the walls of our house. It isn't neat, controlled laughter, not everyday laughter, but *loud* laughter bouncing in all directions. The kind that makes your eyes teary and your cheeks big and red and your stomach ache. I peek around the corner and see my sixteen-year-old sister, lying in front of the TV rewinding a scene from a movie she is watching, laughing on her side, head tossed back, barely even able to hold the remote control she is laughing so hard.

Her laugh is the same as it was when she was four years old—a laugh so suddenly full of joy that she would spring right off the planet if she didn't share it. My little sister's laugh brings memories to life.

Making mud pies in Mom's garden and building forts that we slept in. We dressed in costume clothes and danced and sang songs to our Cabbage Patch kids from morning 'til night. We were the princesses of the world then. Our dreams were what we lived in. There were no doubts and everything under the sun belonged to our happiness.

My sister's laugh settles and fades, bringing me back to the present with a smile. Her laughter echoes softly in the back of my mind, lingering there now, and probably sixty years from now too—always bringing me the happiness of yesterday, as only a sister can.

## A SISTER'S TRAGEDY
*By Anonymous, 16, from a suburb in the East*

An ominous silence always sits at our dinner table with us, a presence that makes us afraid to open our mouths and have the normal dinnertime conversations. There's always a fear about saying the wrong thing, if we say anything. Around here saying the wrong thing can have traumatic results. So we just sit quietly, chewing as softly as possible. The silence sits with us in a heavy, pressing way, almost daring us to say what's on our mind, reminding us that there will be big trouble if we do.

Our overall appearance as a family looks nice enough—a pretty house in a beautiful suburb with nice neighbors. But the neighbors never really talk with us that much. They've seen ambulances come and go from my driveway. They've heard terrible screams and watched things they shouldn't have seen. And a house doesn't look so pretty anymore if you find out what's happened inside it.

My sister sits across from me at the dinner table every night. Tonight is a night just like every night for her, one filled with misery. She's been through almost everything, still recovering from her bulimia two years before and always suffering with mental illness. Another large chapter in her life is about to start tonight, but we don't yet know it as we choke down the cold, stiff meat my mom has made.

"Why aren't you eating?" My dad works up the courage to ask my sister. She's staring at her food as if once swallowed, it would eat her up from the inside out.

"Answer me, young lady."

"I . . . I can't."

I can see my father's face contort with the pain and frustration that has built up over the past couple of years. "Stop messing around, and eat your food," he snaps at her. His fear and concern come across as accusations and my sister gets that look in her eyes.

"You've been losing a lot of weight lately," my mother says as gently as possible. "It'll be okay to have some steak—"

"No, no, no—why are you always trying to force me to do things I don't want? I don't want it! I don't want any of it!"

"At least try." My mom stays calm. "Just eat two little pieces of meat."

"No."

"If you're not in the mood for it," my mom continues, growing desperate, "how about a few saltine crackers? They're practically nothing."

My sister leaps up from her seat, throwing her food onto the floor. "No! I don't want anything! I *hate* you! I hate *all* of you! Why do you want me to be some disgusting pig? Why do you want to ruin me?"

"Honey, we don't . . ." my dad begins, but she's run upstairs. "Come back down here right now. Young lady, *come back*."

Her door's already slammed shut. My mother and father begin to talk in frantic whispers. I sneak away, up to my sister's room to talk to her. I don't realize she is suffering from anorexia. I think she is just being stubborn and mean. I am a lot younger the day this happens, and a lot more ignorant.

"Sweetheart, why don't you eat just a little bit?" I ask, coming into her darkened room.

"Get the hell out."

"They do so much for you and you can't ever seem to do anything for them. Can't you ever seem to think about anybody but yourself?"

We fight, and then she throws me out. I guess I should've expected that.

After fighting with my sister, I do something I hadn't done since kindergarten. I seek refuge in the back room of the basement. My parents had turned the back room into a sort of an artist studio for my sister and me. There are large sketch pads and all types of artist materials. This is where I can be alone for a few moments.

The thing that always reveals my sister is her work down here. My parents have absolutely no idea about this, because they never come down here. But I discover more than enough horrors in her writing and her painting to last me a lifetime. It is down here that I uncover the depths of her mental illness. I read a story about how relief could be found only by slashing her wrists open and letting the bad blood flow out.

*. . . And when life got to be too much, and I could no longer bear the torment of embarrassment and shame, I found relief in my rusted razors. . . .*

In her hidden art, I begin to realize the seriousness of her eating disorder. Propped up on the table, only half-covered, stands my sister's self-portrait. My sister has a great artistic talent. I know it is her portrait right away. As I pull the carelessly thrown tarp off the work, that artistic talent takes me to a place where I never want to go again.

It is a naked picture of my sister. I don't mind the nudity, but she is drawn as a skeleton, skin stretched tight over bones that protrude everywhere, popping up violently all over her body. Tears run down the painting's face, onto the clavicles that stick out so very far, down the breasts that have shrunk from weight loss, and into the deep ruts between the ribs. My own tears fall and mingle with those on the paper. My tears fall down onto those fragile, brittle ribs, taking the black lines that define them across the page.

*. . . When blood starts to gush out of the newly opened veins, all the bad feelings fly out with it and I find release. I find my heaven. If only they would ever let me bleed long enough. They believe they are saving me, but only I know how to save myself. And it would be done, if they wouldn't stop me.*

I cover her painting over again with the tarp, tenderly. I love her. I really love her. And I can't understand. And I wish I could. And I wish I could stop it, and kill it for her, but I can't. No one else can either. And I just don't understand. It's so unfair. Why won't all the love in the world make her realize that she's worth something and that she's cared about? Why can't she see the things we can? I just don't understand. And to compensate for not understanding, all I can do is cry.

When I go upstairs to bed, my sister has smashed her bedroom mirror. There's been a fight, and all the glass has been picked up. Everyone's in bed, so I try to go to sleep, too. I hear my sister in the next room, screaming into her pillow. She's woken up from a dream where she ate half a chocolate chip cookie. This dream scares her so badly she stays up for the rest of the night. I won't know this until the next morning when my parents drive her to another hospital. I hug her when she leaves and feel all the vertebrae coming up out of her back, and a sideways glance will show me that her hair's falling out. I hug her, and try my best not to cry, and tell her I love her and I hope she'll come home to me soon because she's my best friend, although I really don't want her to come back quickly. We don't know how to take care of her here. I say I'll try to come and visit her, but I know this isn't true either. Years ago, when she first started to be hospitalized, I visited her every night, but ever since then I can't bring myself to go near one of those places.

I stand in the driveway as the car goes off down the road. I wait until I'm upstairs and inside a hot shower to start crying. Maybe it will help everyone else to be braver if they don't see me upset and can't distinguish the hot falling water from my tears falling onto the tiles. You can't tell my sobbing apart from the loud and steady hiss of the shower water. My balled-up fists and twelve-year-old body are soundless. I have no tears left by the time I'm done, and you can't tell if I was crying or if I just got soap in my eyes.

I'll write a letter for my parents to take to her, and pick some flowers, too. It'll just be my little brother and me at home in the afternoons now. My parents will be at the hospital every day. I'll have to start to learn how to be a good baby-sitter, and get both my work done, and help him with his. Everything will be okay now: I'm just not going to let myself think about it too much.

# Disintegrating Foundations

≋

I have a mental picture of my parents laughing at me years ago. Their faces are fuzzy; I watched them through blurred, teary eyes. I mustn't have been more than four or so. We sat under a high ceiling, in low lighting, around what seems like an enormous table in my mind's eye. A few of my parents' friends were there. They were all talking about their first or second spouses. Fearfully, I asked my parents if they had been married before. I was horrified by their response: They hadn't. Bursting into tears, I drew the unmistakable conclusion—they were going to have to get divorced. It was obviously the rule: Every adult marries twice.

Instead, my friends now playfully tease me about my parents' affection for each other. I was raised in the security of a stable home.

But, for many of my friends, traveling between their parents' separate houses and dividing up holidays is second nature. Stepmothers and stepfathers, along with half- and step-siblings, are part of their family. New acquaintances seem almost surprised to find out my parents have been married for nearly thirty years and are still happy together. So, at a time when baby-boomers divorce at a rate of over 50 percent, it's not exactly surprising that divorce affects our generation so deeply. We are their children.

Rachel Frazier, a sixteen-year-old from the West, wrote from a point of view seldom acknowledged. Rachel traced the confusing emotions she felt while traveling with her newly separated parents. She wanted clarity from her divorced mom and dad—either split up for good or stay together forever. She summarized her experience in a final paragraph:

I knew they hadn't taken me to the island to eat summer sausage and Swiss cheese. They took me on that picnic as a last-ditch effort to actually be a family. We were no longer three. We were one or two, depending on who stood by who. The person I stood by most was my Mom, and I still stand by her. And it still feels like I am looking at my father sitting alone, ten feet away. Each year the distance grows. He has another family. Mom has built a new life for the two of us. The road ahead is long. I hope someday we'll all be able to meet in the middle.

The first contribution to this chapter captures the sense of betrayal children often feel when parents divorce. Originally written as a journal entry, *A Tiny Crease in the Silence* possesses an unguarded honesty that perhaps only comes when words are unintended for others' eyes. In this piece, Chana Joffe-Walt reflects the secret sentiments expressed by nearly every girl who wrote about divorce.

Nor does Olivia Ramirez's experience in the next contribution, *Disconnected*, stand alone. While convention assumes fathers leave and mothers stay, nearly as many girls wrote about their mothers leaving home as fathers. In the cases where mothers walked away, these daughters internalized the abandonment. They seemed to find it hard to blame their mothers without doubting themselves. When fathers left, most girls expressed less complicated emotions. Some loved and some hated their dads for clear reasons. Some fathers remained loving and loyal. Others had been abusive, and continued to be negligent fathers.

A common theme winds through these contributions: All wish for stability. All feel their foundations disintegrating. The fact that the same tremors tear apart the families of half the girls in the country doesn't seem to make divorce much easier. In this case, maybe misery could do with less company. Perhaps there would be more compassion if each girl's disrupted life was considered personally. I hope these contributions awaken appreciation for each girl's struggle to maintain stability, while trying to find balance in her parents' wobbly world.

# A Tiny Crease in the Silence
*By Chana Joffe-Walt, 16, from a suburb in the East*

My parents are divorced. Separated from one another. Split, forever. But not the "forever" like their marriage. The real thing. All these years my vision has been blurred, distorting my reality in order for me to remain stable. My vision betrayed me: convinced me to believe my stability was reality. Only now, when I think about it too much (or perhaps just enough), I feel so immensely sad. The weight grabs me from the bottom-most coils of my stomach and tangles itself in with the mess, ready to settle. I can't rid myself of its heavy, dense burden and it forces me to travel where, for so many years, I have refused to venture.

We all pretend, us kids. We learn quickly to "adapt" as they say. But they're the fools. Children pick up new languages easily—hear the sounds and imitate. We become so distracted with futile attempts to act as we should, to say what they want to hear, to please, that we forget ourselves and our lives. Next thing we know, there's a plethora of parents, new houses and a formulated schedule for moving between them. We learn to show just how okay we are. For a while, we get nervous, tiptoeing parents, their guilt radiating through the air and piercing our young souls. Then they find new people and can start again, anew. That's exactly when it hits us.

So the tears ooze out, pure and pathetic. Not real. Because the tears do come, filmy and greasy. But these are not what I want. I want more. Tears that I can't stop. Sobs more powerful than the pain. Sobs where I shake so violently that everything else is simply peripheral. But I can't! Because of all these years of self-inflicted, self-taught, self-medicated, containing, compressing, suppressing, rejecting denial. I've shut them away, those emotions. The bottle remains securely shut and I remain fully unable to will it open, to will it to shatter into tiny, sharp, gleaming pieces. After all, I can't unscrew the ten years of diligent work put into getting the lid on as tight as it is now. So when these emotions try to take form, try to haunt me, I stamp on them, stripping them of their dignity and replacing them with the deafening silence of "I'm okay."

The years, the tiny sound bytes of a lost self, threaten to creep up on me. The sorrow swarms over my head, chuckling at my ignorance, at my feeble attempts to smother its powers. We're not so okay. We have no new life, new family. We can't forget our past family because it's our reality. It's our broken weeping family.

## DISCONNECTED
*By Olivia Ramirez, 17, from a city in the Northeast*

*The phone rang.*

"*It's your mother.*" My stepmother said. Then cautiously, gently, "*Your Uncle Ray died.*" Shock. Yet, this was somewhat expected—I had seen him two days earlier, on life support, looking as close to death as one could get.

Oh God, I remembered thinking. It's all over for him and he's only thirty-five.

I took the phone.

People are always telling me I look like her. They can tell that we're related, that she's my mother. Hell, some think she's my older sister. But they could just be saying that. It's true. I've inherited many of her features—the dark, curly hair, the nose, the shape of my eyes, the olive skin. Our hands are even the same.

But the resemblances don't seem to end there. My face is very expressive. I'm constantly making facial expressions, depending on my mood. For as long as I can remember; my father has told me I'm the image of my mother when I make these faces. I have mixed feelings about these comparisons.

I think, "Do I make him sad because I remind him of her?"

I wonder, "In how many other ways am I like my mother?"

You see, my parents divorced when I was two, and it was my mother who walked away.

*What happened?*" I asked quietly, though I already knew what *happened. I just wanted to hear the solid confirmation, the horrible reality of the death of a loved one, from someone who was with him.*

"Uncle Ray died," she said, "about an hour ago, just before I got here."

*More conversation. Expected conversation. Asking what the doctor had to say. Asking if any other family was at the hospital. The bacteria from the infection in my uncle's right lung had escaped and spread throughout his body, infecting and eventually ruining the rest of his organs.*

Yet I wasn't prepared for her next statement:

*"They wrapped him up in a big bag, and I was sitting in the room with his body."*

I was horrified.

Yes, my mother walked away. To this day, my parents have not talked to me or my brother about the separation—no explanation, nothing. Which leaves me curious. This may be unwarranted, but I'm still curious nonetheless.

She didn't go far, however. She moved only three blocks away and even baby-sat sometimes. She didn't totally desert us. To say "it was never the same" would be a lie. I never even knew what it was like to always have her around in the first place. I've never known what it's like to have a mother, a real mother.

*"You were in the room with his body?" I asked incredulously.*

*"Yes," she replied.*

How can you stand that? I remember thinking: If I were in her situation and I had to sit in the same room with my dead brother, I'd be a mess. Here she is sounding merely distressed. Why isn't she crying? Doesn't she feel pain, loss, remorse, anything? She must. I know she must.

Mind you, my mother hasn't had a perfect life, by any standards. In less than two years, she divorced her second husband, was placed in the hospital for a serious ulcer, and now she had lost her brother. Her ulcer was what had me seriously worried.

It happened this past June, the night before my birthday. The pain of yet another failed marriage combined with the pressures of work, going to school, and keeping up with expenses had wound her so tight she was bound to snap. For the first time, I began to consider the magnitude of pain and suffering my mother had endured. The pain of the ulcer seemed only a fraction of the pain she might have already gone through. It was a rare sign of weakness and vulnerability. It honestly scared the hell out of me.

*Then came the silence.*

*I was sad, confused, extremely uncomfortable. I knew she had to be feeling something, She just wasn't showing it. I felt moved to comfort her, to show her I cared, to tell her everything was going to be all right, to tell her I would be there for her, to let her know that she could cry on my shoulder as I had always wished to cry on hers . . . but no words came. I was stuck. Stuck behind a wall made strong with seventeen years of loneliness, lacking and loss, of feeling incomplete—a wall made impenetrable with the tears no one saw me shed and a sadness only few can understand.*

*So I put aside the hope of comforting words, of a teary mother-daughter exchange, and settled for a simple, lame attempt:*

*"Are you all right?"*

And yet, I, myself, haven't been all right. "It" hasn't been all right. "It" has been hard to explain but has something to do with how I compare myself to others, how others speak about their mothers and I envy them. When I was younger this envy was so strong it bordered on hate. My friends spoke of how much they loved their mothers, how much they loved them more than anything, even more than their fathers sometimes, how their mothers were always there for them. Visits to their houses showed these mothers as doting, compassionate, and full of love. I hated not knowing what that was like, not being able to experience that love. I hated feeling uncomfortable in conversations about mothers because I had nothing to contribute, only my father to talk about.

I can remember nights that I would yell and scream at my mother—but only in my head: Why did you abandon us? Do you know what you did when you left us? Do you know what it was like to want a mother, someone to turn to, someone you can identify with, someone who can help you through the tender years of growing up? Do you understand how it feels not finding reassurance, ever? Do you know how empty I feel sometimes? How much I hate you sometimes, for taking away the precious gift of having a mother? Do you know? Do you even care? Are you suffering too?

On and on, I would torture myself. Over and over I would mentally berate her. Only tears came, not answers. They never have come.

What I hate most is when people who live with their mothers, tell me I'm lucky because I have two mothers—a mother and a stepmother. Bullshit. They don't understand at all. Of course I only think this as I politely accept their opinion. I have two maternal figures. Yes. But none to fill this void.

*"I'll be okay," she said. A lame response to a lame question. The wall being put up—almost.*

*I heard a great sob as she finished speaking, belying that she wasn't going to be all right. But wasn't going to let me help either.*

*A wave of almost unbearable sadness enveloped me and I began to cry. I was crying for the death of my uncle, but also because of my mother's sobs. It made me sad; I could do nothing.*

*I don't remember the rest of the conversation. There wasn't much. We bade a hasty good-bye, with promises of later calls, and hung up. I cried for a few minutes, then stopped, and busied myself with other work. I felt small, helpless.*

"I see you in her. You're going to be just like her. A daughter always becomes just like her mother."

The woman who said these words was a friend, the elderly lady I worked for. We talked a lot so she knew a lot about my life, but I didn't like her at that moment. Her comment invoked a surprising reaction in me. I was shocked, hurt, and also scared. I argued with her but she would not back down. I remember those words to this day.

If she sees that, could it be true? Will I become exactly like my mother? Exactly? Will I still be single when I'm forty? Will I leave my kids? If so, will I suffer inside and hide it from everyone? A thousand questions presented themselves. Each more upsetting than the next.

For a moment I was terrified. We do have much in common, so many similarities. But, I didn't want to be like her. I was ashamed to have such a reaction, but it couldn't be stopped.

A little later my stepmother came into the room. I was doing some homework. I was calmer, but still upset about so many things.

"How are you doing?" she asked

"I'll be okay," I replied. I didn't want to talk about it.

# No Safe Place

≈≈≈

I nestled myself comfortably into the maroon-striped train seat. My three-quarter-length skirt fell just below my knees. I admired it, pleased with myself. I had hemmed the too long, awkward skirt to create this one—the perfect length. Trains are pleasant enough, I thought to myself as I unpacked my small box of sushi. And besides, I couldn't eat this for lunch if I was driving.

Two seats in front of me a mother and her two children were not equally content.

"If you don't come here and be quiet right now, I'm going to slap you."

Pause. Sniffling. Tiny voice, "But Mom—"

"Do you want me to come over there and beat you?"

I lost my appetite.

Back and forth, the monster versus the two tiny voices. Threats. Descriptions of the punishments waiting for the girls at home. I sat alone staring at the passing landscape while imagined faces of this monster-mother chugged through my mind.

Then, after a few minutes of relative quiet, two small angels appeared next to me. Beautiful little girls. I was so instantly struck by their delicate features that I complimented them, almost unintentionally.

The older one, about five years old, with eyelashes curled practically up to her eyebrows, spoke with her whole body. She asked, "Hey, where ya goin' to?" her question accompanied by an outward flail of her arm.

I smiled. "I'm going to Burlington. What are you guys doing on the train?"

The smaller girl, about three years old with long braids, looked at me and simply said, "New Jersey."

"Is that where you got on?" I interpreted the information.

Heads nodded.

I calculated their travel time: probably about five and a half hours by now. "Wow, you guys have been on the train for a while."

And then a new voice, the monster's but much quieter, friendlier. I glanced up to see a woman unlike all of the faces my mind had given her. She was pretty, well put together, warm looking. "Gosh, we sure have. I'm sorry, I couldn't help overhearing that you are getting off in Burlington. Are you continuing on to Canada from there?"

I replied, "No, I'm just visiting my boyfriend. He's living in Burlington for the summer."

She smiled and I recognized her resemblance to her daughters. "C'mon girls, let's leave the nice lady alone."

And for a while after they left I just heard quiet giggles and song.

I was eager to make excuses for their mother: It really had been a long ride. Little kids are very demanding. She must be frustrated. I caught myself excusing her harsh words. Then, in a moment of honest reflection, I realized her warm smile and friendly disposition might well mask a frightening reality. Her easily accessed demeanor might actually be the disguise of an abuser. I had wanted so badly to see an ogre face matching the abusive voice. Now, the fact that I wouldn't have been able to pick her out of an abusive mothers line-up shook me terribly.

For the first time, I was sure I unknowingly knew abusive parents. I became aware of a masquerade, where cruel and violent women and men parade around looking like loving mothers and fathers. Prior to that train ride, I believed my experience with abuse-to-be was limited to the troubled friends of friends. My job had been to comfort my "happy" childhood friends who had heard too much and needed support themselves. So many conversations

started with, "Promise me you'll never tell her I told you this . . ."
I took those conversations seriously, but they lacked a certain tan-
gibility. I had always conjured up mythical perpetrators who
looked the part: seedy-eyed with horrible scowls. Suddenly, I felt
unsure. I could not tell by looking who was abusive and who was
not. Walking through a high school hallway, I would never again
suppose that chatting and giggling girls are safe.

Many of the girls who wrote to me about their abusive
mothers and fathers confided how normal their family appears,
and how typical, even happy, they themselves seem. Several girls
asked me to let readers know how many contributions I received
about abuse. They wanted to expose the hidden prevalence of
abuse. Their foresight could not have been more correct.
Submissions about abuse were outnumbered only by those about
eating disorders, and, more happily, were also on a par with the
number of contributions about best friends.

Sadly, tragically, three abusive themes—incest, violence, and
alcoholism—were mentioned more often than all others when
girls wrote about their fathers. Of all forms of father-perpetuated
abuse, sexual abuse was the most common. But, you will not find
any of these contributions in this chapter. Instead, I've placed
these accounts along with other forms of rape.

Mothers, of course, are not immune to abusing. I did receive
disturbing accounts of mothers, as well as fathers, mistreating
their daughters. But in the contributions I received, the abusive
behaviors of mothers were seldom the primary theme.

The writing of all girls who lived in danger demonstrated
courage. A fifteen year old from the South, Jessica Cunningham,
wrote about the far-reaching intimidation of physical abuse. She
and her mother fled from the life-threatening violence of her
father. Time passed. Jessica found friendship and happiness.
Then her security was threatened by a surprise visit:

> My friend Angie and I were home asleep, and someone
> knocked at the door at eight o'clock in the morning. I
> hollered for Darnell to get the door. When he went to

answer it, my grandmother on my dad's side of the family just came barging in. She was saying, "Oh, I finally found Mildred and my granddaughter."

I got to the phone and dialed 911. The police came in no time.

My dad was outside on the porch. So you can see, he finally found us. And for me and my mom, hell has started burning again. As they say, he's started up a new flame. He has me so scared, I carry a cell phone with me. He might just sneak up on me when I'm not expecting it.

The common dignity of these girls who live in unsafe homes is exemplified by the contributions in this chapter. In the initial entry, *"I Dare You,"* Rose R. Stella stands up for herself and for her brother. She confronts her abusive father with proof of her own indomitable merit.

For many girls the substance-abusing habits of their parents robs them of a secure home. Several echoed a shared sentiment of betrayal—"He loves his whiskey more than he loves me." In *Bottled Up Inside*, Erin Fitzpatrick details a saga of illness and divided loyalties. The title for this courageous submission came from Erin's letter. She wrote: "At the time this piece was written, not many people knew what was going on. I was ashamed of what happened at first. After a long while, I realized I did nothing wrong and should not hide the truth. Others should learn that if the truth is bottled up inside, sometimes it can hurt more."

The following contributions are vivid descriptions of abuse that has, in some ways, shaped these young women. Their accounts of the incidents and their reflection upon their experiences are deeply gripping and disturbing. I left these submissions feeling an admiration for their unconquerable power. In contribution after contribution, girls described obstacles designed to break their will and silence them. Yet, they spoke—not with broken spirits, but with the force of authority—saying, as one anonymous author wrote, "I have been strengthened by the abuse in my life. I will be fine."

# "I Dare You"
*By Rose R. Stella, 15, from a small town in the South*

My father spoke to me today. I made him. The last time he said anything to me was three weeks ago.

"Don't you dare interfere again, you hear me? You stupid little shit!" A stinging blow snapped my head around. I felt his grasping fingers around my throat. I would do it all again to protect my little brother. Why must my father pick on the two of us?

That night my little brother, Timothy, ran away. We searched for hours. I knew, concealed under my facade of concern, he was safer wherever he was. I was equally certain, if I discovered him, I would not force him to return. I would hide him. Luckily, it didn't come to that; my mom found Timothy. I fell into an uneasy sleep, hours past my bedtime.

The next morning, I took the SAT I for the first time. My father's ringing words echoed in my head. Could I do it? Could I prove my father wrong once more?

For the next few days, I didn't look at my father. He didn't look at me.

I got over it, like I always do. Then I started greeting him every morning and at every meeting with a cheerful, "Hi, dad!" He stared through me, glowering with the disgust born of the personal resentment that crosses an exterminator's face when he glimpses a roach.

I persisted.

My SAT results returned a few days ago. I pulled in a perfect score in the verbal 800 and a 660 in math. So there—I am not any of those horrid things my father calls me!

I suppose my father had no choice but to answer. I blocked his way down the stairs and repeated the same cheerful phrase which cuts like wind-driven snow when it's whipped back into my upturned face.

He stared, brooding, and paused. Then, slowly, music reached my ears: "Hello . . . Rose." And he walked on by.

# Bottled Up Inside
*By Erin Fitzpatrick, 15, from a small town in the Northeast*

Looking at my father's drooped face and listening to his slurred speech, I could tell it would be one of those nights again. Yelling and screaming, crashing and banging would be heard throughout the house until all hours of the night. Maybe there would be more midnight cleaning madness. Henry would expect the family to leave the warmth and security of our beds to tidy the house. These times had become ordinary. Our family had learned how to deal with them. Then, one day, it got to the point where we couldn't deal with his problems any more.

I knew my father had a disease that was passed on through many generations. I also knew his disease could have been stopped, but everyone in my family had just learned to live with it. People on the outside never really saw all the disruption I had to live with. Except for the occasional unwanted outburst in public, few people knew about my father's problems. I was one of the unfortunate few, who knew too well about Henry's disease. I had learned from a relatively young age about the dreaded effects of this illness.

On the long rides to the Cape, Henry continually promised not to drink. My mom, my sister and brother and I, all knew his promise would be broken. My father was going to be around his friends. All the pressure would make him crack. In front of all his friends and family, Henry regularly made an idiot out of himself, acting like he was in charge. My mother tried to console me and offer some possible explanation, "I don't think that your dad meant to ruin the family outing or to embarrass you. You know what happens when he's like that."

Unfortunately for me, I had learned exactly what happened when my father's disease reared its ugly head. By this time, I no longer wanted to go out in public with him. I made it a point to be "busy" when my dad asked me to do something. I'd "forget" to mark my social events on the family calendar.

Several times family outings had turned into family feuds—nightmares in the clear light of day. On my great-grandmother's ninetieth birthday, our entire family, including nine great-grandchildren, gathered for the celebration. As the children played, tensions mounted between my father and his brother. Tom nagged Henry. When Tom refused to stop, Henry and Tom got into a fistfight. I felt afraid as these grown-up brothers yelled and threw punches at each other. I couldn't image what made family members turn against each other so viciously. I figured it out later: Both my father and my uncle were victims of the same disease, a disease that had also claimed their father.

My father had chances to turn his pitiful life around. As I grew older, I felt his priorities were never set straight. I realized his problems continued to grow out of control. I knew he soon would lose everything he valued. One day, I demanded of him, "Don't you see what you're doing to yourself? To us? Can't you figure it out? We don't want to be around you when you're like this."

"What? What've I done? All I do is bust my hump to give you guys what you need. I just expect a clean house and some respect, that's all." My father's slurred answer made the problem more evident than ever before.

"That's all," I screamed in disbelief. "That's a lot more than you deserve for the way you've been acting. How can we respect someone who constantly makes threats and acts like a jerk in front of our friends?"

Henry couldn't see his life slipping away ounce by ounce, even though my whole family tried to help. After awhile, we felt like our efforts were hopeless. My father made so many mistakes dealing with this disease. We became reluctant to help.

One by one, things started to fall apart at the seams. First, my father stayed away from home, hopping to various places where nobody cared about his disease, or shared the same disease. We hardly saw him. Then, his coworkers noticed dramatic changes in his attitude. They desperately tried to warn him about the danger his condition posed to his job. They wanted him to know he was stirring up trouble with his boss. They told him he would be suspended if his behavior continued. As hard as they tried, nothing registered in my father's thick, denial-filled skull.

He continued to do his job, but his family, friends, and coworkers knew it would only be a matter of time before his disease rose up and landed him in the unemployment line.

For several weeks before everything blew up like an atomic bomb, my family went through hell. No matter how hard we tried to please my father, everything was wrong. He screamed his complaints constantly. "Where are my clean clothes?" "What does everyone do around here all day? Sit on their butts?" "I need to get ready for work." "Is my supper ready?"

By now, all of us, my mother, my siblings, and I felt we could no longer talk or associate with him until he got help. Windows of opportunity to relate to my dad, times when the disease seemed to be in remission, had grown fewer and farther between.

For everyone involved in Henry's sad, problem-filled life, one holiday will go down in history as the worst ever. At this point, his disease overcame his ability to love, think, and act. Henry went insane like a psychotic person. He took the anger that was bottled up inside of him out on the innocent people who meant the most to him. I watched in horror as my father threw things at me, my mother, my brother and sister. He even went so far as to beat some of us. Nothing could stop his rage. He had gone crazy on the people who cared the most.

The sudden blare of sirens was enough to startle me out of my shock. My mom had made the call which would change all of their lives forever. Into our usually quiet neighborhood came four cruisers. Their destination was a place nobody would have expected— our house. The only way to stop my father was to have assistance from the police. My siblings and I went into a state of hysteria. We all shook with nervousness. My sister and I were scared to the point of almost being sick. We went to the safety of the most distant room, all the while quaking with fear at my father's anger. The violence we all witnessed left scars that never healed.

Henry was taken away in handcuffs, cussing at everyone in sight. The police couldn't even question us with my father in the same room. He yelled, "I only did it to protect myself." He insisted that he was provoked by us. After he left, my mom, my sister, my brother, and I were questioned thoroughly by the police officers.

My father was never charged for the horrible things he did that night. We wanted to save ourselves from all the legal fees, bail, lawyers, and waiting for a court date. My father was merely put into protective custody.

My family somehow pulled our strength together to face the next day. My sister and brother and I went to school. Nobody could manage to eat though. No one had slept at all the night. My mom spent the following day at court, trying to find some way to get Henry some help.

Henry was kept in protective custody for thirty-six hours. He was supposed to be released earlier, but his breathalyzer tests showed he was still way over the legal limit to drive. Because Henry posed a threat to us, the police advised my mom to get a temporary restraining order. She filled out the piles of paperwork. My father was not allowed to go to his own house or within one hundred yards of any family member for a minimum of seven days.

When my father came to the house with a police escort to collect all his belongings, he kept asking, "Why? What have I ever done to deserve this treatment?" He was still not completely back to a "normal state." He turned from sad to violent in a matter of minutes. No one in my family was home at the time. The police told us my father had made threats on our lives.

With a week's separation from his family and a clearer mind, my dad realized he did need help. He believed if he got medical attention and put in a minimum effort, everything would be back to normal.

"Things will never be the same," my mom told him. "You've got to get help for this disease or face losing your family. This disease isn't only hurting you. It's hurting all of us. And I can't let that happen anymore."

My dad said the only thing that stopped him from getting help was that he did not want to miss work. My father felt the way to show his love to his family was to work and provide for us. That's what he had learned the man of the house does—provide for the physical needs of his family.

"Too bad that reasoning will never fill the emotional void your actions have left in our lives. I'll never be able to put all these things behind me," I sobbed.

"I will always be haunted with the thought that someday this whole nightmare could happen all over again. I can't wake up and have everything disappear," sobbed my little sister.

My brother thought it best not to speak. Since he was the focus of my father's physical attacks, he didn't know what violence and anger would be released if he spoke.

My father was back in the house in a week. One thing helped to keep his disease to a minimum: Since a minor had been involved in his violent episode, DSS (Department of Social Services) came regularly and checked up on my dad and our family. If my father did anything threatening to the family or drank, he would never be allowed to live in the house again. Everyone walked around on eggshells.

When my father made the first mistake, he got another chance. He went out of his way to prove his innocence, sneaking around the house hiding every shred of evidence.

I thought, You know he is going to keep slipping, if no one sets limits on the number of times he can screw up. I will never be able to trust him again, with all his lies and deception.

When my father was caught this time, he didn't get any medical attention. Nothing happened. Now some of us were angry that nothing was done. My father was given too many chances. He thought he'd keep getting them. My mother tried to explain to me, my sister, and brother that the disease was difficult to overcome, that slips were part of the process of recovery. But we were trying to rebuild a trust. Those slips were the straw that made the tower fall down.

The disease had taken over my father's life. He couldn't face the disastrous effects his disease had had on his family. He wouldn't face the anger he held from his own past—anger that often set off the drunken episodes. My father was in denial.

After a third strike, my father was finally ordered out of the house. If he stayed, DSS would have stepped in and monitored the family extremely closely. They would have ordered him out of the house if my mom hadn't already done so.

When my dad finally decided to get help, he tried to admit himself into a hospital. Unfortunately, the so-called "professionals" declared that he was not sick enough to get in. With this thought, he went back into the denial stage. He stayed at a relative's house for thirty days. He was only allowed to see our family when invited. The idea of not being able to see his children and wife or go to his own house hit my father pretty hard.

"What did I do to be denied the right to see my own children or go to my own house—the house I paid for?" My father complained to anyone within ear's reach.

To deal with his new lifestyle, my father turned completely against our family. He threatened our financial, emotional, and physical security. He tried to prove we were the ones who had made him the way he is. When he did try to fight his disease, he was always edgy. He had to find something to fill the withdrawal. He tried to convince everyone he was dealing with his problem through meetings and counseling. We knew for Henry to recover would require more drastic measures. Henry still needed help. His life might never get better without it.

With my father out of the house, my mom, my brother, my sister, and I could now live our lives without the daily worry of his condition. The agony of the unexpected, unsolicited violence and disruptions was gone.

After my father's month stay at a relative's house, my mother told him to find a place of his own. He never could live in our house again. Everyone thought my father's move was for the best. That is, everyone but my father. He believes he can change the future, but admits he can't change the past. I believe it will take a lot for me to trust in my dad again. Wounds can heal, but it takes more than time to heal them. It takes hard work, commitment, and love. It will take more than just a few stitches to stem the bleeding from my heart and my family's heart.

# Pregnancy

≋

I had to take a pregnancy test once. After purchasing the test at the drugstore, my long-time boyfriend and I waited the five minutes in darkened silence. Before I sat up to look for a plus or minus sign he told me he loved me. He tried to comfort me, "Whatever happens it will be okay." His words did not reassure me. I looked at the result. A single horizontal line had appeared. I sighed a breath of relief, deeper than any I had ever breathed before. Silently, I wondered if anything was worth the anxiety I had just exhaled.

Now, two years later, I remember that fear and relief vividly. All of my sexually active friends have taken pregnancy tests, at least once. We joke about the benefits of break-ups, "Well, at least now you won't have to worry about your period being late." Our playful callousness masks the intensity of our fear of pregnancy.

I remember the day Amy took the morning-after pill. She and Josh went to family planning the day after their condom broke. Then, Josh took her back to her house and comforted her for a while. She felt fine when he left. She phoned me to report, "I'm just going to finish my paper and go to bed." The next day, we met at her locker. Her pale lips, yellow face, and red eyes told me her night hadn't gone according to plan. About an hour after we got off the phone she started vomiting. It didn't stop until she got dressed in the morning. She hadn't slept, and she still felt queasy. Her paper wasn't finished.

In junior high you couldn't just be close to someone, learn

things about them as time went on. Everything had to have some element of drama. Intimacy required shared secrets and personal jokes. Once my closest guy-friend divulged his worst fear in exchange for mine. He begged me not to tell anyone, "I'm so scared of spiders." As promised, I told him my worst nightmare, "I can't imagine having to tell my parents I was pregnant. They'd be so disappointed in me." I am grateful to have never had to.

The contributors to this section confronted my unimaginable fear. In *Stepping Stone*, Amy Salamon takes us through the scenes of her abortion, through her emotional emptiness. Like Amy, all of the girls who wrote about abortion talked about the pain, heartache, and hurt of the experience. None took that choice lightly, blithely, or without respect for life. Each one agonized.

Other girls decided differently. In *Shattered Dreams*, an anonymous writer talks about her attachment to her unborn child. Her boyfriend abandons her. Her mother and friends pressure her to abort. In the end, nature takes over. After a miscarriage, she's left only with her disillusionment. This girl is not alone. Repeatedly girls wrote about simultaneously realizing they were pregnant and seeing their boyfriend with other girls. Others also refused to end their pregnancy, even when their parents and boyfriend pressed for an abortion.

Finally, in *I Will Give Birth*, Netzi Andino speaks up for teenagers who joyfully and responsibly become mothers. Netzi celebrates the baby she carries, looking forward to giving birth and raising a child. She ends this chapter with a self-assertive message: Young mothers are not a burden to society. We deserve respect.

Each of these contributors merits admiration. Whether teenage girls share my fear of pregnancy, survive an abortion, make the best of unexpected motherhood, or relish giving birth, these contributors prove our thoughtfulness. We undertake child-bearing and child-rearing with careful consideration for the next generation.

# STEPPING STONE
*By Amy Jean Salamon, 17, from a city in the Midwest*

I remember how much it hurt. Just like it was yesterday. Not really physical pain but emotional and mental pain. I hated what had happened and I couldn't believe I was who I was. I cried so hard. I cried *so* hard. Grasping the nurse's hand with everything I had, holding her hand so close to my body, needing someone there. Having to listen to that noise was unbearable. I kept thinking over and over that it wasn't me lying there or going through what I was. I could never do something like that. It just had to be someone else.

Ten minutes later they were both gone. I didn't move except to hug my now-worthless self. I cried so hard as I lay there motionless, except for my jerking sobs. The nurse knocked on the door and I quickly wiped away my fast flowing tears. She told me to take my time. But I couldn't stay there anymore. I took my things and left that room. I just wanted to leave, but they took me to yet another room. I sat there for twenty minutes with my mom by my side as I cried. Finally I was allowed to return to the comfort of my own home. My bed.

My room. My emptiness.

I curled up into a ball in the corner of my bed not even changing my clothes. With my shades down and my door closed, I was alone. I cried from the pain and sickness of what I had just been through. I didn't leave the solitude of my room for three days. My family checked up on me, but I wouldn't mentally let them be with me, even if they stayed physically.

A lot changed during those four black, empty days. I haven't been the same since and I never will.

What a stepping stone. . . .

# SHATTERED DREAMS
*By Anonymous, 16, from a suburb in the Northeast*

I first noticed Rob when I was in seventh grade. I was at a dance with my friends. He was there with his girlfriend, making out. His hands were entangled in her long, brown, curly hair. I envied her. It wasn't until a year later that he began to notice me. It didn't take me long to fall in love with him.

I felt so special and important when we were alone together. I idolized him. So, of course, when he suggested that our new relationship remain "between just the two of us," I totally agreed.

That way no one could interfere or split us up. And when he started seeing other girls, I believed I was the special one. I was . . . really.

When we entered our freshmen year of high school things changed between us. Since I was totally in love with him and so sure he was "Mr. Right," I decided to take the big step. I gave myself to Rob—mind, heart, soul, and yes, body. Unfortunately for me, I was a fool. I overestimated him. I always thought he would be there for me. He was, of course, until I told him I was pregnant.

"I'm sorry. Wow, am I sorry."

"What am I supposed to do, Rob?"

"Well, Hon, it's your body, your decision."

With those words he was abandoning not only me, but his baby. I was completely alone and would have to deal with this by myself.

My friends and my mother all had a simple solution: have an abortion. For me it wasn't that simple. There was a little life growing inside me and she was depending on me to survive. How could I kill my baby?

The stress of the situation was wearing away at me. I knew I had to be strong and stand my ground for the sake of my baby, but I was weak and losing my courage. The rejection I would have to face having a baby at fourteen terrified me. I was living in a state of confusion.

Rob's denial that he ever laid a hand on me pushed me over the edge. I crept into the bathroom that night and said a prayer. The next thing I knew my razor fell from my hand and my wrist was slit.

Right away I was filled with regret and remorse. I had forgotten that by taking my own life I would also be taking another. Luckily I had cut myself the wrong way and we both survived.

After the suicide attempt I grew stronger. The reality of the situation became clear to me. I found a purpose to live for—my baby. No matter what amount of rejection I received from Rob, my mom, friends, or society I was determined to learn to deal with it. I realized I was going to have to grow up fast. No longer would I be able to be the selfish child I once was. Nor would I be able to be a carefree teenager. I was taking on the responsibilities of an adult and would be forced to begin acting like one. These realizations made what happened next even harder to deal with.

The doctors said it wasn't my fault: "There was nothing you or anyone else could have done." Of course I didn't believe them. I had lost my baby. I felt it was all my fault. How could it not have been? I was to blame for everything. I made the decisions that led up to this whole situation. Falling in love with a player, giving myself to him, getting attached to the idea of having a baby, and actually believing I could raise her. I had control over all those things. I could have prevented all of it. I just didn't know things would turn out the way they did.

When I was a little girl I had a dream. I would grow up and have the perfect life. I would marry my first love, a man who would not only love me but respect me. We would have beautiful, healthy children and live happily ever after. I no longer believe in happy endings or perfect lives or perfect people. It was all just a little girl's fantasy which would forever be shattered in my mind.

# I WILL GIVE BIRTH
*By Netzi Andino, 16, from a city in the Northeast*

I am a sixteen-year-old Puerto Rican woman and I will give birth to my first child on September 1, 1998. The reason I write to you is because I have been mistreated many times due to my pregnancy.

The church I went to was like a home, but once people found out I was pregnant they wouldn't even look at me. Some said I was a bad potato and one potato ruins the rest. This belief continues to haunt me. I'm not here as a symbol to encourage anyone to do anything. I live my life. I symbolize my own life and the child I carry within me. Whether people see my pregnancy as a mistake or a wondrous thing, I tell people to take it for what it is, to gauge their own lives from what they see when they see me. Take me as I am. Draw your own conclusion.

The way people responded to my pregnancy made me feel depressed. It even made me feel like it was not right to love or feel proud of my child. With the help of the people who did not judge me, I realized my baby was special and he deserves to be loved.

A lot of people like to judge pregnant teens. As soon as they see one, they automatically think she's on welfare, her parents take care of her, she doesn't have a job, or that she dropped out of school. Well, this is my opportunity to defend myself.

First of all, I want to point out that pointing judgmental fingers is not the healthiest way to see the reality. As a teen mother, don't categorize me. Everyday dozens of kids drop out of school. But come to my school and see young, pregnant women trying to make a life, a future for their children and themselves by continuing their education. We hold down a full schedule of classes, go to jobs, have responsibilities at home, and try to keep alive our dreams.

Being a young mother is not a burden upon society. I do, and shall always do, for myself without the help of the society that looks upon us with disdain. We see your eyes, not looking at us but our bellies. We hear your whispers, when we walk out of a room. We feel the coldness that drifts past us, as you refuse to acknowledge us as people, as women, as one of your own.

If anybody reading this book believes I have made a mistake, it is their belief. Mistreatment in this world will not help anyone, least of all my child. I write this to you as an advocate for the thousands who have no time to write, for the thousands who have no way to express their frustrations, and for the thousands more who can't yet speak up for a more deserving life for themselves and their mothers.

# Death in the Family

I keep my collection of *Ophelia Speaks* contributions lined up in hanging file folders. The one labeled "Death in the Family" is among the thickest. Thirty girls wrote to me about the deaths of their mothers and fathers, sisters and brothers, grandmothers and grandfathers, aunts, uncles, and cousins. Death had intruded on their adolescence, robbing them of youthful innocence and leaving a lasting impression. I hope every word I have chosen respects and honors their grief—a grief greater than I can possibly understand.

More girls wrote about a parent dying than about any other family death. The three contributions in this chapter all talk about losing a mother or a father forever.

At thirteen years old, Caren Roblin looks back at her mother's dying and feels guilt-ridden. In *My Mom Was Dying and I Didn't Do Anything*, Caren confesses her sins: wanting to have fun and neglecting her mom. Those sins come with adolescence. I've been guilty of them. Every girl I know has been guilty of them. But Caren's mom died and Caren was left with that guilt, forever. In her unrelenting contrition, Caren hides nothing. With unselfish honesty, she gives us a message: Appreciate your mom.

Like Caren, other girls were left with remorse when death stole a family member from them. A fifteen year old, who preferred to remain anonymous, wrote about the death of her brother:

I was in eighth grade, and he was a mighty and all-knowing senior. He dropped me off and I jumped out of the car, hardly giving him a thank you or good-bye—I had not a minute to spare. If only I had known. If I'd had any clue that would be the last time I would see him alive, I would've told him how much I love and appreciate him. I would've hugged him and told him what he meant to me. He was my only sibling. Now, he's gone.

The next contribution to this chapter, *On November 17, 1994*, fourteen-year-old Karen E. Allen also judges herself harshly. She begins her piece confessing remorse—guilt for not knowing her father had been stricken with a heart attack, for reacting irritably when her mother called from the hospital. Karen takes us with her to her father's side. She helps us understand the horror of seeing him in intensive care. She keeps us with her as her family makes surely the most agonizing of all judgments—when to let a loved one go.

Every girl who wrote about death wanted to feel the continued presence of their mother, father, sister, brother, aunt, uncle, grandmother, and grandfather. In the final contribution to this chapter, *Finding Her*, Susanna Coates searches for and finally finds the ongoing influence her mother left with her.

Still other contributors wrote about missing siblings who had gone never to return. MB lost her brother to a car accident. She grasped at memories in poetry:

now falling at a Lonely Sixteen
time Moves slowly with the company of a Loved one
vague Memories are the Only Images that can be grasped
thoughts left on a Bloody roadways boggle the mind
yearning for the Past that one once had
a beautiful Innocent face Smeared into a puddle of Fear
alongside a car with an ignorant driver
dreams of a Future unknown are what lie ahead for a torn heart
all you can do is watch
what once was yours

and Pray that a Familiar face waits for you in a Heavenly home
and Imagine what you'll Never have
hope pray beg for a Twist of fate that can Never be known
time will Continue
birds will still Fly
new Friends will come Along but none quite the Jewel of your
  Perfect Blue Eye

For many writers death awakened faith in eternal life. Girls felt the spiritual presence of their parents and siblings. Their loved ones had become their angels, watching over them and hearing their prayers.

## My Mom Was Dying and I Didn't Do Anything
*By Caren Roblin, 13, from a suburb in the West*

By the looks of the title you're probably thinking that I'm a pretty selfish person, and you're right. Well, you're right about the person I was. Back then, well, I wasn't exactly the most giving and generous person in the world.

I guess I should skip all of the boring stuff and get to the point, huh? Okay. Basically, the serious, life-altering stuff started at the end of sixth grade. I was in a very rich, very elite, private school called the Meadows. It was considered the best school in Las Vegas. Since I had the mayor's daughter in all of my classes, I believed it was true. Even though I had straight As and was considered one of the smartest kids in my grade, I was an outcast. I wasn't rich and I wasn't famous, but I tried my best to fit in. All of my efforts finally paid off when I started hanging around some of the most popular girls in school. I was very shy, so this was a big step for me. I got crush after crush and all of the usual stuff that happens to preteens. My mom, on the other hand, wasn't doing so well.

I was the child of an affair, so I never really had a father-like figure in my life. Sure, he finally started visiting me once a year when I turned nine. But come on, that's not really a father. So, you could say it was my mom and me against the world.

She always gave me the best of everything. Well, the best she could afford. No matter where we moved, I always got the master bedroom. Whenever we went shopping, 99.99 percent was for me. Of course, I took this for granted. So, yes, I was spoiled. I didn't think so at the time, but as I think back now, I can only realize what a brat I was. My mom put up with it, but she wasn't the kind of person to take my crap. She knew when to draw the line.

My mom already had a broken back. In medical terms, it would be called a compression fracture of the T-12 vertebrate. Either way, it did mean I was doing the chores: cooking dinner, making the beds, dusting, vacuuming, washing the dishes, doing the laundry, sweeping, plus my homework and normal kid stuff. It sounds like a lot, because it was a lot. Mom would apologize occasionally. Deep down, I resented her.

Then she told me what every friend or family member fears. Mom had cancer, breast cancer. She told me in her bedroom while she was resting. Mom convinced me I would be too emotionally distraught to take my finals, and she withdrew me from school. She had some kind of surgery that removed her right breast. I was the only one around to help her with the drainage and bandages. With all of my time being spent helping Mom, I barely had time to just be a kid. It was hard not to show my frustration.

That summer, we moved to San Diego with a couple of Mom's friends, Cricket and Russ. I didn't like the idea of moving into a two-bedroom apartment with my mom and Cricket and Russ, especially since they got the master bedroom. Mom got the couch, and I got the stinky little bedroom with every problem imaginable. The air-conditioning was broken. The windows let in this horrible draft, even when they were closed. And there was only enough room for my bed. I wasn't a happy camper.

Seventh grade started. I guess you could say that it was a year of change for me. I started being outgoing. I loosened up around guys, and my fashion sense improved. In other words, I was rebelling. Whenever Mom wanted me to do something, I would refuse. I could tell we were drifting apart. We used to be so close, but I was too busy with myself to care.

At first, Mom and I had fights every once in a while, then each month, then each week, and finally the tension between us was so thick that you could cut it with a knife. Seriously. Every time we came near, we would ignore each other, or try to win a screaming match. It actually got that bad. Maybe because of that tension, I never noticed Mom's health declining. She couldn't even dress or bathe herself without Cricket's help. As hard as it is to say right now, I did not care. I didn't care that in the middle of the night, my mom would start crying because the pain in her back was so bad. I just considered her a nuisance, a person who kept me from doing what I wanted to do. I regret it these days. But at the time, I was too blind and stupid to even think that my mom was just mortal, that she wouldn't live forever.

Whenever I was with friends, I would complain about how my mom was always nagging me. That started a whole conversation about how my friends hated their parents and just wanted them to die. I never agreed with them, but I never stopped what they were saying either. I didn't want them to think I was uncool. So, in front of my friends, I would treat my mom like crap. They thought it was cool, so I just kept it up.

One day, I think it was a Thursday, I got home from school, and Mom was lying on the couch, just kind of staring at the ceiling. When I closed the door, she slowly turned her head toward me and had this look that wasn't happy, but it wasn't angry either. She wanted to talk to me. I wasn't sure what was going on, but I sat on the floor next to the couch anyway. As she talked, there was this sort of sad tone slipping out. She told me she didn't think that she would make it. I couldn't believe what she was saying. *My mom isn't going to survive?* It was just too serious to really accept, but it wasn't something that I could just blow off. In a couple of days, though, I soon forgot about it.

The next week, Mom had to go to the hospital. The pain was just too much for her. On a low level, I remember being glad she wasn't at home. *Freedom,* I thought. Mom was checked in on a Wednesday. On Friday during math, Cricket came to pick me up. It was only third period, so I had no idea what was going on 'til Cricket started talking about the doctors wanting me to see Mom right away.

The trip to the hospital must have taken about an hour. As we entered the elevator, I had a bad feeling. In the hall, this lady doctor kept emphasizing how "comfortable" Mom was and to not worry about how she looked. Up until I entered that room, I was able to keep perfectly calm. When I saw her with tubes coming out of her arms, an oxygen mask over face, and her short red hair swirled around her head, I couldn't keep myself from crying. Everyone in the room kept telling me to sit next to her. I did it to shut everybody up, but I really didn't want to be there. Mom's eyes were half open and glazed over. It was like she was in a coma. When I was left alone with her she could only blink a little, but she couldn't talk at all. I told her the general stuff—you know, the "You're gonna get better," and "Everyone's waiting for you." I told her how much I loved her. There was just one thing I had left to say. I told her I was sorry. Sorry for all of the back-talking, the harsh attitudes, and all of the times I raised my voice to her. She blinked, and that was it. I couldn't hug her or have her hold me because she was . . . dying. That was when I realized I apologized too late.

I ended up going over to my friend's house, and waited for the call that would tell me my mother was dead. Even with all of that going on, I asked the most stupid, ignorant, selfish, and most regrettable question I have ever asked in my entire life. I cringe every time I remember the words leaving my mouth. Right before I left the hospital room, I had the nerve to ask, "Can I still get my money for the shopping trip tomorrow?" I know what you're thinking. It's the same thing I'm thinking: How can someone ask for money to go shopping the next day in the same room where her mother was dying? Well, I don't know, but if I could have taken one thing I said back that would be it. Cricket just kind of nodded. I thought it was a perfectly normal question at the time. That only goes to show how immature a person can be.

I remember Cricket calling me and meeting me in my living room with my friend's dad at the door. (He dropped me off and was waiting outside to take me back to my friend's house.) Cricket sat next to me on the couch, the same couch where my mom practically lived, and told me my mom was "gone." I don't remember how she worded it exactly, but the main idea was still there. I sat dumbfounded. The thoughts going through my head were so jumbled. I can't recall one single thought except, What am I going to do now? I had nothing left to do, so I cried. Cricket hugged me, and I would have given anything for her to be Mom. I would have sold my soul to have one last happy conversation, one last comforting hug, or even a good crying fest with the woman who had put my needs before hers. It was too late. Much too late.

After Mom's death, I went into a secret depression. I kept my grades up and acted "normal" in front of my new guardians, Cricket and Russ. But in my room, I would sit, blame myself, and cry. I even seriously contemplated suicide. I had the access to get what I needed for the job. And all the while, Cricket and Russ were clueless.

I degraded and punished myself. I felt responsible for my mother's death. I remember one day when my dad had called me. It was the first time since Mom died. His voice was so shaky. I could tell he was trying not to cry. After I got off the phone, I realized everyone was feeling guilty. Everyone must have thought if they had only helped out more, then Mom would still be alive. That revelation didn't keep me from blaming myself, but it did push all thoughts of suicide out of my mind.

It's hard just to talk about my mom. Well, about her death, that is. Even my best friends don't know the complete details of the whole ordeal. I've never told anyone about my past suicidal tendencies. In writing this essay with as much truth as I can possibly dare to remember, I hope those of you reading this will read it again with your parents. I don't care if you're real close to them or not, but you have to know how fortunate you are to have parents, to have that second chance I didn't get. And if you can just bear with me for a second, I would really like to share a poem my mom wrote for me just nine months before she died. It means a lot to me. Other than photos, it's all I have to remember her by.

December 31, 1995

Caren,

I'll be your person of good faith.
I'll take a stand, I won't break.
I'll be the rock you can lean on.
I'll be the fire in your night.
I will defend, I will fight.
I'll be there when you need me.
I swear I'll always be strong.
And that we'll always belong.
When honor's at stake, this vow I
will make. You mean the world to me.

Love,
Mom

I'm now thirteen years old. My mother died on September 27, 1996, when I was twelve. I've changed a lot since then. I can distinguish between what's important and what's not. And disrespecting my mom to "fit in" wasn't important—it wasn't the cool thing to do. I wish I could take it back, but that's the thing about life, I can't. I can only move forward and continue without my mom. She was my support, my backbone, and living without her has made me learn how to become my own support, my own backbone. There is Cricket and Russ, but they're not much older than me. This whole thing has forced me to become more independent. I don't know if that's a good or bad thing. But now, I'm not afraid to tell people what I think. I'm able to accept things more easily. I'm a lot more generous and giving.

So, I guess what I'm saying is: Forget all of the stupid reasons you fight with your parents. It's just not worth it. If you look hard enough, you'll realize everything they're doing is to protect you because they love you. Besides, whether you'll admit it or not, I know you love 'em too.

## ON NOVEMBER 17, 1994
*By Karen E. Allen, 14, from a suburb in the Northeast*

On November 17, 1994, I was home with my little sister Ashley, and my older brother, Scott. We had a half day at school. I was happy to be home around noon, looking forward to enjoying the day. Time passed quickly. It was now 3:30 in the afternoon. My Mom was supposed to be home hours earlier. I was worried and angry at the same time. Where was she? Why wasn't she home yet? I thought, with an attitude. The phone rang. I dashed ahead of everyone to answer it.

"Hello," I said.

"Hi Honey," my Mom's voice replied.

Frustrated and angry at her, I lashed out hollering at her. "Where are you?" My anger eating at me, I was not able to hear the trembling and uneasiness in her voice. She tried lying to me by saying, "Um, I'm shopping." She spoke in a short, choked voice.

Bang! Finally I heard it. "No, you're not Mom. Where are you really?"

Fear was creeping into my soul. The feeling in my stomach was just like I was going down the first huge hill on a roller-coaster ride. I didn't even know why. I knew I wanted to know the truth, but yet I didn't want to know. I just knew it wasn't going to be anything good. I just didn't know how bad.

"I'm at the hospital. Daddy has had a heart attack," she said softly.

I started screaming and crying. I have never been so scared. Why was this happening to me? I wondered. My brother took the phone. I was so hysterical I did not notice the tears streaming down his face and my little sister's face. My brother was trying to be so brave, but I knew he was crumbling inside. My mother explained the details to Scott.

My dad had a massive heart attack while on the bus going to work. A doctor and nurse on the same bus tried to help him right away with CPR. When the ambulance finally arrived they had to bring him back from death with paddles. He was now unconscious and on a respirator. I felt so sick to my stomach. Scott hung up the phone. The three of us grabbed each other in a sobbing embrace. At that point, we were probably closer than we ever will be again in our lives.

Soon my older sister, Jessica, came home with a few of her friends. After learning our bad news, every one of them was sobbing. A short time later my Aunt Sandra was at the door and was joining us in our sob fest.

After pulling ourselves somewhat together, we left to pick up my grandmother and head to the hospital. We had driven on these roads before, but this ride seemed to take forever. I didn't think we would ever get there. The silence in the car was deafening. Deep thoughts were in all of our minds.

Finally arriving at the hospital, we were told to take the elevator to the sixth floor. The arrival of the elevator seemed to take as long as our ride in the car. The tension was building. Although my mom had warned us about the tubes and respirator breathing for my dad, we were unsure of what to expect. Getting off the elevator, we walked into the Allen family, my dad's side of our family. I think that's when it really hit me. I was in a hospital to visit my father who was unconscious, couldn't speak to me, hear me, or see me. It hurt so much. It felt like I had been punched really hard in my stomach. My mom walked with us down the hall toward Dad's room. The walk was like a dream—a nightmare. I felt like I was being held captive and couldn't escape.

Then I saw him. It didn't look like him. "Maybe it was a mistake," I thought. His face was so pale and puffy. He had a million tubes and IVs, monitors with flashing lights, and many other things connecting him to machines that were keeping him alive.

It was awful. I sobbed hello to him, kissed my fingers and pressed them to his cheek. I sobbed, "I love you" and totally lost control. I was half dragged and half carried to the waiting room where my Allen family had gathered. They tried to comfort me, but nothing worked. The only comfort I wanted was for my dad to be okay.

Later that evening, when I had better control of myself, my sisters, brother, and mother took me back to Dad's room. We walked slowly—a very close family. We stayed with him for a long time. I talked to him and held his hand. Deep within my heart I knew we were communicating. I knew he could hear me and he knew I was there with him. I knew then, as I know now, he was in good hands. I could only pray for the best outcome. We had to leave. I said my good-byes for the night.

I went to school the next day, but all I could think about was my dad. I couldn't concentrate on anything. I was dismissed early. I couldn't wait to get back to the hospital to be with him.

That night we were given more information. None of it was good. The doctors were sure Dad was 75 percent brain dead.

I knew at that moment I would never hear Dad's voice again. I would never feel his arm, strongly holding mine, as I walked down the church aisle at my wedding. My children would never know the greatness of having my dad as their grandfather. So much loss for all of us. It felt like my life was over too.

A few days later, after many more tears, prayers and difficult decisions, the respirator was removed from my dad, along with all of the tubes, IVs, and monitors. He was moved to a private room where we were supposed to simply wait for him to die. We never gave up hope.

I only saw my father once while he was in that room. I couldn't stand the pain of knowing what was going to happen, yet seeing him linger on.

My dad died exactly one week after his heart attack. He died at 3:57 P.M., November 24, 1994. It was Thanksgiving Day.

# FINDING HER
*By Susanna Coates, 17, from a city in the Northeast*

Her ashes are buried under a plaque in my church's garden. Her black and white picture is on my desk. Her perfume, the one in the crystal bottle with the blue top, is on my bookshelf. Sometimes, when I feel like crying, I can open the shoebox that contains all the letters she wrote me from the hospital. Her handwriting is on those letters.

My aunt says she saw my mother's image in a stream of light, one December afternoon. My other aunt says she can feel her whenever she makes Rice Crispy Treats with her daughter. I know my father has a home video of her doing needlepoint, and another of her sitting by the fire at Christmastime. But I can never touch her when I watch those tapes.

I've searched pretty much all over the place. I have waited patiently in the garden at dusk, hoping her spirit would make its nightly rounds. I have whispered prayers to her before closing my eyes at night, wishing she would answer.

For my sixteenth birthday, my father gave me her sapphire bracelet. I took her black cashmere sweater from her closet a few months after she died. I remember it always felt so soft on her. I couldn't bring myself to wear it, though, until a year ago. One of my mother's friends gave her a plaid teddy bear while she was in the hospital. I made sure I got it before my sister. I have slept with that bear every night.

My aunt says I look like my mother when I smile. People always tell me I have her voice. My mother's best friend watched me for years, trying to see if I slanted my *e*s as she had. In our living room there's a picture of me at a family party a few years ago. It gives me chills when I look at my hands in that picture. I feel as if I'm looking at hers. I can't even describe the feeling.

A few weekends ago, on Mother's Day, I was in church. I was actually wearing that black cashmere sweater. This man I had never met before came up to me. "I was watching you," he said.

"You have your mother's beauty." I thought to myself, "My mother was beautiful?" I had never really seen her in that way. I remember how her hair was always curled under or how she always towered above the other mothers. I had never really seen her as "beautiful." And here was this man, who I had never seen before and he was telling me I look like my mother.

I have always secretly envied, and even resented, my aunts for having their special "sightings" or "feelings" of my mother. My father told me: A few nights after she died, he had a dream. In it, my mother said, "Come and tuck me into bed." I wondered why my mother had never come to me. Why had I never seen her in a vision or felt her while making cookies. I still remember how completely empty I felt after she died. How my heart was swollen with tears. I wanted to fill that void so badly.

When my father returned from the hospital the day she died, he took my sisters and me upstairs to my parents' bedroom. There was a Tupperware glass standing on my mother's nightstand. He picked it up and showed us there was a small amount of water left in it. Tearfully he told us she had been the last person to drink from that cup. He then asked us if we would each like to have a sip of the remaining water. As that water poured down my throat, I was drinking from the cup of life. If only that small sip could have given me all the things I needed. I imagine now I must have seen it as a glowing, shining cup of liquid hope, somehow passing my mother into me.

This Sunday is my mother's birthday. I'm sure if I took about ten seconds I could figure out how old she would have been turning. But something inside of me will not allow me to do that. By contrast, I am always counting the years, even the days, since my mother's death. My aunt says she would rather remember the joyful parts of my mother's life. But, every year, on the anniversary of her death, I am there, waiting for her to appear to me.

I recently made a big decision about what college to attend. My final choice meant I would not be going to the same college my mother attended. Right about the time I made the decision, I dreamed about my mother. When I woke up in the morning, I was overcome with a somber joy. My aunt says by deciding not to go to my mother's college, I am letting go of a part of myself and my mother I had been clutching since she died. Perhaps she appeared to me to let me know she is still with me, despite the loss I feel.

I have searched far and wide, deep and low, to find my mother. But, like Dorothy, I realize the answer has been right in front of me. My mother is *within*. She is not in a bracelet or in a bottle of perfume. Maybe, perhaps, if I think with my heart and not with my brain, I will see she has been there all along. And, that when I am searching for her, all I have to do is search within *me*. I have spent the last four years searching everywhere but there.

In my dream, the last thing I said to my mother was, "Mom, I need you. Will you help me?"

Now I realize I do not need to wait for her spirit by moonlight. I have found her. She is everything I do. She is in the beauty and the pain, somehow holding my heart and saying, "I'm right here."

# PART THREE

# THE BEST
# AND THE WORST
# OF FRIENDS

≋

# With the Support of Friends

≈

When I was two, my home turned into a daycare. Suddenly, I shared my mom's attention with a dozen playmates. Although one might predict that her divided attention initiated my tears, my tantrums were actually launched by the boredom that followed five o'clock. My new friends were my happiness.

I greeted those toddler days with glee, as my first best friend arrived just after dawn. Jaime was nearly six months older than me. I sensed her superior maturity. Mostly, I admired her way with words. She'd take my hand, motion to a quiet corner, and say, "Let's have a talk-about." Then, she and I would nestle into an intimate space and chat in three-word sentences.

My best friends still bring me incomparable happiness. I'm giddy when they are near, dizzy with delight, warmed by their closeness.

In the fall of 1998, I started college. Most of my childhood friends have scattered, dispersed to various and sundry destinations. But, one day, my best friend breezed into my university's library with enthusiastic ease. Toon breathed life into the stillness of the book-laden building. After repressing squeals of joy, without inhibiting a long-held hug, we escaped to the freedom of fresh air. Once outside, I bounced about, holding her hand and playfully pulling at her. My clunky wood platform shoes hit loudly against the stone steps. In the process of my spontaneous display of excitement, my ankle buckled beneath my body. I fell awkwardly forward. Toon held my hand tightly and pulled me up. With a smile, she steadied my balance.

Here, in this place where few people had known me beyond the six weeks since I had arrived, Toon's presence quieted my anxiety, and animated my giggles. Her excited hand movements, wide eyes and smile returned me to our shared childhood. Her loving sprightliness reminds me of everything good and pure in this world. Our relationship, our shared support, our consistency is unrivaled by any other connection.

Yet, my unyielding appreciation for best friends is a popular passion. Nearly as many girls wrote to me about the support of friends as wrote about eating disorders. I received fifty submissions where girls described the importance of best friends in their lives. Many girls wrote about the comfort they gave, and the affirmation they received, during seriously troubled times. They wrote about overcoming the isolation of HIV/AIDS, anorexia, abuse, and depression. JMK, a fifteen year old from a small town, described how friends helped her through the dark tunnel of a desperately despondent time.

Today I did well. I woke up, showered, got dressed, and went to school. I chatted with my friends on the bus and complained to a peer about a teacher. During yearbook pictures, I smiled for the camera, each of my arms draped over the shoulder of a friend. In class, I took notes, and at the end of the day I packed up my backpack and hopped on the bus once more, finishing my homework on the ride. For some people, this is quite normal every day, but for me, this is an accomplishment. Each day like this one is a new triumph.

Once, I saw things from the other side of the spectrum. . . .

I made the dangerous mistake of keeping my problems to myself. Pushing all thoughts of my friends, dreams, and accomplishments out of my head, I acted on my anger. I swallowed a whole bottle of tranquilizer pills, along with some Excedrin.

I then went to my room and lay down, never planning to get up. I shut my eyes, and got a sudden rush of mental images. First, the faces and voices of all my friends. Then, the image of the silver and blue cross I had worn to the funeral of my friend back in December. She had been brutally murdered, along with her cousin, only one day after my birthday. The rest of her friends and I had vowed to live our lives to the fullest, in memory and honor of her, whose life had been stolen away. It hit me like a brick wall—I was the first to break that promise. I stood up and headed down the stairs, into the living room where my father was, and I passed out.

When I awoke, late afternoon of the next day, there was a phone call from one of my "kindred spirits" on the Net, one of the ones I had met in person. She had called right after I had been taken to the hospital the night before. She knew what had happened. We talked. All that day I spent talking to friends, and all the rest of the week as well. These people cared about me and still loved me after what I had done to them and myself.

JMK's words, along with the contributions to this chapter, demonstrate the life-affirming quality of adolescent friendship. The first captures the fun side of friendship, telling a tale of a clandestine adventure.

In *Cute Memory*, Rebecca Anne Grimes captures the essence of friendship. Her story about her friend's ultimate, self-inflicted bad hair day details the meaning of a best friend. Rebecca knows where her friend will go, what she will feel, and how she can be comforted.

In *Calloused Christmas* Haley Eagers Thompson tells the story of longtime friends whose relationship survives a nightmarish party scene.

These contributions capsulize a truth demonstrated by the numbers of girls who wrote tributes to friendship. During adolescence, friends bring an intimate quality of support that can't be provided by any adult. The comfort of our peer connections is reflected in our most honest and direct hand-holding: When we trip they are the first ones to pull us back up.

# CUTE MEMORY
*By Rebecca Anne Grimes, 16, from a small town in the South*

You can imagine my surprise when I walked into school and was immediately surrounded by a mob of people asking me if my best friend, Kirsten, had shaved her head. Confused, I said I knew nothing more than they did, and excused myself. What an absurd rumor. I walked to first period.

Mr. Jones called roll: "Warren Ames, Gary Bolger, Jerry Dowling, Hanna Fredrick."

Everyone answered to their names. He continued: "Foley" to "Thompson." He paused, "Kirsten Thompson," no one answered. He paused again, this time longer. The silent room echoed in my head.

Mr. Jones lectured on the migration pattern of geese. I followed his drawings, copied them into my notebook, and watched my sketches. They transformed into individuals, lost, flying together to escape cold. I named each goose: Linda, Edward, Ronald, Joan, Kirsten.

I began to think about Kirsten: bald headed. First I thought of the goose in front of me, molted. The naked goose faded into a human body, followed by a head. It was bald but looked as if it belonged that way. Not because of old age, but because of youth.

Hair was a cover, hiding identity. It was long or short, colored or natural, messy or pretty. Nevertheless it was there, judged by people who neither did or would know you. People saw hair before they saw you. I thought about it some more and then believed, myself, that Kirsten might have shaved her head.

"Miss Grimes." Mr. Jones stood in front of me and handed me our chapter test. "Nice job, as usual." He smiled.

Kirsten and I had studied for it together. School came so easily to her. I knew she could have made an A on the test; I also knew she didn't.

Kirsten possessed some strange quality I envied. She studied, learned material, spoke languages, but managed not to care. If she felt she had learned the material and understood it, she was content. She took the test or quiz, filled in just enough answers to pass, and left the rest of the test blank. Grades meant nothing to her. She disconnected her personal knowledge and education from society's measurements. She tormented the education system (because it bored her). Their methods of determining knowledge were proved false by Kirsten. Kirsten's intelligence was there, but they could not get to it.

I once asked her how she planned on getting into college. She looked up at me and laughed. "Don't you get it?" She asked.

The bell rang. I saw Kirsten's sister, Corena, in the hall and called her over.

"I have to go, my class is on the third floor," Corena said. She knew what I wanted to know.

"Tell me now," I demanded.

"Yes."

I grabbed her arm and whispered, "Where is she?"

She answered, in a loud voice. "Kirsten didn't want to come to school so she dropped me off and drove away. Mom's at home so she's not there." She paused and said in a less confident, softer tone, "Maybe she ran away."

Corena ran to class. I stood in shock. I had World History. I knew it was an important class, but Kirsten was my main concern. I put my books in my locker and ran down the hall. Mr. Tass, my World History teacher, yelled to me. I ignored him.

I stopped running when I reached the baseball field. What was I thinking? I just ran out in the middle of classes. I heard a group of geese in the distance and remembered Kirsten. Where would she have gone? I headed toward the Thompsons'. I passed the woods on my way. A fallen bird's nest made me stop. I remembered collecting birds' nests and broken eggs with Kirsten. She took inventory of our findings. She recorded our findings with precise graphs in a blue spiral notebook. An abandoned tree house was the storage room for our treasures.

I sprinted into the woods. The trees appeared the same, the

little stream still rippled beside the foot-worn path. Our favorite climbing tree still stood, solid, youthful, friendly. I reached the clearing.

It looked smaller, weathered, but our tree house still remained in the branches of the dying oak tree. I climbed the ladder. Many rungs were broken. It took awhile to reach the top. I crawled on my hands and knees, entering between the same boards we had nailed in place eight years ago.

Kirsten sat in the middle of the boards, her feet folded in her lap. Piles of papers toppled around her. She wore jeans and a hooded sweatshirt (the hood covered her head). She wrote without looking to see who had entered. She knew.

"You wanna see?" She asked, her voice empty, her eyes concentrated on the paper in front of her.

I shook my head no. She continued to write. I knelt next to her, put my arm on her shoulder. She dropped the pen. Tears dripped onto her paper. The ink ran.

"It's okay," I whispered. "Cry."

We sat on the floor of the tree house. Kirsten cried silently on my shoulder. I glanced at the papers on the floor. She had started to illustrate them. I looked closer. They were my poems. Poetry written when I was ten. On a second look, I noticed the poems had been cut apart and glued together with parts of Kirsten's graphs.

Kirsten lifted her head and wiped her face, mascara smeared down her cheeks. Kirsten's hood fell exposing her shaven head. A stack of papers fell behind us. We are still the two little girls in the shadows of those papers playing dress-up.

## Calloused Christmas
*By Haley Eagers Thompson, 15, from a small town in the Southwest*

I have always been proud of my relationship with my friends. Our friendship is a bond stronger than steel because it is bound with the flesh and blood of seven extraordinary beings, with the will to survive in a small town buried in a small valley in rocky mountain society.

Although we no doubt have our conflicts, we are tight. We understand one another's yearning, our burning desire to shine, to stay afloat above the surface of a tide pool. Society, our peers, our families, everyone desperately pulls at our essence. We have each other, and that is all.

I began high school one year ahead of my girls. When they came into the high school as freshman, I was extremely relieved. I wasn't alone anymore. We were all greatly anticipating the next few years together. Freedom, parties, boys, experimentation, and most importantly our collective growth. It was inevitable: We would meet these possibilities, if not exceed them. We decided our fate. From the day we stepped into that high school we made a pact to have a shitload of fun, even if we had to pay for it.

We all wanted a taste of the *fun life*, but honestly, we weren't invited. No one at our school accepted us. I mean: Come on. We were a bunch of slip-wearing, provocative, against society, outcast lesbians! (The last accusation is based merely on the opinion of the naive.) We basically refused to follow the *All-American*, natural makeup, Gap clothed, basketball-star ruling of the commune our high school had become. We were nothing to these people.

So naturally, we were shocked when about halfway through the school year, a large percentage of the boys varsity basketball team began to show an interest in us. I mean, we are certainly all very far from ugly. I think we're all extremely beautiful people—physically and mentally. Still, this whole thing was very unexpected.

That's why we acted so quickly. I mean we didn't even stop to think what we were getting ourselves into. We were quickly becoming what we ourselves ridiculed, and so often put down.

It was the perfect plan: We would all meet at a house where no parents were present, get smashed off our asses on alcohol the boys supplied, with *our* money, and maybe even get a little lucky. And, we did find a house, out in the middle of nowhere, with few neighbors. And, the boys did supply, more than enough for our young frames to handle, enough alcohol to make that one night a night none of us will forget.

The night began when all seven of us, a truckload of girls, poured into the once desolate house, now full of highly expectant young men. We all positioned ourselves next to the boy we planned on "getting to know." We were all virgins, and had absolutely no intention of losing our virginity that night . . . at least as far as we thought.

The whole evening consisted of who could get what. The arousal of the boys began early. Mia, the crazy muscular blond, whose parents own the house, went to take a quick shower. The boys, well aware that Mia is the most provocative of all of us, tried to get into the bathroom and hop into the shower with her. I hurried to her rescue, and soon realized my aid was almost unwelcome. She was enjoying the whole situation. I soon caught on too. We all rapidly realized that we had the most wanted males in our whole school in the house. We had the ability to get control of them after a few drinks, and do whatever we wanted with them.

I exited the bathroom, my senses renewed, my soul throbbing inside me. This was power: access to the unknown. All around me my friends were milking the situation for its benefits. We each had more than enough attention from the boys who were all too comfortable with the surroundings.

Then began a flurry of mixing drinks, loud rap, and naked torsos running around. I remember downing my third shot as my friend Andrea threw herself onto the couch and a flock of boys followed, grabbing and groping. She was scared, but she squealed with laughter, as they grabbed at the bra supporting her breasts, which greatly exceed the size of the rest of ours. And, I thought I would have control!

But, you see, I still thought I had control. I remember feeling *so* good about myself when I impressed the two boys I was after by downing a shot without following up with cranberry juice. So proud in fact, that I took the bottle of vodka and drank it straight out of the bottle. Only God knows how I actually took it in. I was so numb. I may well have been drinking water.

Soon things began to blur. I know I almost took note of everyone's whereabouts before I really lost it. Joey was safe, having a conversation with the only decent boy in the house. Meg and Lila were dancing in the corner. Both were too intelligent and shy to do much of anything else. Lauren popped up everywhere, laughing and actually seeming to have a good time. Andrea was back in clothes, but *very* drunk with many obnoxious boys still following her. Last, but not least, Mia—she had been discovered in the bathroom with Andrea's boyfriend, by none other than me.

Andrea angrily pounded on the bathroom door, while Mia wept. Lauren laughed. Lila and Meg kept quietly dancing. All tried not to notice what the others were doing. It was a bad dream.

Things got wild. I soon found myself braless, then completely topless. I was, sadly enough, enjoying myself; enjoying myself, but beginning to get scared. I looked to John for support. John's a boy I had been with for a short period of time as a freshman, when I was even more insecure, if you can imagine that.

John has a girlfriend, and I knew it, but I didn't care. I wanted the power and I got it. I would have given him anything at that point: my soul, my essence, my virginity. Luckily he did not oblige me. He refused to take my virginity away in such horrible surroundings. He swore I'd regret it. This, I feel, is the only thing I have to thank him for. The only thing I ever regretted from that moment was wanting to give him so much.

Anyway, I was gone for sure when I began stumbling through the house screaming and bawling for John. I wanted comfort in an unknown place. Finding I had nowhere to turn, I made friends with the toilet. I threw up. Then, I threw up again. This time on Mia's brother's bedroom floor. And, a final time, in a potted plant. All the while Lila tried to calm me. Joey, my best friend, came to comfort me. But I wanted none of it. I looked to the only one who could soothe my pain. But John was busy, stealing the innocence of my dear friend Lauren.

Who's to say what went on the rest of the night. Although I

do recall a cop passing by me as I drifted off to sleep on the couch. I cried in my dreams, being sad because John had left without saying good-bye.

I woke up with a massive headache, and a full bladder. I'm surprised I made it to the bathroom. I found my friends, all gathered in Mia's room, quiet. Innocent, naive, quiet. What had we done?

One by one, the stories poured out. Memories of stupid, drunken nakedness lurked inside us. Mia had been with her friend's love, and lost her virginity to another. Andrea had lost her respect for Mia and for herself. Lauren had been violated, and used, and had hurt a friend. And, I had lost respect for myself by yearning to give myself to John, and then loathing the friend he chose instead. Joey, Meg, and Lila all lost respect and were hurt. It hurt them to see their friends make such horrible decisions, to do such horrible things to themselves.

We all wept, forgave, and wept. Remembered, and wept some more. The months that followed were like blankets covering the pain. We still have each other, but the wounds are there, hiding, taunting. We set ourselves up. We got the night we'll never forget.

# Friendship Lost

≋

Yesterday I sent my copy of Walt Whitman's poem "To a Stranger" to one of my best friends in South Carolina. A year ago, she had given that same poem to me.

Caitlin and I had bonded quickly during our summer away from home. For two months, we lived in the same house, ate the same food, and shared the same perspective. As our summer program came to an end, we sat on the green, spending our last hours together. Reflecting on our sudden closeness, she remembered a poem. Tearing a piece of turquoise oak tag, ripped roughly into the shape of Nevada, out of her notebook, she wrote down the words. It was her favorite poem; she cried when she gave it to me.

When I returned home, I tacked the poetry-inscribed blue tag onto the bottom left-hand corner of my bulletin board. All year Whitman's words peeked out at my desk below.

Passing Stranger! you do not know how longingly I look upon
    you,
You must be he I was seeking, or she I was seeking, (it comes to
    me as if a dream,)
I have surely lived a life of joy with you,
All is recalled as we flit by each other, fluid, affectionate, chaste,
    matured . . .
I am not to speak to you, I am to think of you when I sit alone
    or wake at night alone,

I am to wait, I do not doubt I am to meet you again,
I am to see to it that I do not lose you.

*—Walt Whitman*

Now, after a year of waning communication, I sent
Whitman's words back to her, hoping to evoke, perhaps even
rekindle, our friendship. But, this time Whitman's title, "To a
Stranger," had a profoundly more accurate meaning.

She e-mailed her response: "Nice to hear from you. I'd forgotten I gave you Whitman. I'm good. I hope all is well with you
too. Caitlin."

Most friends grow up and grow apart. In second grade, I
moved to a new neighborhood and made a new friend. Naomi
nearly lived at my house. We bonded like sisters, without the
rivalry, and we stayed tight through elementary school. But,
starting in junior high, our paths diverged. Different friends,
classes, attractions, and habits loosened our attachment to one
another. By high school, occasional hugs and chance meetings
defined our relationship. Then, last summer, we reconnected,
almost accidentally. She had moved to Vermont. I went to
Burlington to visit my boyfriend. Unexpectedly, Naomi and I
found each other. We made a day of playing with a puppy and
giggling. Awed by our ability to return to our nine-year-old
neighborhood friendship, we swore to make up for lost time. Yet,
I haven't seen her since that sunny afternoon.

For the girls who contributed to this chapter, the onset of
distance was not always the result of passive passage of time.
Sometimes, distance was forced on them. With distance came
degrees of abandonment. Thirteen-year-old Kelly Hogan captured the sadness of separation: "I look across the large room, to
see her with her new boyfriend's arms around her tightly, with all
of her new friends laughing and talking to her. Now, all I have are
the memories. With my head in my hands, I cry." This chapter's
first selection expresses similar emotions. In *Confessions of a Best
Friend*, Rachel Wilson puts on paper what she wishes to say out

loud. She laments the intimacy she lost when her friend found a boyfriend. Her confession reflects the emotions felt by many girls when commitment to boyfriends dilutes devotion to girlfriends.

The second contribution mourns a more complex loss—the growing apart of best friends whose lives turn in opposing directions. Choua Vue's letter-like piece, *Missing the Real You,* substitutes for the conversation she yearns to have with her estranged friend. Compassion and sorrow permeate Choua's plea.

In the third submission, titled *Longing,* Charlotte Levy describes a more calculated estrangement, a rejection laced with the meanness of girls bent on popularity. Charlotte depicts a scene I have witnessed and tried to prevent—a clique disowning one of its members. Girls can be cruel to one another. We can circle around, throw girls out of our "in" group, and bury their self-worth. In this piece, Charlotte describes the hurt that is too often inflicted by a sorority mentality.

Sometimes without intention, and sometimes with callous calculation, we lose the friendships once precious to us.

## CONFESSIONS OF A BEST FRIEND
*By Rachel Wilson, 15, from a suburb in the Northwest*

"What's wrong?" you ask me, a puzzled look on your face.

I'm jealous of the time that you spend with Dave. It seems like you are always with him and I never get to see you by yourself. I don't feel like I have a best friend anymore. Every time I want to talk to you about a problem I'm having or about a boy that I like, I can't because you are always with him. I know that you were jealous in middle school because it seemed like I always had a boyfriend, but I never neglected you to spend time with him. Maybe I'm jealous now that the tables are turned and you are the one with the boyfriend. I don't know. But I do know that I miss having a best friend.

I'm happy for you because it seems you have someone you really care about who also cares about you. You must really care about each other, since you two have been together for a year now. But what kind of relationship do you have if you never get to spend time with your friends? Or, at least, the people who used to be your friends before you discovered Dave? What kind of hold does he have on you that you feel the need to sit with him every free period, every lunch hour, and every time in between? Do you feel naked without him by your side? I know that he goes out with his friends without you, why can't you go out with your friend without him?

I never get to see you anymore. I feel like I don't know what's going on in your life. Whenever I want to talk to you, I have to call you or go out of my way to find you at school. Is our friendship more important to me than it is to you? You must not ever want to talk to me because I can't remember the last time you called me. The one time that I did spend the night at your house, you couldn't go the whole night without talking to Dave on the phone—three times, actually. I wish you would need to talk to me on the phone badly enough to call me three times in one night.

I wish you would at least tell me what's going on in your life. I always imagined that when you considered having sex with someone, I would be the first one you would tell. But I had to find out from my mother. Your mom told mine when they had lunch together one day. I can't believe you didn't tell me you were considering sex. I thought best friends were supposed to tell each other everything, especially things like that. I assumed that I would be the first to know, but you don't bother to tell me anything anymore. I know things about you that no one else knows. I know you were a punk rocker in first grade for Halloween. I know James ran by and kissed the shoulder of your coat in second grade, because he had a huge crush on you. I know John was your first real boyfriend. And later, your first kiss. But I don't know anything about you now. And it hurts.

I feel like I'm on the outside looking in. I can see you, but I can't hear what you're saying. You won't let me inside. I know I'm exaggerating how it is a little. I know you still think of me as your best friend. But, this is how I feel inside. I've felt this way for so long that I don't know if I know how to be happy anymore. I'm tired of always feeling bad. But most of all, I'm tired of being invisible to you.

"Nothing," I reply, protecting you the only way I know how.

## MISSING THE REAL YOU
*By Choua Vue, 17, from a city in the Midwest*

Sometimes I wonder what you're doing today. What are you thinking or saying? Are you happy or sad? Staying out of trouble? Are you sitting in school wondering about me too? I wonder a lot, mostly about why things have to change.

Remember elementary school? We played football everyday—you, Sue, and I, with all the other guys. We thought we were tough, tough enough to challenge those guys in any sport, even football. I laugh now thinking about how we carried ourselves with such great confidence. Remember those days?

We became inseparable. Still, we had our days when we fought and argued. I don't remember what it was we fought about so much. It was probably something foolish. Whatever it was, we had Sue to pull us back together. She was the "neutral" one, who never fought or argued with any one of us. She was the one who made us come back to our senses and persuaded us to forgive each other for the mistakes we made.

But then her family moved during one of our little fights. That same year, the new elementary school was built, and we transferred there for fifth grade. We met new people, made new friends, and, without Sue, we gradually drifted apart. We didn't talk again until middle school during seventh grade.

How we stumbled upon each other, I don't recall. Although two years had passed, we found ourselves still able to talk openly to each other about anything. We used to sit outside your house, talking for hours about school, teachers, friends, or life in general. Even though we still had that personal relationship, I couldn't help feeling like you weren't really there with me.

Maybe it was because over time you changed more than I did. We talked to each other at school, but we hung out with different people. You hung out with your "girls," doing your own things. You busied yourself with too much makeup and guys. Every step you took you had to stop and pull those baggy pants back up. Even the way you talked changed. Whenever you spoke to me, I would forget what you said because every other word that came out of your mouth was a form of vulgarity.

I think your brain also started to deteriorate because of all those cigarettes you smoked. I don't know if that's possible, but your grades began to slip. Maybe because you picked up the habit of running away during eighth grade. All the work you missed just dug a hole for you to sink in. But you took everything in stride, never seeming to care that your grades were slipping. Every time you came back from your run away, I always asked you why, but you'd just grin and say, "Hey. Life's too short. Have fun."

I blamed your "girls" for your troubles. I wanted to believe you wouldn't have changed if it weren't for them. I still remember the time when you and your girls beat up that girl. I wasn't there to see it, but I saw her afterward. She didn't look too pretty anymore.

You always had to present yourself as a tough, rebellious girl who always took risks and lived on the edge. But I knew you weren't as tough as you made yourself out to be. Tough girls don't clean up their house as a gift to their mother on Mother's Day.

Soon your running away became a routine. It troubled me. You were the only one I trusted. It was hard to change and make new friends. But you were no longer here, forcing me to find a different crowd.

So when you ran away, you took our friendship with you. You didn't know that I was still holding on to the other end. I was still clinging on to you and what I had left. I hoped maybe it was just a phase, this running away. The more you ran, the more I hung on, and like a rubber band, it stretched until it couldn't anymore and snapped. I tried so hard to keep our friendship going, but you didn't care. You had no clue you hurt me, no clue. I tried so desperately to hold on to you. You went about your life, while I clung on hoping maybe I'd find the old you. But I became frustrated with myself because I knew I wasn't going anywhere. Instead, you dragged me around in circles like a helpless child who couldn't walk. You moved too fast. I eventually lost my grip.

I tried to think of reasons to explain why you ran away, why you changed. I made excuses as a way to build false hopes. Maybe you were still the same, and it was all a phase. I backtracked and reflected on all the time we spent together. That's how I came upon this little memory of the day you came late for school. Rumors already spread that you were on the run again. To our surprise you showed up and ate lunch with us.

This boy across from you started telling you off and calling you names for running away. Surprisingly, you just sat there staring at your food like nothing was going on. I looked at you and wondered why you didn't say something to this idiot. You didn't look up or move. So I turned toward him and told him to shut up. I looked at you again and nudged you to see if you were still awake. You spun around and yelled at me for hitting you! I was shocked at the sudden outburst. Speechless, I left you alone. That incident slipped my mind as the day went by.

It all came back to me again. One day, after school I confronted you. I went over to your house, knowing you'd be outside smoking a cigarette. I asked you to tell me what was going on. Why did you run away? But you wouldn't tell me, so I told you what I thought, my conclusions. You looked at me, hesitantly, and told me all about it. I walked away from you that day, hating your father.

I don't know how you managed to hide it from us. You carried yourself well, never complaining about any pain. I was deeply disappointed though, that you never told me, not until I begged you to. I would have understood, I was your best friend, you know.

A couple of days later, you ran away. This time you left a week or two before the end of eighth grade. Your parents moved out while you were gone. But somehow you managed to find your way back to them. It wasn't until two and a half years later that we saw each other again.

I heard you were in town attending a soccer tournament nearby. I purposely went to see you. I wanted to see you. I searched all over for you because I didn't plan to stay long. I still remember the sight of you that day, dressed in all black with only your hands and face showing under that black outfit. I thought you were crazy, because it was a humid summer day. Two people had already passed out from heat exhaustion, and here you stood dressed in black!

When we spotted each other, we hugged and the first thing out of your mouth was, "Damn, girl, you're still so skinny!"

I looked at you and thought to myself, "Damn, if I'm skinny, then you must be an anorexic." But, not wanting to be impolite, I kept that to myself.

Instead I said, "Damn, girl, compared to you I look fat!"

You just laughed, while I quickly looked you over. I was secretly content you got rid of the massive makeup, but saddened that I could see your cheekbones poking out under your pale, thin skin. I heard people say before that you lost a lot of weight from running, not eating properly, and experimenting with drugs. I didn't believe them. I didn't want to.

All we managed to say was, "Hi" and "How's it going" before you ditched me for your girls. My heart sank and I was crushed because you see these girls everyday. We hadn't seen each other for two and a half years! We only spoke for fifteen minutes! You uttered a promise to write and told me to "take care" before you left me standing there alone.

When I turned around to leave, I caught Sue's glance, and she rolled her eyes. She could see my disappointment, and I could tell she knew you would do that to me.

I left that day realizing that I still had this little bit of hope we could still keep in touch. But now I know it will never happen. Time has changed, and so have we. Sometimes I just don't understand it. We grew up together. I end up with a decent life, while you get yourself in more trouble. Tell me why does it have to be this way?

I've moved on, but I do think about you sometimes. I'm still waiting for that promised letter. I know it might never come. I still hope. I miss you . . . the real you.

## LONGING
*By Charlotte Levy, 15, from a suburb in the Northeast*

Longing. Aching for something you can never have, something you may not even want. It is a disease, an overpowering spirit that takes control of your soul. You find yourself looking at others, wishing you were them, wishing you could feel their happiness. Wishing. Longing.

I was fourteen years old when my life changed forever. It was the first day of ninth grade when my four best friends approached me and told me they no longer wanted to associate with me. In those brief seconds, my world, all that ever had made me happy, crumbled. I was alone, with no one to turn to. I found myself sitting by myself at lunch or, worse, sitting with a group of girls, yet feeling completely invisible. Slowly, I began to slip away, to become a shadow, watching my old friends laughing happily. I felt as though I were seeing them through a glass window. I pounded on the glass, but they didn't hear, didn't even acknowledge my presence.

People kept telling me I shouldn't want friends who would do this to me, who would abandon me without a second chance. Others said I should hate them. Still, nothing could have been farther from what I felt. I wanted to run to them, telling them that I loved them and telling them I would change. All I was doing was longing for the friendship that had made me feel whole. I began to dream something horrible would happen to me, hoping they would understand how much I meant to them. In my worst moments the only thing that kept me from emotionally shutting down was the anguish I would cause my family.

I knew what longing was like. I would never impose that hell on them. It eats at you, devouring you until nothing is left. You become reduced to a vacuous soul.

I began to doubt myself, to question what kind of person I was. All I wanted to do was change so those four girls would want to be my friends again. I didn't care what I became, as long as they wanted me, as long as they ached too for the friendship we once had.

Then, slowly, I began to see things more clearly. I started to understand teenage girls in a way I never had before. I began to see the malicious aspect in so many of them, even myself: The way we can turn on each other, the way we betray a trust. I wanted to withdraw from society, thinking I would never again find true friends, thinking there would always be a secret told behind my back, a trust broken. All I wanted was a friend to talk to, yet I was scared to allow myself to get close to anyone.

My reaction to this pain surprised me. I have always been a strong person: a leader, a straight-A student with a voice. I was always the first to raise my hand in class and disagree, no matter how stupid I looked, or how different my idea sounded. I remember kindergarten. Even then, as a little six year old, I would argue with my teachers, if I felt I had a valid point. When I was older, my father and I would sit for hours having political debates for fun. Nothing gave me more joy than talking or analyzing a situation. I took charge wherever I was. I was never afraid of stating my opinion. Nothing fazed me. No matter what was bothering me, I was always able to debate my position. But suddenly, I was unable to assert myself. Suddenly I was silent, empty. Suddenly, I was no longer myself.

Those months changed me, in many ways. Today, I am a different person. In some ways, I have become negative, suspicious: I second-guess everything and everyone. But, in turn, I see things for what they are. I've asked questions: Why is friendship such an important link in our lives? How can other girls hurt someone so much, causing dangerous thoughts to flow freely through their mind? Why do I long for something I know I don't really want? I want to be popular again and go to parties, to be in the cool clique, but at what price? Is it better to live my life in shallow happiness, or with understanding and pain? Now I know the answer to that final question and it is clearer than anything has ever been. The only way to live fully is with pain and understanding, with truth.

It has been eight months since my betrayal. Even with my new knowledge, I still find myself watching those girls, longing to be with them. But I know now that they are not people I truly want to be with. They aren't nice people and they bring out the worst in me. It strikes me as odd that my brain can tell me one thing, my heart another. I do know the only way to survive this kind of experience is to talk about your pain, to talk about what you miss, what you crave. To keep the feelings trapped inside is a torturous experience, one that empties your soul. I almost lost myself in this experience. Losing friends is one thing; losing yourself is another. For a time, I lost my voice and found myself slipping away. But new friends and my inner strength got me through. The ability to tell myself and others what I was feeling is what kept me from disaster.

If you ever find yourself feeling this kind of despair, talk to people. Let them help you. Express yourself. Be yourself. Because the only people who are worth being friends with are the people who like you as you are.

# When Friends Die

We don't expect to become personally acquainted with death during our teenage years. Yet, few of us seem to escape adolescence without attending a funeral. Many of us wear black to services, grieving for our peers. Girls wrote about friends dying from cancer, suicide, drugs, gunshots, and, most often, car accidents.

In the stories I received, boys, only boys, died in car accidents. Girls talked about seeing shattered glass and tire marks on the road, hearing ambulance sirens, passing police blockades, or glimpsing a body being taken away on a stretcher. Each remembered the moment they learned their friend had died. Each described the shock that immobilized their mind, and the tear-filled grief that caught up to them later. Some, the close friends, described guilt. An anonymous girl from a small town wrote:

> At the funeral, seeing him lying there not moving, not smiling, and not doing what he loved to do best, talking, made me feel all torn up inside. He was dead. I walked past him feeling guilty, crying and thinking, Why wasn't I there for him? Why didn't I go with him? All these thoughts were going through my head . . . I know he will watch over me and someday I will be able to see him and tell him, "I'm sorry."

No matter what the cause of death, many girls spoke about the awakening of their faith. Repeatedly, they confessed their belief that their friend's spirit still lives.

The first contribution to this chapter, *Christmas 1994*, stands as a tribute to the essence of a friend. In this loving memorial,

Tracy Caron takes us through the horror of her friend's cancer, giving us an inspirational portrait of courage and kindness.

In the next, *Flashbacks*, Jenny Joseph describes the depression left behind after a friend's self-inflicted death. By allowing us to see her alone, isolated, and despairing, Jenny shows us suicide's contagious hopelessness. However, she also takes us to the other side of mourning, to her recommitment to living.

In *This One Goes Out to the One I Love*, Liddy! Bargar tells us about her affection for a boy, a potential star, now dead. In sweet words, laced with romantic idealism, Liddy! brings us to the chilling scene of her friend's drug overdose. In the end, she, like Jenny Joseph, turns toward life and chooses happiness.

In the last contribution, Anne Rushman transports us to a scene beyond any nightmare. In *Today*, Anne gives breath to the sterility of news headlines—the horror of a school shooting—the terror of children firing guns, the agony of close-range death, the mourning of a mentor, and the loss of a safe place, forever.

Death during adolescence feels unfair. We're young. We're invincible. Death is supposed come with old age. When death breaks into our lives and steals our innocence, its finality leaves us unnaturally older. There are too many elderly young people.

## Christmas 1994
*By Tracy Caron, 16, from a small town in the Northeast*

It was about a week before Christmas, and I was on top of the world. This was my favorite time of the year. I was all caught up in the mood: buying Christmas gifts, baking cookies, decorating the house, and best of all, having time off from school. So when my best friend, Ali, was absent the last couple of days before we got out, everyone just thought she was taking her vacation a little early. But on December 23, my world fell apart.

That day, while sitting at home wrapping Christmas presents, I received a phone call. One of my other friends told me

Ali was in the hospital. I was a little surprised, but still I did not worry. I thought she was just a little sick or something. Unfortunately, that was not the case. My mother then called Ali's mother, Anna, to find out what happened. Anna informed us that Ali had a tumor in her liver, and she'd be in the hospital for a while. I didn't understand all the complications that went with this diagnosis, but I was still scared, nervous, and upset, all rolled into one. My parents tried to encourage me saying it could just be a harmless tumor and the doctors could simply remove it. At that time, I had no clue what else it could have been. Meanwhile, my family tried to keep me in the Christmas mood, but it just wasn't the same. How could I have fun while one of my best friends was in the hospital? Needless to say, that Christmas was horrible. But little did I know that it was about to get much worse.

Two days after Christmas, I was sitting up in my room writing Ali a letter when my sister came in. I remember the concern in her voice when she said, "Mom and Dad told me Ali has cancer." I had no idea what she was talking about. I started screaming and yelling at her, calling her a liar, with tears streaming down my face. My sister sat there stunned for a minute before she gave me a hug and said, "Tracy, I'm sorry. I thought you knew. But it is true, Ali has cancer." I sat there for a minute, my mind blank, just crying, before I went downstairs to talk to my parents. They confirmed what my sister said was true: Ali did have liver cancer. My parents didn't want to tell me about Ali's cancer before because they didn't want to ruin my Christmas. As if it wasn't ruined already.

I called Ali every day during the vacation, not knowing what to say to her, other than I missed her. Finally, one day we were able to visit her. My mother, my other best friend, Mandy, Mandy's mother, and I, all drove out to the hospital. I remember how frail she looked lying in that hospital bed. Ali had always been very, very thin, but it was quite obvious she had lost weight. Her almond-shaped hazel-green eyes were filled with sadness when she told us, due to the chemotherapy, she was going to lose all her hair. She was trying so hard not to cry when she ran her slender fingers through her beautiful long black locks of hair and she said, "Everyone will make fun of me." I hated the world right then. I hated the world for giving my best friend cancer. I hated the world for not being able to cure her. But most of all, I hated the world for all the cruel heartless people who would make fun of her. Still that should be the least of her worries. I swore to myself right then, I would never let anyone hurt her.

We stayed for as long as we could. Ali had to start her first session of chemotherapy. She was a little nervous. We gave her words of encouragement. I hugged and kissed her good-bye. She held up a necklace with a silhouette of Mary holding baby Jesus and said, "I will never give up hope."

That night I finally got all the harsh details Anna had told my mother at the hospital. The cancerous tumor actually took up 90 percent of Ali's liver. Giving her chemotherapy would hopefully shrink the tumor until it was small enough to cut it out. If that wasn't possible, Ali would have to get a liver transplant. "But there are a lot of complications with a liver transplant," my mother said. "Her chances aren't good, Tracy," she continued gently. "Say a prayer for her tonight." That night was the first night I had prayed since I was little. I continued to pray every night, no matter what—and still do, to this day.

While Ali remained in the hospital receiving treatments, we all had to return to school. It was really different without her. She was one of a kind; she definitely stood out in our grade. Everyone looked up to her. We all called her as much as we could. Most of the time, we couldn't talk to her because she was too sick. I didn't get to visit her again for awhile. By that time, she was already losing her hair. I could tell she was really embarrassed. She wouldn't let anyone except her best friends see her. Then, I came up with a perfect idea. I told Ali, with full honesty, I would shave my head so she wouldn't be the only one without hair. Ali said definitely no. "I don't want you to ruin your beautiful hair because of me. I'll be fine," she insisted. I tried to argue with her, but there is no arguing with Ali; she wouldn't hear of it. I remember her giving me a hug and saying, "Thank you, Tracy. That's very sweet, but I really don't want you to." If Ali wasn't so against it, I was ready to stop on the way home and shave all my hair off. That was the way Ali was. She was used to helping people, not being helped by other people.

Soon after that visit, Ali started coming home in between chemotherapy treatments. She stayed home for a little while, but she still had to go back to the hospital at least once a week for checkups. When she could, she went to school and spent time with us. Nobody made fun of her. At this point, I think she realized what we knew all along: She was beautiful no matter what.

That school year Ali seemed more in the hospital than out. The chemotherapy was working so none of us complained. In the hospital, she did get a couple of famous visitors. Ray Bourke and Johnny Busick stopped by one day and took pictures with her. Having been a hockey player ever since she was little, she was really excited. She also watched a hockey game with Jason Priestly. But meeting all the famous people in the world couldn't make up for all the pain she was going through. No twelve-year-old girl should ever have to go through this.

Ali never complained. She always had a smile on her face. She didn't waste time feeling sorry for herself. She focused her time and energy on getting better, trying everything, no matter how far-fetched it sounded. She also was an active volunteer, assisting in raising money for the Cam Neely House in Boston and for cancer research at University of Massachusetts Medical Center in Worcester. She even helped out at the hockey rink teaching little kids to skate.

Ali took it one step further. Once, the Make-A-Wish Foundation offered to send Ali and her whole family on a vacation, anywhere Ali wanted to go. The Foundation would pay for everything. But Ali said, "My wish is to give it to a child who has less than I do. I've been places, and I've done things. There are a lot of kids who aren't going to make it who haven't had those opportunities."

That April we gave her a huge surprise birthday party. Every girl in the grade was invited. The look on Ali's face when about thirty girls jumped out of her garage is something I'll never forget. I think that was the last time we did something as a group, before her big operation.

In the summer, Ali's parents, Anna and John, had to make the biggest decision of their lives. After traveling all over the country to see doctors, the decision was to try and remove the cancerous tumor from Ali's liver. The operation was going to take place in the beginning of August. We didn't have much time to spend with Ali, but we made the best of it.

In the beginning of August, Ali walked into the hospital, as bravely as she could, knowing in a matter of hours 70 percent of her liver would be removed. I have never been so scared in my entire life. The fear in my mother's eyes, even in my father's eyes, still stands out in my mind. He told me, "This is the big one, Tracy. She makes it through this, and she's doing good." I have never been so happy or relieved as when I found out later that day the operation had been a success and all the cancer was removed from Ali's body.

I knew it was true when I visited her the next day. She gave me a huge smile and reassured me she was okay. Then, she dozed off into a deep sleep. Now, all she had to do was recover. Although it took her a long time to regain her full strength, she was in normal condition by the time school started in the fall.

Ali was back to her old self again. She was going to school regularly, was gaining some weight, even her hair was growing back. She had the cutest little bob haircut that made her look more like a model than ever.

Just when we thought everything was going to be normal, things turned back around.

Around November, Ali started getting pains again in her stomach. The doctors thought the cancer was coming back. CAT scans proved this to be true. On December 23, 1995, exactly one year after Ali was diagnosed with liver cancer: The cancer had indeed grown back. Once again, two days before Christmas, the holiday I now hated, we received more bad news.

Options were limited, and Ali's name was put on the list for liver transplants. Since her body couldn't take anymore chemotherapy, this was her last hope. However, there were many other names on the list. We all knew it would be a while before she got one, if she ever did. That new year we all prayed for a new year of good fortune. But, like always, the bad things seemed to cancel out the good. We all went on day by day, sending our prayers out to Ali and her family.

It was so hard to believe that the cancer was back in Ali. She was looking and acting as healthy as ever. She now had to carry a beeper at all times in case they found her a liver; then she would have to fly to Philadelphia immediately. My heart almost stopped when we were out to dinner one night, our whole group of friends, at a fancy restaurant and the beeper went off. I didn't know whether to be happy or sad when we found out it was just a false alarm.

The beeper never did go off for real. We waited at least four long months.

In March, we received more bad news. Ali's cancer had spread to her lungs, making her ineligible for the liver transplant. All chances for Ali to survive now went down the drain. When she found out, Ali allowed just one single tear to roll down her cheek. She took the news a lot better than I did. When I found out my best friend was going to die, I thought I'd die right along with her. Sometimes I still don't know how I had made it this far. But Ali would not allow any talk like that. She was determined to stay cheerful and make the best of the time we had.

Ali's condition worsened over the summer. By the end of August, it was quite obvious she would not be able to attend high school. We were forced to take one more step in our lives without her.

School and field hockey demanded so much of my time, I barely ever got to talk to her or visit her anymore. That's probably one of the biggest things I regret. I should have made time.

I still remember our last phone conversation. Even though it was only a couple of words, Ali tried as hard as she could to say, "I love you" back to me, but it was so hard for her. She had an IV tube down her throat, making it difficult for her to talk.

By the end of September she could barely get out of bed. Around then, I visited her for the last time. I could only stay a couple of minutes, but I could tell how sick she was—too sick to even give me a hug good-bye. I had to settle for hugging her feet. I'm just glad I got to do that.

When October came, she wouldn't allow any more visitors. She didn't want anyone to see her like she was. She didn't want us to remember her that way. At that point we had to talk to her mother and ask her how Ali was doing. Anna told us Ali really wanted to see snow one more time. She wanted to wait for the snow.

It was a cold brisk day on November 3, 1996, when the first snowflakes fell from the sky. At the same time, Ali gave a faint smile and took her last breath. She continued her journey up to heaven, where she still watches over us. That was the worst day of my life.

Since then, it's been almost a year. Not a day goes by that I don't miss Ali. But, she is still with us. I still talk to her every night when I'm alone, even sometimes when I'm not. And every new step I take in my life, I'll always take her with me—her kindness, her unique sense of humor, and her graceful smile. But most of all, I'll take all the memories we ever had together. Those memories I'll treasure for the rest of my life.

*This poem is dedicated to my best friend, who succumbed to liver cancer November 1996*

## Ali

Ali is the deep blue color of the sky
She is the voice in my head that tells me not to cry
Ali is each and every star that twinkles into the night
She is the voice I hear when I try with all my might
Ali is the shape and form in every white cloud
She is what makes me stand tall and proud
Ali is the beautiful orange color in the moon
She is what helps me believe I'll see her again soon

Ali is the warmth in each ray of sun
She is what tells me to go on and have fun
Ali is each little glistening snowflake
She is within every fresh breath that I take
Ali is the big splash in every puddle of rain
She is what keeps me from going insane
Ali is the breathtaking assortment of colors displayed in the
　　trees
She is the words that come to me when I'm praying down on my
　　knees
Ali is the exotic rainbow that stands out in the sky
She is everything that shows me she did not truly die
Ali is and always will be my best friend
She is the part of me that knows our friendship will not end

## FLASHBACKS
*By Jenny Joseph, 17, from a suburb in the Midwest*

Darkness silenced the wary depths of despair I dwelt in. I sat
upon a cloud of loneliness, secluded from my family and friends.
I was in my room, devoid of light. I huddled in a little corner
with my head hung. How I wanted to reach out to others—this
emptiness in my soul craved another human being.

My best friend, Lindy, committed suicide. *Stop!* It's all over
now! I shook my head violently and took a deep breath. A soft
knocking came on my door. My sister peered in slowly.

"Um . . . Jenny, mom wants you to come down to dinner."
Lucy glanced at me. She paused. "Are you okay?" She looked nervous.

I nodded as she went away.

I stayed huddled with my memories. There were so many
and Lindy was a part of all of them. Ever since kindergarten,
Lindy had come in and out of my house with a smile on her face.
My family and I adored her. She was full of life, always cheering
people when they were in their worst of moods.

But now, she is not here. There was no one to cheer me up. That's not exactly true. There were so many people to help me, but I pushed them away. Just like Lindy pushing me away when she took that knife and plundered my perfect world. The frustration, anger, and resentment reared its ugly head again.

I remembered the day one phone call changed my life, for a really long time.

"Hello? This is Jenny. Is Lindy there?" I asked Lindy's mom. I was at school and needed a ride home. Lindy had her car, so I figured I'd call her.

There was an odd muffled noise at the other end of the phone, somewhat like she was crying.

"Mrs. Thomas? What's wrong?" I remembered how my voice shook.

"Oh, my God, my baby ... she ... she ..." Mrs. Thomas sobbed so loudly. I was worried by her reaction.

"What happened to her?!" I yelled out at the top of my lungs.

"She's dead. My baby is dead. What am I going to do?" Mrs. Thomas went on and on, but I did not hear her. The receiver had fallen from my hand. My breathing decreased. I trembled, not knowing what to do myself. People surrounded me, asking what was wrong and casting worried glances at me.

After I found out Lindy committed suicide, depression took my life by storm. Darkness became a friend to me. I shut myself in my room, all the time. I did not want anyone or anything near me. I cherished my privacy and my journal. I wrote about Lindy and me and the world. I thought about suicide myself.

My family worried about my sudden mood swings and angry outbursts. I built a wall to keep anyone who tried to get close away. I laughed at my psychologist when he told me he understood how I felt.

"Excuse me. You wouldn't know crap by just looking stupidly at me."

After much denial, I realized he was truly trying to help me. The thought of slicing my wrist became unappealing. I remembered how angry I had been at the whole world for taking her away from me. I realized she had taken herself away from the world. It was then I decided that the cruelest, most selfish act is to commit suicide. When you kill yourself, you kill others—emotionally anyway. I was rescued from an avalanche of snow. I sat huddled in the corner of my room. I saw myself climbing unsteadily toward the top, afraid and lonely.

A year had passed when my sister called me out of my seclusion: "Um . . . Jenny. Mom wants you to come downstairs to dinner."

When I came downstairs, my parents and my sister were laughing with each other. I loved seeing them happy, even though I felt I was totally the opposite. My mom noticed me and her smile looked forced. I felt so sick to my stomach.

I was quiet during the entire meal. My family talked, but no one said a single word to me. I really wanted to reach out to them, but I couldn't. The pressure was too much for me to bear. I raced upstairs and ran to my room. I wanted to cry and cry and cry and cry, until I reached a place where no more tears were left to shed.

After some time, I glanced out the window. What I saw took my breath away. There was a multitude of colorful butterflies everywhere! They looked so beautiful frolicking by the drooping lilacs and scarlet roses in the lazy afternoon sun. I wondered why no one was in the garden, my garden, the one I had grown. People admired that garden because it was so heartbreakingly beautiful. I remembered how proud I had been when my family exclaimed over my creation. But, now I was not in my garden. No one was there.

My mother came into my room. "There's someone on the phone for you," she said, smiling.

I was about to say my usual refusal. Then I realized how long it had been since I had seen my friends. I wondered how long I could keep straying from my loved ones. Until there was no one left for me to love? It suddenly occurred to me, my life didn't have to stop because Lindy died. She wouldn't want that. I just had to accept the facts. I have to move on, without Lindy.

I picked up the phone. "Hello?" I asked.

It was my friends asking me if I wanted to go to the mall with them.

I said, "Great!"

As I hung up the phone, I really did feel great. The chains that had once contained me, broke loose. I was liberated from the invisible claws of depression and brought back to my haven once more.

My whole family came into my room. I stared at them and they stared at me. We all knew how that one phone call changed my life—this one for the better.

I reached the top of the mountain, and I want to stay here. Lindy will always be remembered in my heart. I won't forget her. Neither will anyone else who ever got to know her.

# This One Goes Out to the One I Love
## One Girl's True Love Story

*By Liddy! Bargar, 16, from a small town in the Northwest*

Today I feel like that shoe. You know the shoe—the one everybody has hiding in their room, too ugly to bring out in public, worn, with that telltale hole in the toe. The shoe someone loved, once, some time ago. The one long since lost under the bed, sentenced to live with the dust bunnies, a few Lego's, and a wool sock.

Yesterday I was a girl. A girl who loved a boy. The boy nobody could break. A boy strong and shining among a crowd. I watched him lean against a wall and smoke a cigarette. I watched him, quietly hoping he would forget I was there, and he would look up. When he lifted his head his eyes would fill my heart, ask me questions, make me feel alone.

The boy had brown eyes as do I. His were far more striking. I am just a girl with brown eyes and hair to match. Not too fat and not particularly thin. My clothes bear the badge of the Salvation Army. He dressed with style. He didn't dress to show off his wealth or his beauty, though he had both. He dressed to show who he was.

I danced with him, once, on a rooftop. It was drizzly and cold. We climbed up there to smoke. I sat shivering and smoking. He reached out a hand and said, "Dance with me." I looked around to see who he was talking to. Only I sat on that rooftop. We waltzed above the skyline stumbling and giggling.

"Wear that to my funeral." He whispered. "You look beautiful."

I felt beautiful. I promised him I would, never believing I would have to.

I talked to the boy one night. It smelled like spring that night. I crouched behind my house smoking. I lit my cigarette with a little pink lighter I stole from the boy. Out loud, but whispering, I begged him to prove to me that he was watching and knew that I was listening. The boy I loved never knew that I loved him. I strained for something to happen. I put my senses on high, aching for a sign. A bird was staring me down with a hungry glint in its eye. I guess that bird was my sign. I hate birds, they scare me.

I had watched him hold his "baby," and gently caress it. I see him still. His baby has no heart, no eyes, only spice, a soul. Wrapped in plastic, his "baby" quietly cries for him. I smell him. He is emotion. He is a robot. The boy I love wraps leather around his arm. His body tightens. His beautiful lips curl. The rush flows from the needle. I can feel it dancing, sweating inside him. This river is sex, climax, and cigarette. His eyes glaze, then smile.

The boy I loved died last night. He died with a spike in his arm, injecting venom into his body. He died alone. He closed those brown eyes and died. Poison killed him. The boy I loved did not love me. He loved the evil potion that made him fly free.

I dreamed of the boy I loved. I was wearing a ball gown, with flowers entwined in my hair, walking on a spring morning. I walked too far and fell into a blue lake. I am beautiful in my dream. I fell into the blue water. I opened my eyes as I suffocated, and there were the boy's eyes pushing me up. I breathed fresh air at the surface. The boy was there drowning me. He was toying innocently with my life, my soul.

If only I could have saved the boy. If only I could set him free.

I have always wanted to be free. Soaring, alone, without inhibitions. I tried to fly away from his funeral. It was classic—raining, hailing maybe. I drove up the hill, the boy's house looming ahead of me. His house with the father inside. He got those brown eyes from his father.

I pulled up, girl music playing behind me. Something pulled me from the car. I started walking. The boy said I looked beautiful in these clothes, these shoes. I was wet and cold and not pretty. I am ugly when I cry. My feet hurt. I sat down and smoked a soggy cigarette. I walked three miles that day, before I went to his house and looked into those eyes, his eyes, the father's eyes.

Then, I was alone. Alone was bliss. Alone was power. Alone was self-loathing, hatred. I had forgotten how to be with people. I walked, voices and faces were a blur. A hand reached out to me, I pushed it away. I didn't need help. The world was spinning. My eyes burned red.

Summer comes. The air was fresh, but somehow bitter. I walked with flowers entwined in my hair. The pain was far less intense now. I don't think the hurt had actually faded. I think probably I just forgot how it felt to be normal, happy. I felt guilty when I laughed. The boy I loved will never laugh again. It was summer, but I was cold.

Tonight is New Year's Eve. Those eyes, his eyes, the father's eyes still haunt me. I suspect they always will. Over too many glasses of champagne and a pack of cigarettes, I made a resolution: I will be happy. I will not forget the boy I love. I will allow him to become the boy I loved once, a memory. I will celebrate his life, not mourn his loss.

I will be happy!

# TODAY
*By Anne Rushman, 15, from a small town in the Northwest*


Today
In the noisy music of my room
I cry; tears pouring;
I can't control my emotions,
today has been so sad.
I've lost so much,
but I don't know what to do with myself.
I've lost a friend, not a best friend,
but someone who could perfectly explain life
in just a few words:
A big mess!
I can't believe how children can kill children,
like one has done today.
So many kids injured
in a place they should feel safe: school.
The realization of life may have hit today,
with the bold thought of death,
I feel like our society is crumbling under my feet.
Am I the only one falling with it?
I wonder how it's possible
to make it through this
long miserable journey
called life.
Where to begin the adventure?
and where to end?
Music. Loud.
Tears, they're gone.
They're all on paper now.

# PART
# FOUR

# TOUCHED
# BY DESIRE

≋

# Innocent Attractions

≋

I practically skipped into my house. A file folder labeled "The Crush" was tucked under my arm. With a nearly giggly enthusiasm, I announced, "I love these contributions."

While compiling *Ophelia Speaks,* I often found my spirits sinking. Though I felt uplifted by the contributors' strength, I felt pulled down by the unfair weight of their circumstances. This chapter is an exception.

Its contributors returned me to my daydreaming days, to a time before the objects of my affection had facial hair, a time when just a smile could induce sweaty palms. I am happy with my "mature" relationships, but I am remarkably nostalgic for those one-sided, silent affinities, those never-to-be-realized romances. In junior high, one of my best friends had a remarkable ability to turn her terribly unrealistic crushes into actual flesh and blood boyfriends, but the real boyfriend-boy was never as much fun as the fantasy version.

I love every entry in this chapter. Each one playfully demonstrates how intelligent we really are. Even when, maybe even especially when, we appear silly and ditzy and brainlessly infatuated with some terribly undeserving individual, we know exactly what we're doing. The girls in this chapter talk from both sides of irrational affection—from the side that feels totally consumed by unreasonable attraction and from the side that knows objectively the limits of romantic delusions.

In the first, *Reality Bites Is More Than a Clever Name,* thirteen-year-old Laverne Difazio expresses her irrepressible personality, telling us about her incorrigible fascination with an unlikely recipient for her affections. She knows the object of her desire is oblivious, unavailable, and not particularly attractive. Yet, she adores him, dwells on his image, and rejects other suitors. She keeps the potentially scary "real boy" experience at bay, while allowing herself the satisfaction of an unredeemable fantasy.

Next, Mireille Latourers Hyde offers a peek into her diary, where she confesses to indulging in her own brand of forbidden fruit. In a poetic stream of consciousness, she confesses her attraction to a boy who's simply not her type—an artsy boy with a bad attitude. In the last line, she tells the truth concealed inside her fascination: She wouldn't want him if he wanted her.

This final contribution is truly a love story for our technologically advanced generation. Willow confesses her clandestine affair—her all-night Internet rendezvous—with the boy of her dreams. *For Trevor* displays the connection between mental affinity and physical fantasy.

Together, these three pieces represent the innocence of secret loves. In these butterfly-tummy times, we surrender more to our own emotions than to the actuality of another person. We revel safely in our own love of love without the dangers of anything too real, too scary. Fantasies can be perfect. Reality is often unbearable. Crushes are fun. They allow us a momentary escape—like reading a page-turning book or crying during a movie. We are not giggling girls without grounding, but sometimes we do need a break from our often too harsh reality. Sometimes nervous queasiness and sweaty palms can be our escape.

## REALITY BITES ISN'T JUST A CLEVER NAME

### My Venture into Reality and the Important Conclusions I Have Yet to Make

*By Laverne Difazio, 13, from a suburb in the East*

Okay. So last night was frightening. Very frightening. I've lived my girl life in reality, for the most part, but one or two parts of my life were always left to my imagination—boys and drugs.

"Drugs" is such a general term. I'm not too excited to start them. Yes. I'd like to try them and probably will, later. Still, sometimes you know excess isn't for you. I'd like to think I won't become addicted to anything. But, bullshit surveys say my personality is quite addiction-prone—not to mention alcoholism runs in my family. I'm not trying crack or heroin, or coke, ever. That's just not my lifestyle. Perhaps being a drunken, depressed hooch isn't my lifestyle either. But, I'm not as wary of a bottle of Southern Comfort as I am of a hypodermic needle between my toes.

But, I digress. The reality I encountered last night was free of narcotic fun. No, it was simply a boy. Simply.

My friend "Janet" met this boy "Brad." She was upset because Brad likes her. And, she's not allowed to like him because her friend "Satan" (sorry, I don't like this girl) likes Brad. I think it's unfortunate you're not allowed to be with a boy you like and who likes you, if a friend likes the boy in question. He becomes a prize, then a symbol, and finally a beast. In reality, he's just some guy who'd be better off ditching the whole scene. Nobody can win by sticking around this sordid kind of triangle. Well, it's not really a triangle. I don't know what it is.

Back to my story.

Brad called up Janet from his friend "Frank's" house. They talked for hours. And, Oh no! They like each other. So Janet is stuck with a guilty conscience—but, not horrendously guilty.

Janet invited Brad and Frankie over to her house along with my friend "Columbia" and me. Well, Brad had to go to the movies with his grandparents, but Frankie could make it. Janet, Columbia, and I waited outside on her front steps until Frankie arrived. Then everything got awkward. Columbia went home to take a shower, and I went up to Janet's room. Frankie followed. Looking at the graffiti-covered shelf above her bed, I wrote something scary about when the object of my affection, "Scoliosis Boy," gets out of the hospital. (He's still in the hospital and won't be returning to our dandy middle school until September.)

Well, it was all uncomfortable for about fifteen minutes.

Then Frankie and I just talked, listened to Santana and played wall-ball. (Fun, fun, fun!)

Finally, Janet, Columbia, Frankie, and I took a walk. My clever little friends kept saying Frankie and I would be a good couple. Frankie's not a scrub. He's a nice looking and very built guy. But, Frankie and I talked about his friend and my crush on his friend, Scoliosis Boy.

So, what's to be done with my fatal attraction to Wonder Boy? He's still getting operated on. Maybe I'm in love with the idea of him. But I think he never loved the idea of me. I still like his squinty green eyes and deep sort of John Henson voice, and his long, unkempt brown hair, and . . .

This must be unfathomably boring to all of you. It's like a Harlequin historical romance novel description, except Scoliosis Boy looks nothing like manly blond warrior hero, Roen, or mysterious, gaunt, dark-haired DelFonza, the Italian pirate.

Back to reality. Frankie is such an Abercrombie model. You should see him. Anyway, he even told me I'm attractive. I told him he's also attractive. But, I wasn't going into cardiac arrest over that. It was a fabulous adrenaline rush, but I wasn't really in love with this Frankie character.

I've had this stupid, stupid, stupid crush on his friend for eight months now. And, instead of replacing Wonder Boy, Frankie just added reality to the whole situation. I'm glad he did. I'm not expecting Frankie to fall in love with me. But, Oh, how I miss my Scoliosis SweetTart.

I wasn't kidding when I told Frankie, and everyone, that I like Boy Wonder. I like him: his crooked spine, his crooked teeth, his pale skin, his amazing, sick, hilarious sense of humor—a humor exactly like mine except he's brilliant and a million times better at being funny—his Japanamation shirts, the way he wanders around the room for no reason, his (pardon the adjective) manly nose and chin, his slacker philosophy, his profile, the way his feet inadvertently tap the floor at all times, his fabulous ability to use profanity in a natural way, the way his voice softens when I oh-so infrequently talk with him. I don't care about his teeth or hair (it's kind of oily), or his tendency to drop things on the floor, then hit his head while reaching out to pick them up. I don't mind that some girls say he's a loser—whatever that means—or that Katie called him that "kid with the long oily hair." What I care about is: Maybe he just won't ever care about me and my unrequited love for him.

Frankie told me the latest news about Boy Wonder, "He can bend over, walk, and stretch, and stuff. But he has to keep the metal rod on his spine until he stops growing."

Now my major question is: So what next, you idiot savant? (This is how I address myself) Frankie thinks I like him. I think I love his Scoliosis Buddy. But, when my dear Chicano partner in crime, named "Ruby," told the object of my affection about my attraction to him, he replied, "That's nice."

What next, indeed?

In fact, right now, in this very moment, Frankie and I are in the same room. I came here, to the library, to think, make up overdue homework, and listen to a mix tape of Bob Dylan, Bob Marley, and Neil Young. But, oh no . . . Frankie has come over twice to talk with me, and I feel like a bitch and a half for not being happy to see him. But, I'm not happy to see him. I'm slacking, wishing, and hoping, Oh, Frankie, please, please leave, just kind of fade into the dark.

I can't deal with him now. He's beautiful, but boring. I want my Scoliosis Boy, but he'll never be mine. Oh, somebody do away with me. I don't deserve Frank's attention. I crave my Boy Wonder. Frank's a great guy, but I don't want him.

Isn't that silly? I had a theory. I'd go out with any boy good enough to like me. But, this wasn't what I had in mind. I didn't know I'd fall head over heels in love with a comic book monger who has a severe case of Scoliosis. But, I can't be in love with him, because, believe me, it would scare him more than the decline of anima in Western Civilization. You just can't tell a thirteen-year-old guy with intimacy issues, "Hey, I'm crazy ass in love with you, and want to be your girlfriend." I know. I know. I'm only thirteen. He's only thirteen. We can't fall in love anyway. But I have issues with reality. So, that explains that.

I've been getting counseling from my ring-a-ding, coo-coo, all-in-all brilliant, compassionate, kick-ass therapist, and from this eccentric, loud, vulgar, but sensitive guy in homeroom. We'll call him Rocky. He used to be shy, like me. Now, he fits the description I gave him—but he's really nice. So we talk about my making an effort to talk more, and it's hard, but I'll try. If I had talked more, maybe I could have been Wonder Boy's girlfriend by now. Oh, the reality! The reality! The complete logic of it all astounds me. Cause and effect.

Oh dammit. Frankie just came over and talked to me. He's fine. I'm fine. We're all so fine, I could vomit. He's really nice. He's really hot. And, I'm so stupid I could scream. Oh, well, I'll get back to ranting later. Might as well walk home now. To quote another of my antiheroes, "Death to the weird."

I have no idea. What next? Well, I have ideas, but I can assure you—they're all backwards and wrong.

In conclusion: I'm better off alone. At least until Monday. . . . The Ominous End. . . .

## CRUSH

## A Diary Entry, April 1997

*By Mireille Latoures Hyde, 16, from a city in the West*

This is not what I want to want.
I want to want a macho jock, who's sweet (at heart), and naive about what's important.
I want to want someone with whom my friends get along, someone who cuts their hair short, someone who picks me up in a car and takes me to a movie and back to his house to kiss under his bedcovers and pretend it's *forbidden*.
. . . To you it isn't, is it? Somehow, I imagine that to you sex is natural, easy, necessary, nothing to giggle about, nothing to wonder about.

You are shorter than I'd expect; you seem to be more of a man to
    me.

I love the dark, the stubble, the thick slits of black eyelash with
    your white-toothed smile, your carved-from-granite jaw.

You bite your nails.

You wear fuck-the-world clothes; your hair is too long for my
    taste.

You make me think—taut pliable tan, stretched over juicy
    muscle, clinging to a steel skeleton.

You are too into music and film, you make me feel dumb for
    thinking *I'm* "artsy". . . . I've always said that art-guys bother
    me.

I don't like a lot of your friends.

I don't like that you are into (heavier) drugs.

I love that you make me laugh.

I love that you smell like cologne and soap and thick smoke.

I love the color of your skin.

I love your smile. (*Love!* your smile! It's amazing. . . . !)

I love that you can be immature, while still you remain one of
    the only mature ones to me.

I hate that some of my friends dislike you, that they would go so
    far as to say you're arrogant, simply because you're nice to
    them or maybe it's because you never speak to them.

I love that you are someone who I imagine would hold me
    roughly against the wall with one hand, but softly hold me
    with your other hand while you kiss me, if you kissed me
    . . .

I love how shockingly gentle your touch is—yet it's sensual,
    sweet—I love that you touch me at all.

I love caring what someone thinks again.

I hate that I am probably not what you want to want, one girl in
    a group of many, all in jeans and colored tank tops and
    Lash-by-Lash mascara, a girl who can't decide between
    little-girl-cute and true woman's beauty (ick), and therefore
    has neither.

A girl who says she likes film, but only sees every other

Hollywood because-I-was-with-friends movie.
A little too ditzy, a little too naive, a little too obvious.
(I'd love to feel I exude unattainability . . . )
I would love to have you want me.
It would almost surely cure me of wanting you in the least.

# FOR TREVOR
*By Willow, 17, from a suburb in the Northeast*

When I think of him, I see a picture—two years old, maybe
more—printed from the blood of a cheap ink ribbon, pasted into
my diary beside a poem he wrote for me, in the early-morning
beer-hazed hours of New Year's Day.

Then I am lost, haunting the hallways of years past.

I feel soft, synthetic fibers squishing between my naked toes,
as only soft, synthetic fibers do. I feel my heart shuddering,
lurching forward, clutching at Cloroxed ribs, then thudding back
again in rhythm with every creak of the hidden floorboards, every
shift in my home's well-fleshed skeleton. I can picture threads of
sound linked to my parents in the bedroom below. One false step,
one abrupt jerk on aural cords, and the marionettes will be acti-
vated.

With a gasp, I collapse into my threadbare seat.

From my distant state of nervous agitation, I hear the
Windows 95 start-up sound heralding familiar news: Yo, Mom!
Yo, Dad! It's two o'fucking clock, and your goddamned pathetic
daughter is at the computer—yet again!

I flinch.

But this time, the guards are asleep at their post.

I wiggle my ears into varying positions, feeling the skin
draped over my cheekbones pulse in tempo with my attempts to
hear any movement downstairs. It's hopeless. I can never tell the
difference between the wheezing rattle, the dying breath of a fan

and the freeze-dried ocean captured in a little black box, sent express from the Sharper Image, to help my mother sleep.

The screensaver casts an impatient spotlight on my uncertainty. 3-D shapes gyrate around the log-in sign, occasionally pausing in their travels to point an accusing red triangle at my nose.

So I try to enter my name and password, but it feels as though I have jammed my fingers into the heart of the San Andreas fault. The energy of the earth's core, of all creative and destructive forces—not to mention of my own melodrama—is being channeled through my hands. I am trembling.

Then the cacophony of modems chattering, gossiping, blathering makes me long to curl up into the fetal position beneath my desk. It's sounds like I'm back in a fourth grade lunchroom—I swear I can hear my name being chanted. That inherent urge to hide was never quite buried in passing years. But as always, there's no room for me down there, beneath my desk.

He isn't here. But we're both insomniacs. He'll come. I'll wait.

We'll talk about free will versus determinism. We'll discuss religion. We'll debate the merits of Sartre and Nietzsche. We'll talk about books. We'll wonder about the true nature of time.

I'll whisper, "I love you," but only the computer will hear, and I alone will care.

And then I'll sleep, maybe an hour or two before school, trying all the while to turn a pixelized graphic into flesh, typed words into warm breath against my throat.

As always, I'll fail.

# Seduced by Sex

≋

The first time I had sex it was unplanned and unprotected. I thought I was ready. After all, I was a mature fourteen. Ha. Soon after, I found a magazine article during study hall: *Of sexually active girls the average age of first intercourse is fourteen and a half.*

I had been just a month shy of fifteen. I neatly creased the thin shiny paper, ripped it out. I laminated it onto half a note card with clear tape and placed it in my wallet. I held on to that magazine clipping for years. I validated my passing milestone with the statistic hidden behind my high school ID.

A year later, I described myself as having been "just a baby" when I lost my virginity. But, my young age was not particularly unusual or surprising—we grow up immersed in a sexually titillating culture. We hardly expect to be "sweet sixteen and never been kissed." Instead, the majority of us intend to be sexually active in our teens.

I survived my first serious relationship unharmed, perhaps even a little stronger for the heart wound I braved. I never lamented the decisions I made. Instead I valued the lessons I learned.

Many girls, however, do not escape early sexual activity unscathed. For them, the benefits of self-reflective hindsight do not easily soothe the pain. Most girls who wrote about sex wished they had waited for a more perfect time. Some simply realized sexual initiation is seldom perfectly timed. For these girls, sex was laced with regret. No one wrote about feeling satisfied by first-time sexual relationships. Instead of feeling love and commitment, girls consistently reported disappointment and disillusionment.

Tara, a seventeen year old from the East, wrote contrasting her fantasy scenario with her actual experience. Many of us innocently fantasize our first sexual experience. Tara described a story of anticipation and disappointment. She innocently fantasized her first sexual encounter, then wrote of the stark contrast between her dreamy anticipation and the disappointing reality:

> Me in a silk nightgown, rose petals covering a bedroom, and candlelight—my impression of what the most important night of my life was supposed to be—the night I would lose my virginity. That picture stuck in my mind since I was younger. When that magical night finally arrived, it was nothing like what I pictured. I built that one evening up to be so much. When it wasn't what I imagined, I was disappointed. That night there were no rose petals or candles, only Matt and me . . .
>
> Unfortunately three months after we made love together, we broke up. I don't really know what exactly happened. Sometimes I hung up the phone hating him. He tried to make me jealous by saying "Megan called me today" or "Katie called me." I guess Matt was too secure with our relationship and felt that he could treat me badly. Half the time I loved him to death. The other half of the time, I hated him. It's so ironic. I thought by having sex together we would become closer; instead it tore us apart.

While Tara traded in her fantasy for unanticipated distance, another girl, who wished to remain anonymous, told another typical tale of disillusionment:

> I simply didn't believe it. Why would someone like him go for someone like me? He was gorgeous. He had an

incredible physique from head to toe. He was an All-American soccer player. . . . He caught the eye of every girl he passed by. . . .

This date seemed like any other . . . at least at first. The heated events that could lead up to lovemaking were always cut short by my incessant excuses.

"Josh, I'm sorry, I'm having my period," I pleaded.

"Aw, come on, you said that last week," he said in an annoyed tone. He pushed me down onto the floor and grabbed his shirt from the bed. "I'm tired of this shit. It's been eight months and we're not even having sex yet. What the fuck is your problem? Any girl would love to be in your situation right now!"

What an asshole, I thought. "Excuse me? Did I just hear you right? Why don't you just fuck yourself," I cried.

Going out with Josh was actually the best thing that ever happened to me. No way will I ever base a relationship purely on sexual attraction and lies.

While these two girls wrote of more typical adolescent sexual experiences, the contributors to this chapter speak from a darker reality. For the anonymous author of *Another Milestone*, a first sexual experience is remembered as mundane, marked with no date. Instead, she grapples with the physical failure and emotional upheaval of the second night. Sex does not awaken her sleeping beauty, instead it accentuates her self-loathing.

*The Test*, the other submission in this chapter, drags us to the scene of our generation's most dreaded consequence—HIV/AIDS. Jenae Green shows us the other side of Planned Parenthood—the side where an embarrassing admission of unprotected sex is required and death is feared more than new life. In this piece, Jenae reminds us that we are growing up in a sexually treacherous time.

This chapter passes without any flowery odes to passion, without one word encouraging a younger sister to abandon herself to desire. Yet, speaking from experience, no contributor preaches an out-of-touch abstinence message. Instead, these girls take sexual reality seriously and hand over their hard-learned wisdom.

## ANOTHER MILESTONE

## An Undated Journal Entry

*By Anonymous, 17, from a small town in the Northeast*

And another milestone passes without a hint of sorrow or a mark of passage. No ceremony. No dwelling. Only a brief, unsuccessful attempt at trying to forget it ever happened. Of course, I am no longer a virgin, ta-da? And how funny those words sound, look, written in blue ink on paper—as if they are something, as if they mean something, as if I should feel their weight within these pages. It is with pretension, a bit of pride, fear, relief, confusion, and some joy.

Joy? I said it would be good. I would make good choices for myself. How wrong I was. How wrong. I say it. Write it. Truth? I am embarrassed.

It was Friday. November 22. If I can't mark it on my skin, at least my journal can.

But somehow, more important was the next night. After washing dishes, and drinking wine, and going to bed. And the same pattern repeating itself: me, silent and passive, feeling passionate but driving the passion completely inside, expressing nothing, letting myself be groped, fondled until I am no longer wet, no longer turned on (hurting). He stops, not because I say anything, but because he knows. And I know. Therein lies my double-bind, my inefficient consciousness, trying desperately to learn, to assimilate, to construct, to understand, to reconcile. I can't allow myself to think I am anything. It is only a disappointment. My rotting insides are visible on the surface again. I fall apart. Entropy increases.

So I cried. I sobbed, screaming, wailing out for something.

For death, for pain, for anything I could define and squeeze into a little box.

But it didn't come, and I shook with the power of the voices inside me, all ripping at the physical shell. All trying for dominance. I knew for once all the selves inside me, the fifteen year old and the eight year old, and how they are me, and how I've come from there, and how they still exist within—hurting, feeling—because I have never processed anything. Like a ghost who has to find their killer before they can rest in peace, I am just not the nice, sweet, perfect, honest, true being I claim I want to be.

So he held me while I flipped out, gargling with my own tears, trying to keep him away. I am, after all, disgusting.

My pen will never keep up with my thoughts, they rush at my hand. My nerves make emergency decisions as to what gets said, and what remains forever locked within my skull, buried or forgotten.

So the question remains, what do I do? What is good for me, can I actually make a good decision for myself? I don't know. And I want so much, but I don't know what it is, or how to ask for it, or how to ask for what I really want, and not some other lame excuse for a desire. I almost completed this entire journal entry without mentioning what a dramatic twit I am. Oh well.

## THE TEST
*By Jenae Marie Green, 17, from a suburb in the East*

My throat was dry, as I said to the lady peering through the plastic window at me, "I'm here for an HIV test." The waiting room was messy with information, posters and pamphlets scattered about. The walls were a soft peach color. Were they supposed to make me feel like I was outside on a warm spring day? Oddly, I gained more comfort from hearing the arguments made by the talk show host, blaring at me from the turned-on TV.

"Hold on, let me buzz you through." With a loud buzz, the door unlocked and I stepped into what seemed like an ordinary doctor's office. A woman with dry blonde hair and brown oval tortoise-shell glasses rolled her chair over to me and asked, "Now, why do you want a test?"

I felt completely humiliated, but refused to let my composure turn to mush. Replying as nonchalantly as possible, I spoke, "Well, I had unprotected sex with an older guy, who's had intercourse with many women."

"Uh-huh."

What else did this woman want from me? My sanity? She continued to wait for me to say something else, even though I didn't know what, so I rambled on. "I cheated on my boyfriend and I'm worried about the diseases I could contract." While I was wondering if I had given enough information, she showered me with forms. Thankful to be out of her sight, I returned to the comfort of the waiting room with the TV and other women. I didn't feel alone. I was sure there were many secrets in the room along with mine.

How did I end up at Planned Parenthood? I used to be the really shy girl who hid behind her blue-framed glasses. What happened to me over the last few years? Obviously people change and make mistakes. It's remarkable how fast time goes. It feels like just yesterday, I was flirting for the first time. I had been nervous and tried all of the things my girlfriends and I had read about. I smiled, and even batted my eyelids. But it's long past those days.

My blood has been at the lab for the past week. My body is tight and shaking as I walk toward Planned Parenthood to find out the results. I can only think, "Nothing was worth this fear."

# Diverse Sexualities

≋

For a straight girl, I am more than comfortable with diverse sexual preferences. My three closest friends are lesbian or bisexual. I've had privileged access to the post–coming-out collisions of their heterosexual and lesbian worlds—the senior prom meets the girlfriend, jockey boys meet the girlfriend, straight friends meet the girlfriend. Circles, straight and gay, usually came together well, overlapping without much more than a nod of recognition. But, growing up gay in my town is somewhat different than other places—*The National Enquirer* once designated the neighboring city as the "Lesbian Capital of America." My friends and I were sheltered by our exposure to a lifetime of gay mentors and couples. Still, even here, being lesbian or bisexual puts girls in a minority. In too many environments, girls in that minority face prejudice.

Newly felt physical attractions and sexual arousal throw nearly all of us into confusion. When those feelings don't fit heterosexual expectations, fear often transforms into upheaval. With few exceptions, lesbian and bisexual girls described a period of terror-stricken isolation. The realization of their sexual preference brought on a time of unrelenting anxiety, filled with self-doubt about their own normalcy and apprehension of others' judgments. The longer and more carefully they guarded their secret, the more self-destructive they became. While trying to stay closeted, girls reported drinking excessively, cutting themselves, and attempting suicide. Once they came out to friends and family, the prejudices and judgments they faced were far less damaging than their self-decaying prison. Yet, for some, the bigotry they faced was considerable. Still others encountered unexpected acceptance. One girl's childhood friend sighed with relief, "That's all? You sounded so upset. I thought you had cancer, or something."

In the first contribution to this chapter, *On the Other Side of the Rainbow*, Lauren Manley writes about her effort to appear straight, and her success at maintaining the illusion of heterosexuality. Talking as though to a trusted friend, she tells us the reasons why and the ways she conceals her identity. She ends her submission with a question, "So much pressure. So much pain. When will it ever end?" In a note to me she answered her own question:

> Since writing this piece, I've been to a meeting for gay youth. I realized I'm not alone. And, I'm not a freak. There is no reason for me to hide who I am. There is nothing wrong with me. And, if you disagree, that's your problem, not mine. I'm not hurting anyone. I don't need closed-minded people in my life. My name is Lauren Manley and I am a lesbian.

Like Lauren, Becky Shain writes about the relief and self-affirmation that comes with honesty. In *Call In Queer Today*, she faces the intolerance of our society with strength and humor. However, for the next author, the prejudice leaves no room for laughter. An ambush waited for her outside her closet. While M. R. Swoboda finds comfort and love in her relationship, she is besieged by name-calling and hate in her school.

All of us—whether gay, straight, or bisexual—explore the exciting, scary, and fragile feelings that sexuality awakens during adolescence. These three contributors teach two lessons: how society takes the joy out of this adventure when it christens us abnormal, and the complete normalcy of discovering sexuality along the way to growing up.

# ON THE OTHER SIDE OF THE RAINBOW
*By Lauren Manley, 15, from a city in the Northeast*

*Fag, Dyke, Fairy, Lezzie*—I've heard them all. Of course, no one
would ever think about saying these things to me. The thing is, I
make everyone think I'm so wrapped up in the male species. The
thought they might be staring into the eyes of a full-fledged
homosexual never crosses their minds. Truth is, each one of these
words slices through my mind. I'm amazed that this generation,
my generation, is supposedly more opened-minded. Go figure!

It's hard to go through the day with a mask on. With only a
couple of people there that really know me for me being out, I
sometimes feel like I'm gonna go crazy. I can't be myself. I spend
the whole day lying about who I am. Why should I have to sup-
press who I am? Who I have feelings for? No one else has to.

When you live your life as a lie, you are constantly in a state
of confusion. Who can I really trust? Why do I have to hide
being gay? Why do I have to be this way in the first place? Is
there really something so wrong about it? Am I a freak? A per-
vert?

Homophobia never even really started to bother me until a
few months ago. Then, I started to come out to some close
friends. I was like a wild animal, getting a slight taste of blood. I
craved for more, craved so much that it hurt. A burning pain
crept into my heart. I wanted to go on a rampage and tell everyone, but my own fear stopped me from doing so.

No matter how many times I try to tell myself, Fuck them, if
they can't accept me for who I am! Who cares? The truth is, I
care. A big city high school is hard enough, but when the student
body totals in at a whopping ninety-eight, and half of the school
is known for being back-stabbing, catty mutants, you start to
wonder who you really want to tell. Do they even deserve to
know?

I've been lucky to have supportive parents (my mom and my
"second mom"), but if anything, having gay parents has caused
me even more problems. Some people I have told don't even

believe me. They just blow it off and say, "It's just because your mom's a lesbian." Uh, I think not. I think I know better then they do, don't you?

Then there is the ever-popular response, "But if your mom is gay, how'd she have you?" I don't know. Spontaneous combustion, perhaps?

It's hard enough to have to go to a high school with people knowing my mother is gay. They all stare and think I'm a freak of nature—a sideshow. Come see the girl who was hatched. But what would I do if they knew the whole story?

Having to hide behind this facade is both aggravating and painful. I want to break out, but I can't. I'd be faced with rejection and loneliness.

I know I don't do much to help myself. I just keep creating a bigger and bigger character for myself. I spend my days talking about guys. I constantly talk about this one and that one, until the point where I get on everyone's nerves. I make people believe I am completely obsessed. Like guys are my life.

I've tried to give people subtle hints though. At one point I had a rainbow ribbon on my bag and I still wear a rainbow bracelet everyday, but kids are either too ignorant or too dim-witted to realize. (You think I'm a little bitter?) I don't know how to let people know without walking around with a big sign.

It's funny. They are all so sure they can spot us in a crowd. (Ever hear, "You act so gay" or "I can tell they're gay. Look at them"?) Well, spot me. One of my ex-boyfriends prides himself on being able to spot a queer, and yet he couldn't tell even when we were kissing. I think we were close enough, don't you?

Then there is the whole issue of finding more friends like myself. I don't want to have to go through this alone, especially while I'm starting to come out . . . slowly, but surely. I want to be able to talk to someone who knows what I'm going through.

I know I have someplace to go. In fact, I know exactly where and when, but I'm scared to go there too. What if they don't accept me either?

I mean, I'm not even sure how to explain myself. The best

description I've heard so far is "lesbian bisexual." I don't see why I have to choose who I'm going to fall in love with because of their gender. It's about what's in their mind and their heart, not what's between their legs.

Living as a fifteen-year-old lesbian can only be summed up in one word when you live in the closet: *fear*. The fear of rejection. The fear of loneliness. Emptiness. Denial. The loss of friends. I just don't want to end up spending my life alone, forever rejected by the world for not wanting to conform. From this fear stems many other emotions. I feel anger, betrayal, sadness, and repulsion, but fear is at the root of it all.

I don't even know what I expect to come from writing this piece. Maybe some girls will find out they're not alone. Maybe someone I know will read this and spare me the agony of having to hide from them. And maybe it's just a way for me to get my thoughts out, before I explode. So much pressure . . . so much pain. When will it ever end?

## CALL IN QUEER TODAY
*By Becky Shain, 17, from a city in the Northeast*

I received an e-mail from a friend a few weeks ago. In it was this quote taken from the New York Times: "If homosexuality is a disease, let's all call in queer to work: 'Hi, can't work today, still queer.'"

I diagnosed myself long ago and am still waiting to be wheeled away. I suppose that would have happened by now if it were going to happen at all. Ironically, the ease with which my sexuality has been accepted has been most surprising. Virtually every gay adult I've met has remarked on my courage for living openly out of the closet. I believe the period in which my generation grew up has made it less difficult. With homosexuality in the media on the rise, along with a growing network of gay and lesbian supporters, being a teenage lesbian in 1997 has been the most mirthful experience of my life.

When I first realized that I was gay, I was horrified. At fourteen one can't even admit to themselves they're attractive, let alone attracted to members of the same sex. After years of making succinct excuses as to why I never talked about boys, never brought home any male "friends," never even seemed to be remotely interested in what the phallus had to offer, I was exhausted. Any of the lurid excitement I once felt at the thought of simply being myself had vanished with my friends' perpetual loquaciousness around boys. Not only was I uncomfortable being with them, I wasn't comfortable being with myself. It wasn't reassuring to know there were people out there like me. The way I saw it, they were just as damned as I was. My misery could've cared less for the company of a dozen other reticent adolescents—all scared, all aberrant to the existing heterosexual social hierarchy. I didn't *want* to be like them. I didn't *want* to find a community. All I really wanted was to live out the rest of my high school days in silence. Only after my escape, diploma in hand, would I pursue myself as I longed to be.

I remained loyal to that silence for another year. I got a boyfriend, grew my hair long, wore makeup, and formed friendships based on Saturday-night parties. I hadn't forgotten my attractions. I just sort of put them on hold until I was sure I couldn't get my boyfriend's best girl-friend into bed with me. Then I began to give up. It was easier that way—living a pseudo-sanguine existence filled with ephemeral satisfaction, than to live honestly and be belittled.

But, as time went on, I began to see a change in the people around me. After openly announcing my obsession with Madonna's music (truthfully, it was Madonna's sexual core), conversations with some of my friends took slightly different turns. "I'd fuck Madonna!" was one of the most satisfying phrases I had ever heard exit the mouths of pals. Though I knew my friends were only kidding around, it meant a kind of vague acceptance of bisexual curiosity. I pressed my friends for more significant statements, but never really received what I had hoped would be a confession. I realized the confession I was constantly searching for was my own. I made a decision to find myself.

By the summer before my junior year, I was more than ready to try new experiences. What I figured I had to do to *truly* consider myself gay was to *act* gay. Through my own desperate attempts and with the help of some lesbian matchmakers, I filled the void that had enshrouded my life.

It has been almost a year since I came out of the closet. I will always remember New Year's Eve, 1996. On that night, I made the mother of all confessions: "Guys, I have something to tell you . . . I'm . . . gay." My friend Lauren's reaction was unforgettable: She shrugged and asked for more champagne. That has been most everybody's reaction. I'm still debating whether it is open-mindedness, or indifference—a denial approach to what they don't understand or don't *want* to understand. In any case, I have no secrets for the first time in years. And whatever secrets I may acquire cannot match the one I've put behind me.

If you were to ask me three years ago, what I thought my life would be like at seventeen, I think I would have said, "I don't know. I can't see that far into the future." Well, it's the future *now,* and I'm looking, looking, looking into a further one. I think that's what has changed. I can envision my life as I live it now. With a little gray in my hair or a fold in the lines of my face, but it will still be me. It'll always be me looking into my future, where I won't have to call in queer to work. I shouldn't ever have to.

# UNTITLED
*By M. R. Swoboda, 16, from a small in the Midwest*

She is my comfort factor and so much more. She is Alex, my soul mate, the One. She is the pick ax that chipped away the boulder in my tunnel. She is the cheerleader who cheered me on from the sidelines to keep going, keep playing the game.

March 11, 1996, was a Monday like no other. It was the product of years of slowly falling deeper and deeper into a "chemical imbalance." It was the Gettysburg of the war inside of me, and an unforgettable landmark in my life.

After a weak attempt at suicide by means of chewing a handful of aspirin (my intention was to consume the entire contents), I received my first hug from Alex. Many more would come afterward (though not for two years), but none would surpass the precious first. Tears streaming down our faces, our bodies meshed in our first embrace. We clumsily fumbled, our arms around each other. I gently squeezed her to my chest. Her body wasn't limp, but unreceptive. She seemed neutral, not necessarily refusing the affection, but showing no signs of welcoming it either. Despite her body language, somehow I knew inside she had longed for that touch, that embrace.

In everything we did, I knew we were connected in some way. My best friend, Tiffany, had told me long before about the concept of soul mates. She explained soul mates as two people whose souls were meant for each other. To justify the closeness and oddity of my relationship with Alex, I once threw out the idea that we could be soul mates. At age thirteen, we both succumbed to the exciting notion. Our relationship had previously been inexplicable, but now had a title, something to call ourselves.

We addressed and signed our in-school notes to one another: "soul mate." We also began to use the cliché, "I love you," though strictly in written form. Rumors flew about the school. Alex was gay and I was her mark. People talked of her fantasies of kissing me. Though no one was quite sure whether her fantasies were rumor-invoked or true. I never paid much attention to them, although I knew full well they weren't merely gossip-produced fables. One would think it would bother a person to be the subject of a same-sex obsession. It didn't bother me in the least.

I began to question the validity of my assumed heterosexual preference. Whether the talk in school influenced this uncertainty or a few other factors, I'm not entirely clear on. It was probably a mixture of everything.

Alex persistently tried to sit next to me, or lie by me, or touch me lightly on the arm. I always resisted, shaking her off. I was at war with my own misgiving. I continually tried to convince myself I was at war with society, but the war was really with my own mind. It was "wrong" to be in love with someone of the same gender; everyone knew that. Or, that's what I thought, anyway. So any time she would touch me, though it was the soft touch I craved and loved, my mind would snap to reality, and think, What am I doing? And I'd shake her off.

For two years, through mountains and valleys in the landscape of our relationship, I denied my true love for her. To this day, I'm not sure why I held back my feelings. Society made it abundantly clear how it felt about homosexuals. But I knew right from the start I wasn't "gay." Sure, I had my doubts at times, before I fully understood the situation. Who wouldn't question their sexuality, when feelings of desire for someone of their own sex became natural? What I realized and others have to understand is: Love is not based on gender. The natural instinct of any species is to reproduce with the opposite sex, but love is an entirely unrelated issue.

Everyone asks me if I'm confused or mixed up. To those people I say, "I've never been so sure of something before in my life." But they all have their doubts—every single one of them. I don't need a sixth sense to perceive their suspicion. Most of them voice their pessimistic opinions loud and clear, trying to make a point, to prove me wrong. Others just aren't very talented at the art of hiding their feelings. Smirks and grunts show it all. One person's eyes rolled so far to the back of their head, I was almost scared they would remain that way.

And then there are the people at school, the really openminded type—they see us walking toward them in the halls. They say, *"There they are."* As we pass by, we can hear them chiding, *"They're soul mates you know,"* and a chorus of chuckles echoes down the corridor.

As with all things, some days aren't as bad as others. On rare occasions I can go through a whole day without being asked about my "girlfriend." That's putting it nicely, though. They could (and do) use much worse terms, such as my "woman," "bitch," or "dyke." But their favorite line is, "How's your little lesbian friend?" Depending on how many times I've been asked the same or a similar question, I answer with, "Oh, she's fine," my infamous hyena-esque laugh, nothing at all, or, "Shut the hell up." If it's been an exceptionally bad day, I take my seat, bury my head in my folded arms on the desk, and try to keep the floodgates closed. It doesn't always work, though. And those are the moments I wish all human existence would perish except for Alex and me. I know it's a terribly selfish thing to wish, but I can't help it. It's just the way I feel.

She is my comfort factor and so much more. Our bodies have grown to know one another. When we hug there is no fumbling around, not knowing where to put our hands. Every limb knows exactly where to go. We fit together as if we were made that way—only separated at some later point in time. She is Alex, my soul mate, the One.

# Manipulated And Controlled

≋

Good girls get snared by bad boys and sleazy young men. All the girls who wrote about self-destructive relationships described falling into a well-set trap. Lured by sweet compliments and wooed by unwavering attention, they fell in love. Once caught, their seducers turned on them, eating away at their self-worth. Candy-coated charm turned into tyrannical manipulation. Most, but not every one, escaped. The determined ones recognized their misery, freed themselves from their oppressors, and vowed never to be trapped again.

Although none of my relationships have been abusive, some have been terribly unhealthy. I was willing to give up too much. I stayed in detrimental situations for too long. If my relationships had been controlling or manipulative, I probably would have lingered anyway. For a while I'd do practically anything to feel loved by my boyfriends—I'm thankful my willingness was never driven to self-destructive subservience. I may have fallen.

Kit Dewey wrote to me, making clear how frequently girls find themselves dominated by boys who treat them badly. Speaking from experience, Kit commented on relationships where vulnerability exposes girls to manipulation:

The true tragedy of my story is not in what happened to me. The true tragedy, instead, lies in the fact that variations of this story happen to so many girls. So many are dominated and mistreated. They are unwilling to realize it. Like me, these girls are held by potent words. They are told that they are loved, that they are beautiful, and that they are special. In today's world, these words are so rarely spoken and so often misused that they hold tremendous power when they are spoken.

The first contributor to this chapter, who wants to remain anonymous, details her seductive and destructive story on one poetic page. This selection, *A Smooth-Talking Guy*, arrived with a note:

> This boyfriend I had was a manipulator. He could talk his way out of anything. When we first met, he enchanted me. . . . He led me to think we were perfect for each other. Now I know that no one who makes you feel two inches small is worth caring for. There are wonderful men waiting for wonderful women. I learned not to sell myself short.

In the second contribution, *Do Not Fret Over Evil Men*, Maria Fedelle illustrates her ex-boyfriend's "ugly need to control," scene by scene. When finally he pushes too far, she breaks free. But not every girl frees herself from the bondage of a boy bent on total domination. I received a strikingly similar contribution from another girl. She, like Maria, described a boyfriend who chose her clothes, isolated her from her friends, and frequently flew into jealous rages. She predicted he would continue to make her cry and fill her with self-loathing. Yet, she confided in me that she would never leave him. She vowed undying love. Her submission came without a name and I never heard from her again.

I am inspired by the girls who are determined to never allow themselves to be mistreated again. I am scared for those who remain at-risk. We should all fear for their future.

## A Smooth-Talking Guy
*By Anonymous, 15, from a city in the Southwest*

He's such a smooth-talking kind of guy
a suave Southern gentleman like
a gallant cowboy riding into guaranteed trouble
he's kind of a blanket
who invites you to join him
from a fierce winter cold.
he thinks about you,
and the shapeliness, or unshapeliness
as the case may be
of your body
and the sweet and sour smell of your
hair and strawberries.
he's the one
touches you in all the right places . . .
and your thighs—
makes you forget how mean he can be
when he's jokingly teaching you
against your will
self-defense
and makes it up to you
by touching your thighs
and smiling


## Do Not Fret Over Evil Men
*By Maria Fedele, 18, from a rural area in the East*

There he goes again with his "How can I trust you speech." Of
course, it's all over a friend, a male friend, his best friend, merely
saying "Hello." In his world "Hello" translates into distrust.

So I cry and give another apology. Tomorrow comes, he
offers a red rose and a quiet dinner out. And, I, with a picture-
perfect smile, get ready to go.

"What will the lady have this evening?" The waiter inquires.

I skim the menu and say, "Let's see. I'll have—"

"She'll have grilled chicken and potatoes. That's her favorite. Right honey?"

I shyly bury my face in the menu and agree, "Of course, you know all of my favorites."

As the meal goes on barely a word is spoken. When dessert arrives he gives me the sparkling look—the perfect gaze for getting his Friday-night way, the way to my bedroom.

With the rising of the sun, the morning breaks. At home, I quickly and quietly slip out of my bed, grab my clothes, and head for the shower. I step onto the shower mat, dry off, and dress. With a knock, he opens the bathroom door.

"Hi Sweetie," I greet him as I reach out to give him a kiss and hug.

He grabs both of my arms and turns my whole body around, so I face the full-length mirror. "What do you think you're wearing? You know if you wear that skimpy skirt guys will look at you. Are you trying to do that?"

"Of course not, Honey. If it's going to cause you to be mad, I'll change my clothes."

With disgust in his eyes, he walks into the bedroom and grabs a pair of jeans off the floor and hands them to me.

"Here, wear these. Baggy clothes look good on you. You know that, right?"

I begin to put them on and reply, "Yeah. You're always right."

I give him a reluctant kiss.

He walks away saying, "I love you, you know that."

"Of course, I know, I love you too," I echo, as I take one final look in the mirror and toss the skirt in the garbage can.

With winter on its way, so is wrestling season, a world I help him through. The losing weight and tiredness create new burdens on our relationship—mood swings and a nasty attitude. I become his number-one fan. With an attitude like his, I'm his only fan.

Without a friend to be found, I tell myself, At least I have him, right?—always with a question, always knowing it really wasn't right.

As the new year arrives, wrestling disappears. By doctors orders he quits.

With this breakdown, his ugly need to gain control, to overpower me, rears its tyrannical head. I knew it was coming. I felt it all over. We were finally near the end.

That cold day in March, he pushed so hard—the hardest mental push I had ever felt. There we stood in the mall. His orders hit so hard, "Just put the shirt in your bag! Do it for us."

Threatening words I sadly obeyed. I listened out of fear, fear of his anger—a madness lasting for hours.

And when the police came and the handcuffs hit, I cried and so did he.

As he looked into my eyes, while the officer spoke, he asked, "Will we be all right?"

I just turned my head in disgust, and every time our eyes met he said, "I love you."

When my parents arrived, Daddy didn't yell. He told me, "This isn't the way someone shows their love. We trusted him to take you out and protect you."

The punishment came. I wasn't allowed to see him for a month. That month of crying and soul searching disguised a blessing. I now knew, he had broken my heart. He ran my life. My mind could no longer accept his rule. Still, when he saw me in school, he said, "I love you. What are you wearing tomorrow?"

At sunrise, that morning in April, I knew it was time. Perhaps it was the smell in the air, or the glow of the sun at 7:00 A.M. Something was calling out my name to be free, to free myself of this so-called love that felt like a dead weight.

It was time put to rest all the talks of high school sweethearts and graduation engagement. It was time to put his commands— "You can't wear that. Don't look at him"—into perspective.

I evolved that morning on the way to school. The more I thought and planned it out, the firmer I gripped my Civic's steering wheel. I was exhausted from being driven by another. I was tormented by the demands. I wanted a different prom date. I wanted to come home and have no one to call. I wanted to walk to class alone. I wanted to talk with some girlfriends. It had been so long. I needed to remember how to be myself.

Maybe it was the sun's glow that morning in April. Maybe I wanted to be as bright and free as that very sun—shining so happy and independent. I had no identity. We had become one— one by his rule.

The breakup came. With rage, pain, and butterflies in my stomach, I told him: "Good-bye." Together again, we cried, for the last time. He said he couldn't let go. He swore he'd kill himself. I tried not to hear him, and walked away.

By the time the sun set that night, I had gathered its power. I, proudly enough, had become sunshine. I was again me, the dead weight was finally gone. It felt good to be back.

Now months later, I am without him, and, of course, he is still very much alive. Ha!

# Broken-Hearted Independence

≋

Alone in my room, only the lamp behind my head glowed. It was late and a school night. That light was hardly visible from the door. Passing by, my parents wouldn't notice I was still awake. Once upstairs, they wouldn't hear an after-hours call. I wedged the phone between my ear and shoulder. My body bowed around my hopeful heart, I dialed. He answered from his distant dorm room. Despite our recent break up, I retained a fantasy of our year-and-a-half long relationship conquering all. As we said good-bye, I told him, "I love you." His response: silence, then scuffling. Girlie giggles in the background became more distant. I heard a door close, and I pictured his temporary exit from his room. In a whisper, he said, "I love you, too." I hung up the phone knowing the girls in his room didn't know about the serious relationship he left at home. He didn't want them to know. I wailed involuntarily. My parents came running from their room to find me in a quivering ball on my bed.

But they had warned me, "You're not going to marry him. Breakups are inevitable." I knew they were right all along, but that inevitability didn't soften the blow. The logical assurances of dismissive adults—"Oh, you're too young to know about love"; "There are plenty of fish in the sea"; "In a week, you'll forget you ever met that one"—didn't console me. Audra M. Hopf, a seventeen year old from a rural town in the Midwest, knows how harshly the clanging words of adults can ring. She wrote of her parent-enforced breakup: "In the end, I was forbidden to see Luke. Every gift I had received was to be returned. Every memory I had was to be forgotten. Every instinct of love was to be smashed, because I didn't know what love was. Apparently, I hadn't come to the almighty unspoken age of officially knowing what love is."

The feelings of first love are stronger than reason. We hear the warnings of our parents, our friends, even our own minds, but our emotions will rarely be restricted. We lose ourselves in love. We love with abandon and, then, love abandons us. Lauren Alysia Norkus, a seventeen year old from a small town in the Northeast, understands. She confided her difficulty in getting over lost love: "Everything, absolutely everything, reawakens the memories."

I was sixteen then. My room, my furniture, my possessions, my house, all reminded me of him. That night, and the nights that proceeded and preceded it, were among the most painful times in my life. I had invested myself solely in a wish for unconquerable love.

Hillary Wright, another sixteen year old, shared the devastation of this illusion. She wrote: "I think this is one of my first 'adult' realizations: Nothing conquers all."

Still, I defined myself as his ex-girlfriend. I knew that was not who I wanted to be. So with our separation, I forced myself to face the dependence that left me alone and broken with our breakup. That confrontation was frightening. I was not brave in the usual sense. I cried often and hard.

But instead of lonely isolation, I read and wrote and thought and thought. I buried myself in Virginia Woolf and Alice Walker, Margaret Atwood and Maya Angelou, Sylvia Plath and Toni Morrison, and I wondered why women I had never met knew me so well. With these women I was not so alone anymore. They understood my emotion, if not my literal situation. Like their characters, we are often left lost and broken.

Now we've been broken up for longer than we were together. I have moved on entirely. My heart is fully healed. Years later, collecting contributions to *Ophelia Speaks*, I have found my experience echoed in the writing of other girls. Acquiring lonely independence is not a lonely subject. However, most of us gather the strength to pick up the pieces of ourselves and puzzle together a stronger identity. In the end, we are often better for being broken.

Yet, after letting go of romance, few of us celebrate. Reasserting independence seldom feels like a victory of feminism over oppression. Instead, most girls wrote as though they were crawling out from under a complex web of affection and alienation, woven largely by their own insecurities, fantasies, and confusions. In the end, most walked away accompanied by unpredicted emotions.

*Defiance,* the first contribution to this chapter paints a portrait of that emotional unpredictability. Like a perfectly written screenplay complete with flashbacks, Jennifer Barnett shows us the scene of her final good-bye. Coming from self-admitted insecurity, Jennifer wants to hold on. The boy pulls away, leaving her revitalized by unexpected relief.

In the second contribution, Jessica Titlebaum grapples with the anguish of crossing the emotional line between friendship and romance alone. *I Wanted to Know His Truth* shows how the pain of being told that love will never happen rivals the heartbreak of knowing it will never happen again. Fantasies never fulfilled ache differently than memories never repeated. But, both hurt terribly.

Next, *Glimpses into the Heart of a Girl* gives an accurately twisted view of the possessiveness we often retain of our exboyfriends. Without censoring her emotional reality, Honey displays raw feelings secretly harbored, seldom admitted, and only acted out by the truly violent and troubled.

In the final contribution, *A First-Person Narrative on First Love,* Lucy Jane Lang begins her story with secure clarity. The romance is gone. She made a wrong choice. She's bored. She wants out. For Lucy, the insecurity comes later. After months, she misses him, demonstrating the power of first love, even when we wanted out of first.

These four contributions astutely demonstrate how much of our selves we attach to our first loves, and how much we lose when love leaves. Yet, one unifying theme is woven into our differences: We learn from leaving relationships. We grow stronger and wiser as we establish our independence. We can love ourselves outside the affirmation of others.

## DEFIANCE
*By Jennifer Barnett, 16 ,from a small town in the Northeast*

"Do you want my opinion?" I asked him. He nodded his agreement. As I continued, my voice began to shake and my face became fluid.

"I wish we could have had a chance," I began.

He looked at his shoes and pretended to be interested in the zipper of his jacket, then spoke. "I want to apologize for what happened last weekend. I guess things just got out of hand. I never meant to make you feel guilty."

He looked up and I couldn't stop myself from staring. I wondered what he was thinking. As I watched him, I realized I would never know. He was so unpredictable, but I couldn't deny the attraction I felt. I explained myself, "If you regret what happened, then there is nothing I can do to change that. I just want you to know that I wouldn't trade that night for anything."

He nodded his head, as if he understood. "I'm sorry if I hurt you. I never meant to lead you on." As he spoke, he stared at the floor, afraid to look into my eyes and see the pain he had caused.

"I know." I said. "It's not your fault I believed I had a chance."

"Don't!" He interrupted. "It has nothing to do with you. I just need to fix things with her right now. Ever since she found out about that night you and I were together, she's been . . . different. I need to know she's going to be okay." He ran his fingers through his dark brown hair and I could feel him watching me.

"I know," I replied. "It's just . . ."

I thought back to the first night we kissed. I had never expected it to happen. I pictured him standing in front of me, smiling as he brushed my dirty blond hair from my face, exposing hazel eyes—eyes that trusted every word escaping his lips. I could remember the way he tasted and the way he smelled. I could still hear him whispering into my ear. I had opened up to him and told him things I couldn't tell anybody else. But I had been the fool. He had been committed to a girl—a girl I couldn't even compare to. His girl was beautiful, thin, and happy. Things I could never be. Not that I hadn't tried.

My mind drifted back to the time I had gone days without eating. I had been determined to be thin. Cigarettes became my nourishment. After a couple of days, I forced myself to believe I was strong. I felt unstoppable, but in reality I had become what I promised myself I would never be—addicted. I despised being controlled. Yet with every passing day, two empty cigarette packs stared me in the face, reminding me that they had won. I began moving on to other drugs, hoping to hide myself from the pain. My world seemed to be crashing down around me, and I felt completely alone. Day after day I would find myself in the same situations. Ones I couldn't control.

He spoke, bringing me back to the present. "We'll have our chance, Jen. I promise. And, it'll be great."

I longed to reach out and touch him, just one last time. I couldn't wait for him anymore. I knew this time I would have to let him go.

My eyes traced all the features of his face. I searched for details I knew I would never find. Closing my eyes, I imagined gently pressing my lips against his. I hesitated before I opened my eyes, almost as if by opening them I would lose the feeling I had when thinking of him.

I paused for a moment more, and suddenly I felt his warm breath on my cheek. I turned toward him and our lips touched. His tongue caressed the edge of my mouth and I felt as if I were melting into him. I gently touched him, trying to memorize his face with my fingers.

"I wish things could have been different," he whispered. He kissed my ear and began working his way down to my neck. He lingered for only a moment before he pulled away.

"I'll never forget what we had," I said as tears slid down my face. He grabbed my hand and pulled me toward him. He wrapped his arms around me, holding me so tightly it hurt.

"I should go," he said. After a few seconds, he turned and walked toward the door.

"Please, don't leave me. I need you," I pleaded.

He hesitated as his hand touched the handle of the door, but he didn't turn around. I leaned against the cold, damp wall and let myself slide to the floor. I wiped away the tears with the sleeve of my shirt, then pulled a pack of cigarettes from my pocket. The red and white design seemed to rise off the box and the cellophane wrapper crinkled under my touch. I removed a cigarette and let it rest gently between my fingers. Reaching back into my pocket, I pulled out a black lighter. Lighting the cigarette, I pulled the smoke into my lungs. A tear slid down my cheek, but I didn't brush it away this time. Instead I let it roll down my chin and drip onto my jeans.

He had appreciated my insecurities, that allowed him to become a part of my survival. I knew he enjoyed being needed. And maybe that was just part of the game. In the back of my mind, I sympathized with the girls that had fallen into his trap before. I considered the reality of his influence, and I realized I had finally found a way to reclaim myself.

I could see the pattern clearly now. Endless nights he would come to my window, begging to come in out of the rain. I'd smell the alcohol on his breath and give in, allowing him to use me one more time. Afraid to lose him and everything I had worked so hard to change. Each night I'd watch him slip further away and promise myself it would be the last time. But I knew I'd take him back.

I heard him start his car and panic surged through my body. I realized this had been the last time I would ever see him, no matter what he promised. I took another drag of my cigarette and let the smoke escape from my mouth.

I finished the cigarette and left it still burning on the floor. I opened the door and stepped onto the sidewalk. The air was cold and I felt more alone then usual. I walked to the edge of the road and stared at the tracks leading away from me, challenging me to follow. My throat tightened, although what I felt wasn't sorrow, but relief. With a defiant step I began to walk in the opposite direction, leaving my uncertainty behind.

## I WANTED TO HEAR HIS TRUTH
*By Jessica Titlebaum, 16, from a suburb in the Midwest*

I wanted to hear his truth, but I wanted his truth to be what I wanted to hear.

So I sat confused.

I watched him walk away and I knew what he meant. I couldn't move, not yet. I don't think I wanted to. I think I wanted to sit on that wood bench and watch him walk away, because I knew I never could.

The shade of darkness made it impossible to translate what he was trying to say. If he didn't leave when he did, too much would have been said.

He looked back once, as I watched. He didn't say anything. He just kept taking his small steps away.

I sat still, knowing he had just done the bravest thing either of us could ever have done. Deep down neither of us wanted to walk away.

I think he wanted to keep going on the way we were. I couldn't. Too many words had been spoken. Too many glances had taken place. His thoughts had explored far beyond the boundaries that lead us astray, even if his hands hadn't.

But then, I couldn't leave either.

I couldn't let go of his words, even if they were only words. I couldn't erase his touch and his good-byes. I couldn't blot out those unusual moments of truth and honesty.

So there I sat, wondering what the hell had happened in the last ten minutes of my life. Confusion still lay as a concrete foundation, but it was the tears forming in the corner of my eyes that made the situation a cold life lesson. I didn't want to let them fall, fearing that once they did, they wouldn't stop.

But, then again, what could I do?

I sat frozen on a park bench, watching lifelessly as a piece of my soul broke off and walked away.

I tried remembering what he had said, and what he hadn't. Everything was jumbled, torn and scattered on the ground. The circle of circumstance that surrounded me, suffocated me into a jar of heated reality, too harsh for my own eyes.

And in the end, I still sat there. I think I was afraid to move. When I left that bench, I had to face the world. Alone.

I wasn't experiencing a breakup. Although, hell, I wish I was. No, that would be too simple, that would make our friendship definable. As of then, we were undefinable. Our relationship was unique, incredible, and somewhat imagined. We concocted this past, full of false memories and unspoken speeches. We both had seen what we wanted in each other. Now we paid the costly price. Our relationship lay broken on the floor.

I think I was supposed to be picking it up, trying to glue it back together. However, just like all the king's horses and king's men, I couldn't run after him, and put Humpty Dumpty together again.

Not that running after him would have helped one bit. I had no clue what the hell I would have said when I caught up with him.

I started laughing at one point, not out of funny ha-ha jokes, but because of something I pictured. I thought of catching up with him, looking into his brown eyes, and realizing his eyes were closed.

Which was true, they were, but I couldn't ever say that to him.

With his eyes closed how did he see this fine line was crossed? How did he notice me when I made that daring step across his bridge, when I didn't even realize I had taken the challenge?

That's just how he is.

And I am an idiot because I had all these things; I wanted to scream. All these questions he needed to answer, but I couldn't find a voice to ask. Where was that crucial heart-stopping moment?

Why couldn't my voice have disappeared all those times I told him I loved him, or all those times I told him that I needed him, or all those moments that I just wanted his attention? He could hear the calling then, why couldn't I find my voice now?

I knew why. I was afraid of the truth. I was afraid of hearing when everything had changed. I was afraid of learning when his "I love yous" became lies, and when his touch became false, and his smiles became deceitful, and his kisses became poisonous. I didn't really want to know.

I wasn't strong enough.

And then he came back.

I didn't see him walk toward me, or hear him stand next to me, but I felt him. I knew he was sitting on the bench next to me.

He just sat there, in the same pool of confusion I was drowning in.

And he smiled.

I knew it was sincere. He showed me his teeth. His eyes opened really wide and his mouth turned upward. A smile appeared on the face of an angel.

He didn't need to say anything, because I had no clue what I wanted to hear. He didn't have to touch me, that was too familiar.

I wanted to agree on indifference. We did.

I looked at him smiling, and all I needed was for him to keep silent. I needed him to look at me, because I knew my face couldn't hide what my heart had muffled for so long. I still don't think I had a voice to produce the speech that could have prevented what happened next. But it was okay.

He held my hand. He just put his callused hand over my small one, and made his presence known. Not by his touch, or words, or even body language. For we never communicated on that level before. Until then, we had misread signals, and learned from mistakes, that we could never be reality. We had to play out our fantasies in a fantasy world. We could never blur each other's lines of reality.

It didn't bother me, and it never will.

Compared to him, I was nothing.

However, when we stood together, I stood alone.

And recognition made all the difference as he walked away again, for the last time, the second time that night.

An eternity held us together, but the world kept us apart. Only in my mind did that make sense.

As he walked away that night, I finally was able to comprehend his truth.

The truth will always lie open in his eyes, a collection of brown dust memories.

I sat crying. It wasn't what I wanted to hear.

## GLIMPSES INTO THE HEART OF A GIRL
*By Honey, 15, from a suburb in the South*

I want to kill a girl a named Debbie. I want to kill her, and watch her die. I don't have anything against Debbie personally. She is just the unfortunate one my boyfriend picked. Excuse me, my ex-boyfriend (I can't get used to saying it). I am not psychotic, I simply want to kill a girl named Debbie.

He picked her, after me. Less than a week after me, in fact. That's why I want to kill her. Someone said she looked like me. They wondered if that was why he picked her. I wonder if that is why. I was talking with him on the phone the other day. He said, "I still love you." "I still need you." "I still can't live without you." And then he said, "I am seeing a girl named Debbie." I wanted to kill her then. That was the first time I wanted to kill her. It hit me like air-conditioning out of a building in 100-degree weather. Moments before, he was professing his love for me, and then— *bam!* What was I supposed to feel like?

I know I do not love him. But he is a part of me. And I cannot let that go. I believed it that night, when I said, "We're finished," I would have truly believed myself. But inside I went on thinking it was all right, we were still together. So when he told me about her, I wanted to kill her. Something inside of me was hidden so deep I didn't know about it, until he said the name "Debbie," and I wanted to kill her.

I hate him, I always have. I told him I never loved him. That started all of our problems. But, no, I don't truly believe I hate him. I think I did love him, for one very brief moment in time. But love is love, even after it turns to hate. So why was I compelled to end it? I can never find the answer to that question. I have the most precious memories treasured in my soul, yet some are dark and hideous. I do not want him back. He is too much of a child for me, even with his seniority of three years. I could go on forever about his faults, but that is not what I care about. I care about killing Debbie. I hate the very essence of her name. It has an evil ring. Though I hate her with all my power, I could never extinguish her life.

At night, before blessed sleep comes and whisks my fears away for a few precious hours, I think about her lips touching his, her hand caressing his, her arms around his body. And, I want to kill a girl named Debbie.

In my mind, that girl does not deserve to live. No one deserves to have him but me, but I do not wish to have him. What am I saying? I am too good for him. He is so immature, such a spoiled child. I always did hate it when he would sulk. But I do not want his hands (hands that touched me) to touch anyone else. He is with her now; I know it. He does not answer when the phone rings, and rings, and rings. My heart tremors in my chest, and tears spring to my eyes. My worst daydreams surface, and in my mind's eye I can clearly see the two of them, together . . . What shall I do?

*I want to kill a girl named Debbie.*

Sometimes my mind clears, and I know why I want to end this girl's life. I want to be the only one he ever believes in, the only one he ever loves, the only one he ever longs for. But then things jumble together again, the sky of my mind becomes cloudy and overcast, and all images of sanity are washed away to reveal pure madness, except for one clear thought.

*I want to kill a girl named Debbie.*

That thought surpasses all with its strength. I want him to suffer with his emptiness. Except for me. I want his life to consist of nothing but me. So why do

*I want to kill a girl named Debbie?*

Do I not care for him? Don't you always hear of psychotic ex-girlfriends that hate or try to kill their ex's new girlfriends? But in all those cases, whether true or Hollywood-influenced, the girls truly and madly loved their former boyfriends.

*And I do not love him.*

So why? Why do I want to kill a girl named Debbie?

I loved touching his stomach, running my hands over its flat, smooth surface. Does she love his stomach the way I do? Or does he miss my touch? Does he tell her to feel his abs? Does she wonder why? Or has he forgotten all about that little quirk of mine? Most likely the latter, he never could figure out why I did it. But then, I never told him. I just loved to feel his bare skin beneath my fingertips, I loved touching him. Physical touch was something I had never experienced much of with a boy before. The simple act of holding hands sent chills down my spine.

*Thinking about killing Debbie.*

Him and her made me so unhappy and helpless. To reassure myself I was in control I burned little smiley-faces into my fore-arm. The physical pain helped take away the emotional pain; at least for awhile. But the burn scars were totally inappropriate; smiling was the thing I felt least like doing. I thought it was too bad lighters didn't come in different shapes; I could tattoo the shapes I felt were proper into my arm, like lighting bolts for anger, teardrops for sadness, and a long, jagged blade for

*Killing Debbie.*

My more violent illusions. But it was not the shape that sat-isfied me, it was the deep searing pain. And it satisfied me, it occupied my thoughts completely, leaving no room for depres-sion. That was how I got through the long days that followed my knowledge of Debbie's existence.

But now it has been almost a week; my best friend is seriously worried about me. Even my parents are noticing something is wrong. I know I cannot go on like this. I haven't left the house once, but to work. I am drowning deeply in depression. I can barely lift my head to smile. I will make him pay for bringing this girl's life into my head. I will make her pay for the scars on my arm, the ache in my heart, and the confusion in my mind.

For now I must retire. Tomorrow I will again continue my wretched plan to

*Kill a girl named Debbie.*

Make them suffer. I will, somehow, make him realize he can have no one but me. And then I will break his heart, tell him he can't have me either. But he will be so hurt he will live in solitude for the rest of his days. And I will have completed my mission.

## A First-Person Narrative on First Love
*By Lucy Jane Lang, 17, from a suburb in the Northeast*

And sometimes I opened my eyes and thought, "Why the hell am I kissing a stranger?" The thought made me laugh. He once had said, "Thanks for knowing me better than anybody." That was the silly irony of his himness—there was just so little to know. Back in the days when I liked kissing him because he was a stranger, I just couldn't wait to know it all. And then I came to know it all, and none of it was very interesting.

I had known from the very beginning all I wanted was to create something that was forever. From my earliest knee sock–wearing days, when it was still okay to shower with mom, I had lusted to fall in love. Not just a tomorrow kind of love, but a tomorrow's-tomorrow-and-then-some kind. What made me different was I didn't just think about it alone at night. I consciously looked for it. I heard its voice in opera and in Shakespeare. It was a sprightly nymph, a decadent myth that I sought.

Oh. Here's the deal on boyfriend boy. I had been indefatigably pursuing the legendary love—a little more than an abstract concept to my adolescent self. Suddenly, I rounded the corner at a summer camp dance, and there it was—my ideal staring at me. Being full of youthful zeal, I pounced on the elusive sprite, closed my eyes, and kissed him. I kissed him, and kissed him, and thought my heart might burst.

Two years later when I opened my eyes, I was shocked and appalled to discover, I had captured the wrong nymph.

You see, he looked an awful lot like my fantasy. But, I had confused a football player for a fairy. It's funny how that happens sometimes. He tasted and cuddled and even smelled like love. But at second glance, I noticed his blood ran about ten degrees cooler than the life force which coursed through the veins of my self-envisioned Hamlet. His blood was too cold, and his eyes too empty, and my lips too tired of saying the same thing. Frankly, I was bored.

My predicament reminded me a lot of that Barbra Streisand movie, where she spends her whole life convinced she's in love, until it suddenly hits her that she's only in love with wanting love. That was where I stood—at the threshold of seventeen, feeling like a thirty-year-old yenta in a film that perfectly compliments a pint of Rocky Road, kissing the love of my life who has nothing to say.

I said to him once, "Don't you ever get, you know, bored?" He hadn't even paused to think, "Only in class." Aha, I thought. "Why, do you?" he asked. "Uhhhh . . . ," I explained, "I think we need a break. I just want some space. To know myself, okay?" I said something like that, and dream boy didn't cry, or flinch, or even agree. He just explained to me—he loved me because we never fought.

"Yeah, well strangers don't usually." And I got in the car, and drove away, and wanted to turn around more with every passing moment. I knew I was right. My mom reminded me how many damned fish there are in the sea, but I felt too weak to swim, and almost wanted my boring old fish back. After all, he was on my speed dial.

The months passed. I remembered I had a life and treading water isn't so bad. My long-awaited nymph was on vacation.

I went on a date with a boy who wore sweatpants and wrote love songs, but I didn't take boyfriend boy off my speed dial.

And a hundred parties and kisses and term papers later, I was alone.

Well, I don't know quite what became of starry-eyed Ophelia. Even now I sometimes secretly wish to run to his comfortably boring arms and just dive back in.

# PART FIVE

# OVERCOMING OBSTACLES AND COMING INTO OUR OWN

# The Academic Squeeze

≋

"So, stop by the coffee shop tomorrow, if you have a chance," I said to my friend as I left her house.

"Yeah. I'll try to come by your house tomorrow."

Confused, thinking she hadn't understood, I corrected her, "No, no—to the coffee shop. I'll be there doing work."

"I know, Sara. The coffee shop *is* your home."

She had understood. I nodded. "Ah, yes."

Indeed the coffee shop was my second home. I spent practically as much time pouring caffeine down my throat, plugging away at my laptop, making to-do lists, downing my final 10:00 P.M. "Ed's Study Aid" (a large coffee with two shots of espresso), as I did eating and sleeping at my house.

At the start of my junior year, I made a commitment to myself to excel in school. With that promise, I unknowingly signed a pact with the caffeine devil to always work harder, to strive for less sleep, to never be quite satisfied.

So this section is quite personal to me. Sure, I wanted good grades. Certainly, I was determined to work for them. But, my motivation was not so simple. I made a decision to do whatever it took to be a straight-A student, because I believed my dwindling confidence resulted from my dwindling grades. I had always said I could get the grades if I wanted them, that I just didn't care enough. For a while I believed it myself. I knew I was smart. I didn't need grades to tell me I was intelligent. Or, did I?

At some point, I began to doubt my assertions. Could I really make the grades? Even if I wanted to? I had to prove to myself that I could. I was testing myself, learning to measure my self-worth by the red penned letters on the last page of my papers. Every assignment turned into an evaluation of my intelligence, my self-discipline, my personal value. A preposterous idea, I know, but an occupational hazard of many students.

School is, after all, our work; and grades are our compensation. We are the children of working mothers. Growing up in the age of post-liberation, we take our work seriously—often too seriously. For the girls who wrote to me, academics was synonymous with pressure. High school academic achievement was the gateway to a prestigious name on their college acceptance letter, then to the best graduate, law, and medical schools, and finally to the secure world of a good job, a stable income, independence, and prosperity. Of course, I'm oversimplifying, but not as much as it may seem. At the height of my Ivy-aspiring phase, telling me, "where you go to college won't change the ultimate course of your life," didn't help my parents' cause. Rationally, I knew they were right, but emotionally, I invested both my self worth and my future aspirations in which envelopes arrived in my mailbox come April.

The following contributions illuminate our awareness of the pressure we place on ourselves. But, further beneath the surface stress, the sheer pressure we put on ourselves is telling of the importance we place in the payoff. These contributions describe our constant stretch toward scholastic perfection, or at least betterment, and our unyielding dissatisfaction with the results.

In the first submission, Hilary Menges models the internal pep-talks we give ourselves during times of high stress. This piece, accurately entitled *The Facade*, represents the discrepancy between our outward look of competency and our inner feeling of incapacity.

In *No Pain, No Gain*, Marianna Racz specifically details the stress of applying to college. She shows how she organizes every detail of her day-to-day life with college in mind, mobilized by the "importance" of acceptance into a short list of highly selective schools.

Finally, these stories come to their logical conclusion. In her personal essay entitled, *Yellow*, Mimi shows the self-destructive results that come from giving a college the power to assess our value. Receiving a deferred admission to an Ivy, she attempts suicide.

The pressure can be too much.

## THE FACADE
*By Hilary Menges, 16, from a small town in the West*

The pressure was always there, always behind me. I could feel it. I could feel it as I sat in class, my head propped up with a limp hand, the only thing from preventing my face from falling flat onto the desk.

*Is it possible to sleep while awake? I've done it many times.*

When my eyes are on the clock, the hands creep by at the slowest pace imaginable. I couldn't concentrate on chemistry, or the Puritans.

*I have to study for the SATs when I get home, and I have to write an English paper, and I have to finish my German report, and . . . oh God! Was today the day I promised to take my brother to the mall?*

It builds, slowly. Teachers thought I was immune. Many didn't sympathize at all. The counselor looked at me searchingly, when I went in to talk about colleges. "Are you all right?" she asked. I smiled. "I'm fine."

*Just keep up the facade, keep your nose to the grindstone, don't think, don't eat, just work continuously. Maybe if you don't pause, you won't fall apart.*

This past year, during the winter, I worked myself into an illness; then I missed a week of classes. The toll is taken quietly, softly. Most people don't notice because they are so wrapped up in their own agendas. The eyes lose a bit of light. The mouth turns down at the corners. In general, the face looks drawn, worried, stressed. Smiles occur less frequently.

*Just keep it up, keep playing, stay in the game. Smile. Laugh. Do what you have to do. Keep the facade going; people won't notice the difference between a grimace and a giggle.*

"You need to relax," my friends said. "You're driving yourself crazy." But the truth is: They were even worse. They stayed up even later. Lauren goes to bed at 11:30, then wakes up at 2:30 to study, then sleeps for another hour, gets up at 4:30 to finish her Spanish, sleeps until 6:00, then sets her alarm again and finishes her homework.

Can this be healthy?

*Smile, laugh, flirt, keep the gears running, drink caffeine like it's water. And be sure to watch your weight. No chocolate. Funny how everybody thinks life's dandy. Funny how the cracks just don't seem to show.*

What difference does 20, 30 points on the SAT mean, anyway? Will life be ruined if I can't break into the 1300s?

Failure, always so close. Whoops, can't pause—history worksheet to complete.

"How late are we looking at, honey? You really should get some sleep."

"Goodnight, Mom, don't worry about me. I'll go to bed soon."

Three hours later, at 2:30 in the morning, crawl into bed.

*All you have to do is keep the pressure at bay. Just keep it one step behind you, and you'll be fine. Make sure it doesn't get to you. Otherwise, you'll explode. "Work a little harder, darling. It'll all, pay off in the end." You'll live through this. Heard senior year was a breeze.*

# No Pain, No Gain
*By Marianna Racz, 16, from a city in the East*

I sit at my desk procrastinating over my history paper. I have to hand it in after the too-short weekend. "The Best 311 Colleges" (the book my mother has been absorbed in for the past few months) stares at me from the corner of my room. This 707-page book with "the inside on getting into the most selective schools" has become my life without my consent. The "college process" is the most horrible, intricate procedure in my life thus far, and I have not even started actually applying to the schools. I always assumed my teenage years would be carefree, full of fun and excitement. At certain times they are, but it has become difficult to enjoy the weekends and vacations. There is something constantly shadowing over me. The worst part is I have no one to blame for my lack of fun and abundance of stress. I completely put it upon myself.

I went into the summer of '97 without anticipating the workload of junior year and the stresses of college preparation. Of course I brought a few SAT workbooks on my two month getaway, but they just ended up gathering dust on a wooden shelf. When I returned from camp at the end of August, my friend told me about the SAT tutor her mother got her. I became intensely nervous. I told my mom to call Princeton Review. . . . quickly! But I knew that my SAT scores were not the only thing colleges looked for in an applicant. They could not measure my personality, aspirations, or my deep interests. Then I became *really* nervous. I was not an actor, a singer, an artist, an athlete, nor had I won an award for discovering a new element. The truth was I had no incredibly real interest outside of academics. I knew colleges really looked for that kind of extracurricular obsession.

But I did love being with people and working with other people so I volunteered for jobs working with disabled children and the elderly hoping these activities might satisfy the extracurricular section of my application. But no matter how much I enjoy myself at my volunteer jobs, the question always lingers in the back of my mind: Is it enough? I constantly fear no college will think I am gifted enough to study there.

Friday morning rolls around and I am overwhelmed with happiness. Thankful that for the next two days I don't have to wake up at 6:45 A.M. and watch the sunrise from my window, as I slowly dress for the long day ahead. Grateful that for two days, I don't have to sit through class after class taking notes furiously so

I don't miss something important for the test next week. But then, at 6:00 P.M. Friday evening when I arrive home from my community service at the Y, I realize I have two essays to write, three midterms to study for, and pages of SAT homework for my tutor on Tuesday. My hopes of partying over the weekend are soon suppressed by my extensive workload.

Not everyone is like me when it comes to work, in fact many people are not. I can never fully enjoy myself when in the back of my mind I have hours and hours of work waiting for me on my cluttered desk. My weekends over the past four and a half months have consisted of going to sleep late, waking-up early, and working all day, Saturday and Sunday. Sometimes I look forward to Sunday night. By then, all my essays will be written and safely tucked away in my Jansport backpack.

When I speak to my friends and fellow classmates they never seem to have as much work to do. Some even make fun of me for studying as much as I do, and for always being so paranoid. But I honestly cannot help feeling the stress. I can't stop putting it upon myself.

One morning on my much anticipated winter vacation, *Admissions Essay Ordeal: The Young Examined Life* was laying on my desk with the note, "Marianna, read!" It was one of my usual late starts and I was looking forward to a day full of nothing to do. But once again my mother had gone beyond her duty as a nagging parent, and placed this enormous burdening issue on my desk. What was she thinking? During vacation? As I gazed over the title it rang in my ears as something I should stay away from, at least until after my time of freedom was done. But I sat down on my pink and white striped beanbag chair and read it over and over again until I became fully sick. A girl in the article even wished someone she knew would die so she could document it for her college essay. I prayed that when it came time to sit down and write this fifteen-hundred word story of my life I would not become as desperate as some of the students discussed in this article.

But who is to blame for my pain and suffering? Is it my

mother for being the overly pestering parent and never getting off my case? Is it my school for giving me endless hours of homework? Is it society for trying to ruin my life? Or is it me for letting all these people and establishments get to me, and for taking it way too far? When it comes down to it I put the stress on myself. I worry about what others are doing; what their PSATs are, who their tutor is, what grades they have. I constantly worry that I am behind and try to run (sometimes too fast) to catch up. The speed is both difficult and unnecessary.

At this point, I guess, I am supposed to come up with a solution to solve all my college stress problems. But there isn't one; anxiety and apprehension come along with the territory. It's one short (although it seems like it will never end) part of my teenage existence. I have to get through it without any shortcuts. It's like skiing. You'll be on your skis, gripping your poles, dreaming of a steaming cup of hot chocolate to soothe the freezing feeling you have in your right foot, and you'll see a huge hill in front of you. Sometimes you can go on the sides and avoid actually going down the hill but sometimes the sides are too icy. You have no choice but to go straight down. This is just like one of those huge hills. I know the sides are way too icy. There are no shortcuts. I have to keep my goggles tightly fastened around my head, grip those poles firmly, deter the hot chocolate image from entering my mind, and go straight down the hill that will eventually lead me to college.

# YELLOW
*By Mimi, 16, from a city in the West*

I had applied to Yale. In December, I was deferred admission.

I wanted to kill myself. I tried. A slice, two, three, four, five. Flesh parting cleanly under the fragile, tiny razor blade. Instantaneous little streaks of pain. Negligible. Unimportant. Then bright red beads, welling up, swelling, joining. I saw the blood, coming, coming, in spurts and trickles. I was so proud. I thought it had worked. I had to show someone. I felt my heart-beat, pounding in my ears, penetrating my bones, and imagined it slowing, slowing, and stopping at last.

Then, impressions of cold, of voices, of tears. And it was over. My brief madness (or perhaps my only moment of sanity) ended. I walked away.

I was standing alone on a dark street, at midnight, on a silent winter's night. All alone, without even a passing pair of head-lights, or the rumble of a truck out of sight. There was no emo-tion. Perhaps there never had been, but whatever had been there was replaced by utter calm and clarity of thought. All the things I had wondered about, all the things I had known, poured back at me, to be seen in a different aspect, to be held up to an unwaver-ing new light, unclouded for the first time. I had no desires, not to live, and not to die. There was the cold, and snow on the ground, frigid white to the extent of purification, and no more.

I walked home. It was cold; I could feel my skin going numb. I should have been shivering, but only my legs moved. Everything was so sharp, so strong, even the silence engraved itself into my brain. I started to remember what had happened, what had been a blur, a mist, "resolved itself into a dew" and every sound, every ges-ture, every touch replayed itself, like a movie without music.

I reached my house, walked up the steps, and opened the door onto a warm pool of yellow light. My mother was sitting there, waiting for me. I held up my left arm, pulling up the sod-den sleeve of my sweater, revealing streaks of dried blood. She screamed. I went to bed.

Only to be woken. I was in a pit of blackness, oblivion—yes, but without finality—fragile darkness broken by a door being flung open. And my father was shouting. In the background: crying. And then the phone rang. Silence. Then ring. Then silence. Then ring—cut off. Conversation. Silence. And then it started again. Shouting. "How could you do this?" Shaking. "Are you crazy?!"

The clarity is gone. The thinking is gone. Emotions come flooding back. In this heat, my dew evaporates. If death is to escape this, then yes, I want death.

In Chinese, blood and snow are homonyms. For me, blood meant death, and snow, cold. Pursuing one to escape the other, I wandered, hoped, and despaired. There must come an end to everything, but this time, it was not my life that ended. It was my search for an end. I looked at the pieces, so recently broken and scattered, and started gathering. Mix blood and snow, and the result is neither one nor the other. Not red, not white. Oddly enough, it's yellow.

# Depression and Therapy

The worst night of my life I envisioned my own funeral, my death by suicide. I curled up in a tight ball, paralyzed by my imagination. Scene after self-destructive scene reeled through my consciousness. My parents were the only people who cried at the service.

Writing here is only the third time I've confessed those deathly images. The next day, I tearfully told my tenth-grade boyfriend. Later, I confided in my journal. Now, I tell you.

Although I crashed that one night, I had been falling for months. Since the end of my tenth-grade year, self-judgment had tugged at the upturned corners of my lips—that's why my smile looked forced, and my bottom lip often quivered. I didn't like myself. I only saw my weaknesses. I heard only the abrasive tone of self-criticism.

I understand depression. I deeply wish I didn't.

Like sixteen year old Alethea Beatrice Trorrier Barbaro, I felt alone and invisible. Alethea wrote as she sat on her friend's bed, "No one can see me today. I don't mean the superficial, look-in-the-mirror, type of seeing. I mean really seeing, feeling, understanding." I didn't think others saw the sadness that consumed me. I thought my smile looked real. I masked myself in the same self-contradictory disguise as an anonymous seventeen year old who described herself this way: "I was a lacrosse girl. I was a superstar eleventh grader. I was a girlfriend who wanted to have sex. I was off to Europe in seven weeks. I was happy . . . or was I?" My strained smile perpetuated my feeling of isolation.

Fifteen-year-old Joisyphene Poe captured the escalation of this despondency in a single sentence: "Loneliness makes depression feel like insanity."

I recognized my downward spiral. I knew I needed help.

In an effort to learn to like myself again, I enlisted the help of women who didn't insist that I smile back. An occasional tear didn't cause them concern. The salty drop just left a wrinkled dot on the page. Virginia Woolf, Maya Angelou, and Alice Walker became my most trusted companions. They didn't know I existed; I couldn't disappoint them. We spent most of our one-sided relationship sipping coffee at a table for one. I have a journal filled with my reactions to their wisdom. Sitting in coffee shops, I could read and write and think with anonymity, free from others' expectations. I became more comfortable in the impersonal chatter of strangers, and the milling of coffee grinders, than in the company of those who had once known me. Alone, nameless to others, I could concentrate on my own self-healing. That was the semester of Me. I learned a lot about myself, by myself. All by myself. Intense self-analysis, self-therapy without a second party, can be terribly lonely.

But I was the child of a therapist, not a patient. Perhaps that is why I refused to see someone. Or, perhaps it was simply my habit to refuse help for practically anything important. I mean, I wouldn't even let my parents read my term papers for grammar mistakes, let alone let someone help me reinvent my self-esteem. Now, I am grateful I was able to do it myself.

Though the images of my own suicide seem distant, the resurrection of my self-worth is still the accomplishment I hold dearest. But, with the benefit of hindsight, I can honestly say I shouldn't have done it alone. I did find strength in my solitude, in my gratingly close proximity to myself without the comfort of companionship. Still, I think recovering from my depression would have been easier with a therapist.

In the four contributions to this chapter, girls write about emotionally difficult times. Like me, Iris Martin Cohen found solace in the pages of a book. *To Brooke,* was originally inscribed on a gift to a friend—Iris found her self-therapy in the pages of *Les Miserables.* In her self-revelatory poem, Iris revisits her depression, and demonstrates her own self-inspired way out.

Unlike Iris, the remaining contributors to this chapter received professional psychotherapy during their times of crisis. Each tells a different story. Each demonstrates the importance of finding the right help.

But, not all help is helpful. In the *Psychiatrist's Garden*, Willow allows us into her mind as she reacts to the deafening buzz of an absurdly ill-suited therapist. Resisting this woman's irrelevant intervention, Willow shows her strength and her humor. She demonstrates the need for each of us to find a therapist who relates to us honestly.

*Paris, Idaho*, the third contribution, is a travel diary through the sights and sounds of residential treatment. Melissa J. Bentley's words perfectly evoke her melancholic surrender, as she passes her school vacation in a psychiatric ward instead of in Paris. In one well-studied comparison after another, Melissa resolves to make the best of her "vacation" and learn the most from her visit to this unwelcoming destination.

In the last submission, *Some Years Are Better Than Others,* T. P. recounts the pressures that threw her into a downward spiral. She enters therapy and shows how, despite her initial resistance, her psychologist has helped her to lift herself out of her depression. T. P.'s optimistic story illustrates the support every girl should insist on receiving from therapy.

I hope this section will encourage other adolescent girls to seek the help I avoided. I also hope more parents will make an effort to support their daughters' need to find helpful professionals sensitive enough to be instrumental in the recovery process.

# To Brooke
# On Giving Her My Favorite Book

*By Iris Martin Cohen, 17, from city in the South*

You know the real me?
That wondrous, true Iris that Cory is perennially searching for,
that phantasm of projected attributes—mysterious,
     sophisticated–
elusive,
Well, here it is, the *real Iris*,
and all that lay at the bottom of the seemingly endless
     speculation
was this—an old, cheap, gray paperback.
—a bit of a let down I guess—
But, to explain—I must go back,
through the black sludge of school years and summers,
through the terrifying mess that was Simon's Rock,
through the desperate giddiness that was high school,
to the pink tipped beginning of my years at Country Day.
To that tremulous and impressionable age of eleven
when, suddenly, but with absolute conviction,
I realized,
I was all wrong.
From my chubby fingertips to the deepest recesses of my heart,
from the brand of my jeans to the passions that guided my life,
all of it was horribly and contemptibly wrong.
(Don't ask me by what standards, at that age we think in
     absolutes.)
So I set about destroying myself from the outside in,
with an intellect advanced enough to be ruthlessly efficient
and an emotional state simple enough to follow with blind
     devotion.
In a master stroke of displacement,

I became not only the victim to my own executioner,
but the multitudes cheering him on as well.
I'll spare you the gory details, my premise was simple.
If it comes from me it's wrong. And worse than wrong,
    contemptible.
I shed my interests, my loves, my thoughts, my dreams,
furtively, ashamed.
I broke my own Spirit with a calculating cruelty worthy of
an inquisitor or a fascist.
Those were bad years.
It was during this period that I read *Les Miserables*,
and because it sparked something that glowed fiercely
in the part of me that I was rapidly dismantling;
I lunged for it,
with the raw and bony hands of a prisoner of war,
and deemed it me.
Like a soldier facing a firing squad who leaves his dog tags
    behind,
or a suicide who leaves a note,
I grabbed this object as a chance to leave evidence of the part of
    me that was dying.
I poured all parts of myself that I valued into this book,
locking my soul inside the inanimate pages,
where it would be safe,
put the book into my bottom drawer,
and threw my empty shell to the wind.
I stopped fighting and watched,
as the relentless wind that blew through the hallways of my
    school,
ripped parts of me away.
At first I hated my teeth and felt each loss like a gaping wound,
leaving me hurt and angry.
Then I stopped caring and just watched, impassively,
as the cold wind peeled away layers of myself that were already
    dead.

Then I forgot, I forgot there was even anything missing.

Well, almost.

Except late at night, sometimes when I'd got to my desk with ashy gray skin

and hollow eyes,

feeling a weary specter with no tears left to cry,

and cradled this book with an intensity I no longer understood.

Like a living skeleton, I'd press this book to me

and feel such emotions I didn't think my chest could contain them.

Feelings that left me breathless,

but whose identities had been lost in my depthless misery and indifference.

Like a freezing vagrant watching a fire through a closed and frosty window,

what I had put in this book was no longer accessible to me.

I could only see and be aware of its existence, but at least it was preserved.

By placing it outside myself I had saved it,

and I carried this awareness around always,

it kept me from killing myself and increased my torment.

So I floundered for the next seven years,

making mistakes everywhere,

thrashing my head against these paper gray walls I had erected,

scraping at them until my fingernails bled,

tears, razors, shrinks, confusion.

But, you know, all things must come to an end.

And perhaps the mere fact that I'm writing this dedication shows

I don't need it anymore,

and letting go is sweet release.

So, take it.

Even if you don't like the book, treasure the volume for me,

and as long as it sits on your bookshelf, you'll always have a piece of me nearby.

I love you dearly,

Iris (or Iris)

—and if this is all too pseudo-psyche-angsty for you, just read it. It's the best book ever written.

## PSYCHIATRIST'S GARDEN
*By Willow, 17, from a suburb in the Northeast*

I am seated on an ancient-looking sofa, overstuffed with polyfill, covered with coffee stains and Victorian blue roses. The latter pair wage a two-dimensional battle over the surface of the couch. Otherwise, I have it all to myself.

The woman is standing behind me. If she would keep quiet for a moment, I could pretend the stink of heavy perfume is coming from my resting place—from my little bed of roses. I could seize each wrinkle of fabric, crush it between my fingers. But she is watching my every move right now, pen in hand, so grasping for the flowers in the floral print probably isn't too brilliant an idea.

*I feel like an exhibit in the flower show from hell.*

Behind me, she drones on and on, until her words are lost in the buzzing of insignificant sound. Funny, isn't it? A drone—a male bee among flowers. Strangely appropriate. I consider sharing this thought with her. But if I spoke, it would only give her an excuse to move closer, to strangle me with the scent of fake flowers as she tries to plug herself into my brain.

Though I'm sure she could come up with a million great theories. Maybe my thoughts indicate a subconscious belief that men, like bees, sting the hell out of any girl who gets too close. Maybe it means I'm afraid to love. Maybe it means I'm a lesbian. Maybe it means there is some kind of weird bug colony nestled between my ears.

Or maybe it just means she's boring me to death. I decide to remain silent on this point.

The sound of brisk footsteps. Against my better judgment, I raise my eyes. There she is—Freud in a granny dress. A dress covered with violets and roses. She bends down, looks into my eyes:

"Are you all right, dear? I'm sure this is a terrible shock for you." I glance momentarily at her face. Her glasses reflect a graveyard of synthetic petals. I shift my gaze to the floral wallpaper growing behind her. My mouth remains a folded bud.

She sighs. I sigh. *This is a good sign,* she thinks.

A large packet of paper, "my intelligence report," hits the couch beside me.

Momentarily, I consider swatting her with it. My hands twitch longingly, then resettle in my lap. And she drones on. She tells me my verbal skills are high. She tells me my math aptitude "leaves much to be desired."

*Yes indeed they must be, if after all these years, I still can't come to a conclusive answer by adding "X" to "Y,"* quoth the little voice in my head. I silence it, and continue listening.

With the great mystery of my intellect resolved—plotted points on a cheap paper flyswatter—she moves on to my psyche. She informs me that my life has not been a very good one. She tells me that I am very morbid. Yet, with the same radiant smile a young girl gives a flower she's about to tear from the earth, she says that there is good news hidden in this situation, because I am not alone.

*I can't help but wish that I were. These flowers are driving me mad.*

She says there are names for my conditions.

*Yes. Yes—my name is among them.*

I don't speak. She does. Out comes a long Latin phrase.

*I have never taken Latin, but it seems to have taken me.*

"Do you know what that means?" she asks

*Yes, God damn it, I do! I have lived it for sixteen years! I have breathed it, eaten it, walked it, spoken it, lived it!*

I look at her, my eyes unreadable, and I read her eyes. She is absolutely dying to tell me why I am who I am. She is desperate to tell me all about my experiences. Her hands are trembling so violently, the coffee stains have just gained a permanent advantage over a particularly riotous patch of the sofa's blue roses. So I shake my head. No.

The beehive reactivates.

My ears, however, short-circuit.

Without reason, I begin thinking back on all the soap operas my mom has seen over the years. How I used to laugh at them. She laughed too. She found them ridiculous, she said, but she only said that during commercial breaks. Otherwise, her eyes remained glued to the set. I half expected her to stop blinking. Sometimes, she did.

My life—a soap opera. I am suddenly a script written on a flyswatter, a bee-killer. I am nothing more than a life that has suddenly been written into a purely fictional account. Suddenly, this all becomes incredibly funny.

*But I don't dare even crack a smile, for fear that I will crack in turn.*

## PARIS, IDAHO
*By Melissa J. Bentley, 16, from a suburb in the West*

The flowers were from a friend in Wisconsin. I was allowed to take them to my room because they contained no wires and were in a plastic, not a metal or glass, case. They were yellow and reminded me of Impressionist sunflowers, although they were probably daisies or mums, I'm not sure which.

I took a class about Impressionism last year. No, it was just last semester. It seems so long ago. The class was going to Paris that spring. I was going to go too, but didn't make it that far. Instead, I was sent to the University Neuropsychiatric Institute, on the East Branch of Boise. The two destinations are not so different as one might suppose. Certainly the cost of living is comparable.

In Paris, I have heard, they have lovely cafes that overlook colorful, well-peopled city streets. And so we have here. I am a "Day Glow" today, which means I've gone to groups, set goals, cleaned my room, and haven't said "fuck you" to any of the social workers. As a Day Glow, I am allowed to go down to the cafeteria to get a drink at mealtimes. Some patients even get to eat down there, but I eat under observation.

I move my magnet on the sign-out board to the space marked "cafe" and wait for a tech to come open the door and walk me down. We aren't allowed to wear shoes because they make it easier to run away or to hang ourselves. I suppose that's good, because one of the patients did try to hang himself with a belt. Still, going without shoes is embarrassing: Everyone in the halls and cafeteria knows the people in stocking feet are crazy.

Laura is the nurse today. She frowns at me and mutters something about "special privileges." Gary, the tech, finally comes. We walk down the cold stairs and into the dining area. A huge window on one wall looks out over the city—Boise, not Paris. I get a Diet Pepsi. Wishing they had Diet Coke, I begin to go back upstairs. I meet Laura in the hall.

"You forgot your medicine," she says.

"Sorry. Thank you for bringing it." I reach to take it from her outstretched hand, but she drops it on the floor and goes to talk to Gary while I reach down to pick it up.

"Come with me, Melissa," she says. "It's not fair that you should get to make a special trip down here when you have to eat on-unit anyway."

I don't go down to the cafe anymore, but I'm sure some people in Paris don't get to go out to eat either. They probably get sick and want to stay inside, where it's comfortable.

I had planned to visit the Louvre while I was in France, but we have artwork here as well. We made a self-esteem collage with magazine pictures this morning. I cut out three pictures: a tall model in a red dress who was walking a poodle, a pair of jeweled high-heeled shoes, and a picture of the Eiffel Tower. I also cut out a picture of a woman with red hair who looked something like my mother.

Chopin was from Paris. I have been learning *Etude Opus 10. No. 3 in E Major*, which he composed while there. Here we have a boom box in the Commons Room. I sometimes get to choose what we listen to, but I am afraid to ask for classical music. Grunge or rap is more acceptable to the other patients.

I may get to go outside tomorrow. It looks warm; sunlight is baking the autumn-colored leaves so that now they're almost brown and turning the endless stretch of lawn a tired yellow. I haven't been out since an ambulance came to get me at my home last week. It was cold then: A device inside the ambulance told the outside temperature. It read forty-two degrees when we were moving and forty-seven when we stopped.

The hospital the ambulance brought me to was tall: It could have been a building in Paris. My room was on the fourth floor. I was fed through IVs. It was hard to pretend I was eating rich French pastries, although the dripping, chalky liquid probably had as much fat. I don't care for food much anyway. I've been here now for twelve days.

I'll probably be leaving the hospital in a few days, if my vital signs are stable and if I gain a few more pounds. I don't have any souvenirs to bring my friends or family from this journey. I could give my brother the *gak* we made with Borax and glue. *Gak* is a sort of slimy stuff that's supposed to help relieve stress. I wanted to give my mother a French perfume or scarf, and my dad some expensive wine or dark chocolate.

It's Friday night and we get to watch a video, the new remake of *Sabrina*. We could see an eclipse of the moon for a while, through the window. But then cloudy sky made it hard to see. It looked very far away. My pulse slowed and was irregular at bed-time vitals. I'll have to be on bed rest tomorrow. I think it has started raining anyway. I've heard it rains a lot in France.

I had hoped to visit Paris to escape my life for a while, and to be an actress, a poet, in love: a beautiful cultured person in a beautiful place. Instead I had landed in a place where life is more real—and therefore, harder—than I had ever known it could be. I had wanted to learn something of a different people and a differ-ent way of life; to study a foreign land that could teach me a new way of thinking about the world and about myself. I have not been disappointed. Really.

# SOME YEARS ARE BETTER THAN OTHERS
*By T. P., 16, from a small town in the East*

Some years are better than others. But how do I deal with three bad ones in a row? I was a little down during my freshman year. The next year my mood dipped even more. During that sophomore year, someone listened to me and I received help. Slowly I improved and learned that you have to help yourself, and also, let others help you.

Why was I depressed? It seemed I had no reason to be: I lived on a beautiful street with my mom. My grades had always been above average. I enjoyed sports and was pretty good at softball and tennis. My violin had earned me two trips to Europe. I had three best friends and a boyfriend. Looking at my life that way, there wasn't much to be unhappy about. Still, for a while, my thinking was not so positive.

Why do people die? It never seems fair, especially when a young friend dies. John Nolan was hit by a car during my freshman year and died before his life had barely begun. He never went to a prom, never got his license, and never played football in his first homecoming game. I wasn't close to John, but he was an acquaintance. It was a huge shock to me when he died. I've often thought about him since. That same year my Uncle Bob died. He was a classic Catholic Irishman, minus alcohol and smoking. He even went to school to become a priest, before he fell in love with my Aunt Mary. Ironically, he died of lung cancer. To be honest, I was angry that he had to die. There were so many evil people out there who were perfectly healthy, yet had extremely unhealthy habits—smoking, drinking, and taking drugs.

It is very normal for people to be depressed, especially when a loved one dies, but I felt depressed all the time. Not only did I think of John and Uncle Bob, I also obsessed about every person that I knew who had died. I was constantly thinking of Father Michael, my priest who had died on Christmas Eve, or my mother's friend, Cathy, who died when I was in middle school. I seemed to want to be depressed.

Meanwhile, my older sister fought with my parents constantly. She moved out a couple of times, and was even kicked out. Sophomore year, my dad moved to New Jersey and my sister went to college. I felt alone and scared. The change was more than I could handle. To make things worse, my parents decided to get a divorce and sell our house. I didn't know how to handle anything, so I decided not to. I thought I would deal with my feelings later.

I found myself getting into lots of trouble, first by getting drunk, then by throwing up. I didn't care if it hurt my throat or if it killed me. At that point in my life, I wouldn't have minded dying. I didn't feel there was anything worth living for.

Halfway through my sophomore year, my mom found a letter I had written to my sister in college, telling her that I had been purging. Shauna had written me back to give some "big-sisterly" advice. I hid the note in my underwear drawer until my mother just "happened" to find it. She was very upset and made an appointment for me to see a doctor.

I was incredibly angry at my mom for invading my privacy, and scared that she knew I had been throwing up. She was very upset. She wanted to know why I was doing it, but I didn't want to talk to her about it. She paid close attention to what I was eating and what I did in the bathroom.

A couple of months later my mom took me to a psychologist. I told this doctor things I had never shared with anyone before. There was a lot of crying, but it felt good to finally get it all out. She mostly listened, but she also asked questions about my family and how I felt about Dad leaving. I told her how I felt before and after I threw up, but I couldn't give her an exact reason why I was doing it. She gave me ways to manage my time better and to keep my concentration during school. I learned how to block my family out while I was in class and just to get my work done.

At the end of our meeting, she invited my mom back in the room. The doctor said that I was clinically depressed. She thought it would be a good idea for me to take an antidepressant to help improve my mood. She described it as though I was in a deep hole and couldn't climb out by myself. The medicine would be like a ladder to help me. I still had to do all the work, but the ladder was there when I needed help.

It has been about a year since I first received help and now I rarely make myself purge. I say rarely because once in a while I feel myself slip, and I throw up. But I have improved dramatically. I would like to be totally better. Sometimes I wonder if it is normal for my mood to change so much. I change from happy, to confused, to extremely sad, and then to angry. Is it healthy, or should I not feel this way? I don't know. I can't say whether the medicine really worked. I don't know how to determine that.

I can say, however, that therapy has worked. I love having someone to talk to who listens and doesn't yell, like my mother. The doctor gives me advice and helps me to learn things about myself I never knew. She has shown me that I try to please everyone, often an impossible task. From our sessions, I have learned that I need to decide when it is time to just worry about myself and do what is best for me. I'm glad, in a way, that my mother found the note in my room.

# Race, Identity, and Prejudice

≋

When we were in second grade, my best friend's parents didn't speak English. When I was in fourth grade, my first boyfriend was African-American. By the time I got to seventh grade everyone at my lunch table looked and talked just like me—we wore Gap jeans, had braces—and spoke only English. Every table had a distinctive ethnic or racial flavor, as though color and speech served as criteria for cafeteria seating.

With the terrible importance of "fitting-in" comes adolescent self-segregation. Our racial and cultural identity is often one of our few outwardly visible traits. In the highly superficial world of junior and senior high school, the complicated search for community is often compromised. We usually settle for people who look like us.

At a summer program after ninth grade one of my roommates was an African-American girl from Florida. We became best friends that summer. When she asked me if any of my best friends from home were black, I was reluctant to tell her the truth. My best friends looked basically like me. I tried to sugarcoat my answer, "Well, none of my *best* friends, but definitely a few of my good friends." That was almost true, except they weren't really even good friends, and their real friends looked just like them, too.

The summer before my senior year I took classes at a university. A few of the people I actually liked looked different from me. When they called home, some spoke languages other than English to their parents. Karina and I had big plans to make me a fluent Spanish speaker by summer's end. Hassan had the same name as my first boyfriend's little brother. For the first time since elementary school, I enjoyed the freedom of picking my friends from an unbounded cultural pool. I thought growing up finally meant overcoming the bondage of appearance.

I was mistaken. Age doesn't yield openness. That fall, I went back to the university to visit a friend from home—a white friend. I sat on the cold steps of the main building, my body relieved after dancing in a party's suffocating heat, watching an appealing mix of people pass. Laughing and chatting with my high-school friend, I heard my name called. I glanced toward the mesh tables overhead. "Hassan!" I leaped up, eager to see my summer friend, eager to introduce him to my friend from home. However, in the next few minutes I realized their awkwardness was magnified by an invisible color barrier. When Hassan invited us to a party sponsored by the Black Student Union, my white friend told me he would meet up with me after.

Now I realize that the look-alike tables in the cafeteria can become a permanent seating arrangement. The contributors to this chapter have experienced difficulty successfully desegregating those metaphorical tables. They have all faced prejudice. In each case, the intolerance came from unexpected sources, making the hurt and the confusion all the worse.

Karisima Amelia Rodriguez's *Reflections* begins the chapter. After illustrating the powerlessness of women in Latino culture, she writes: "Here, in the United States, you are still worthless for being a woman, and also despised for being Latino. Your fault doubles." Karisima takes us to work with her, where she is subjected to the prejudices of her employers.

The second contribution, *My Loss*, tells a story of peer betrayal. Adrienne Boyd, a Native-American/African-American girl, grew up innocently in a small white-majority community. She did not know she was surrounded by bigotry until she dated a white boy. Confronted with ignorance and hatred, she wishes she could return to her naiveté.

In the final submission, *The Only One,* an anonymous author faces the prejudices of other African-American teenagers, boys who label her a "sell-out." Contemplating their verbal assault on her "blackness," she values her uniqueness.

A single theme repeated itself in the submissions to this chapter: Girls wanted to be appreciated as individuals. They appreciated the ways the color of their skin and the origins of their ancestors support their distinctiveness, but they loathed the twisting of race and ethnicity into self-denying stereotypes and bigotry. Although I have never been the subject of such prejudices, their ideal of individualism without preconceived judgments is a popular goal. We all want to be seen as individuals; we should treat each other accordingly.

# REFLECTIONS
*By Karisma Amelia Rodriguez, 15, from a city in the West*

I never wanted anyone to open the door or pull out a chair for me. I thought these rituals were created by men to prove women invalid and useless. True horror stories of my grandma's tortured life made me a stubborn and independent young girl. Knowing the hidden truth created rage and sorrow, battling inside me, silent to the world.

I never knew my grandma. I only knew what my mother told me. After my grandma had two children—my mother and my uncle—her family forbade her from having any more children. Still, she got pregnant with a third child. Then, my grandma's own brother forced her into an illegal abortion.

After the forced abortion, my grandma woke up with nightmares, woke up screaming through the night, "My son! My son! Where is he?"

My mother and her brother, who were younger than I am now, knew nothing about the abortion. They both came running to my grandma's room. My uncle held her shivering body tightly in his arms. Trying to comfort her, he assured her, "I'm here Mommy. I'm here."

But, my grandma could not be comforted. She said, "No. My other son. My other son."

Confused, my mother and uncle thought my grandma had gone insane, until they learned the truth. My grandma's unborn son had been taken from her.

After a life of endless demeaning and insulting abuse, my dear *abuela* (grandma) died a horrible death from breast cancer at age forty-eight.

I never knew her. I never kissed or embraced her. I've seen only one sweet picture. I never got to wear one of the many frilly dresses she adored making. I have only her black silk shawl.

In Latino culture, if you were a woman, you were worthless. You could be sold as a maidservant/slave to a man for the rest of your life. You had to do everything exactly as you were told. You were at the mercy of your master. Your dignity was hidden, if not destroyed.

Here, in the United States, you are still worthless for being a woman, and despised for being Latino. Your fault doubles.

## In America

Last summer, at fourteen years old, I came to know the difficult bind of being a strong-minded independent Latino woman. I had never imagined the ignorance and hatred that exists in the "real world." I thought prejudice was a thing of the past, an attitude diminished over time. I heard about racism on the radio, and saw it on TV. Truthfully, I did experience intolerance where I live, in poor neighborhoods. And, I had seen the bigotry that comes with trying to interact with wealthy people. Still, I somehow managed to convince myself that prejudice could not succeed in a stuffy, middle-class office. I assumed the people would be too smart to allow its existence . . . I don't know how I came up with that one!

Back to my story. I was going to work. I was so proud. Proud and nervous. The job didn't matter. It wasn't my career, but it was real work. Real work, for the first time. I would earn real money. I could buy lots of new things to replace my old raggy clothes, backpack, and school supplies. I could help out with our financial difficulties at home. I could return to school in the fall, ready to work hard and maintain my 4.0 GPA. Then, I could brag to the world and they wouldn't put me down. They'd have to set aside their stereotypical categories.

So I began work at a school for special-needs children. My job was in the office, helping an Asian lady and man. Since the lady already had help, mostly I worked for the man.

He liked me at first. I usually impress people because I'm intelligent and a hard-worker. And then, he also thought I was white. In his words, "most likely French."

One day, after I had been working for him some time, he was browsing through the file the work program had sent with me. They make resumes for us. He read it. Then, he mocked me because I hadn't had much experience besides volunteering at the school library. I wondered, What does he expect? Fourteen is the youngest age you can work. I frowned, but ignored my thoughts.

"Oh, you're Mexican!?" He questioned me in a confused, shocked, and disappointed tone. I knew immediately that he had discovered my last name. I thought he'd found it long ago. He asked, "How do you pronounce your name?"

I pronounced my family name and then added, "Yes, I'm Mexican, and Puerto Rican and Cuban."

For the next few weeks he'd ask me stupid questions about "how" and "why" I was "Hispanic." I didn't how to answer. Should I say the obvious, I was born that way. What would he do if I made him feel dumb? What did he want me to say? He'd sporadically come to me and say, "So, you're Hispanic." Then, he'd sigh or make some strange noise.

"Yeah," I'd reply, more annoyed each time. I hated it when he used that word. "Hispanic" would roll off his tongue slowly, like peanut butter or sticky caramel he was trying to remove. He couldn't think of anything else to say, so he'd leave and conjure up his next interview, which was usually the same as his last.

I wished that another nice lady at the school was my boss. She was so kind and sweet to everyone. Her voice was like an angel and it calmed my anger. She was white, but tanned with layered blond hair. She had a soft, comforting smile. But she often worked in other office areas and during those times my supervisor would continue his investigations.

One day he finally blurted it out. "But why are you so light? I saw your mother bring you here. She's not even as white as you are. How about your dad? Is your father white?"

I was confused. At a loss for words, I tried to think of something say—something that would make him shut up. Thinking back to the one time I had seen my father I answered, "No. He's dark too. Much darker than my mom. Everyone in my family is at least two shades darker than me." I wondered silently, Now. Will that end the conversation?

But he persisted. "Oh, but that's great. You should be glad. It's *very* good you're so white. It makes you look *cleaner*." He emphasized the last word *cleaner* and looked straight into my eyes with a strong stare that said, *Understand?*

Although I was taller than he, and he had sat down in his cushioned, adjustable chair, I felt like he was ten feet tall, looking down his nose at me, talking down to me. He had repeatedly tried to humiliate me before. He had tried to make me feel little and insulted, but I had never let him—never until then.

I remembered my world history teacher explaining how the early Americans despised the first Mexican immigrants because they were dark and appeared to be permanently *dirty*. I thought of my sweet, innocent brown-eyed cousin Lidia who dreams of America all the time. I remembered my mom telling me how no one would hire her as anything—even as a deli worker. She behaved American, but her last name stood out on her applications. They questioned her ability to make a sandwich, but never let her make one.

I stood there—in the doorway of his evil office—without moving. I didn't want to cry. He would win if I shed tears. Then, he would ask me, "What's wrong with you?" There was nothing wrong with me. I restrained myself from making a tight fist because then he would see my anger. I wiggled my fingers. A slight sound came out of my mouth. Then, I left his doorway solemnly with a thousand thoughts and retorts swimming through my head. And that's where they stayed until I got home.

This man didn't like who I was, but he tolerated me. He excused my heritage because, according to him I "had the looks," and "could be a model." He took pleasure in watching me. I *hated* every inch of him. He stared at me and sometimes smiled. I got this creepy feeling. The same one I get when old men gawk at me down on the street, or when guys driving cars make crude, vulgar noises and offensive vulgar filth pours out of their mouths. I was so uncomfortable. I felt on display.

When he came close to me, I often was afraid he would touch me. He never did more that pat me on the head. I washed his touch away with all the shampoo left in bottle. They say "These days girls cannot avoid being harassed—it's a common as eating." But, I avoided being touched wrongfully.

On my last work day, my boss and the other girl boss took me out for lunch. He said, "It's your choice," but he dismissed me when I suggested a Mexican restaurant. He said, "You should try something new." I wondered why it didn't apply vice-versa. They had both eaten soup and rice with chicken every single day, except for the day they went to an Asian restaurant and ordered rice with some other meat.

My lady boss was behind me at the Soup Plantation. She tapped me on the shoulder and pointed straight ahead. "Look, it's a *Mexican* guy," she informed me, dripping in disgust. I looked at him to see if he had a big chocolate stain on his apron or evenly cut spiky hair. But, there he sat, the clean-cut cashier. There was nothing wrong with him, only with her. I don't know why she surprised me. She had always been so nice to me—nice under false pretenses. I wondered, What will happen if I blurt out, "*I'm Mexican*." I said nothing.

When were leaving the restaurant, the same Mexican guy came to pick up our trays. In a snobby tone I had not heard from him before, my boss said, "Oh, a tip." I looked back at the Mexican man apologetically. I wanted to say something, but what? Something in Spanish? Could he know I was Mexican? I was with only Asians. Could he tell me apart? I said nothing.

At the end of that day, my last work day, my boss gave me a plastic bag with a T-shirt from the school, a mug, and a card. He explained how he didn't know what to get me, what I would like. I told him seriously, "It's fine." I didn't want his gifts. All I wanted was an apology.

At 2:30 P.M. I said good-bye to everyone and left. The minute I stepped outside the door, into the fresh air, the chains were removed—taken off my wrists, ankles, and, most importantly, my chest. I felt light and free, like I could fly, soaring down the street. Having left the heaving feeling behind, in his office, I smiled uncontrollably, deeply.

In Puerto Rico, they say: *Lo que no te mata, engorda*—"What doesn't kill you fattens you." I say, You learn from your experiences. You become a stronger, more beautiful person.

## MY LOSS
*By Adrienne L. Boyd, 16, from a small town in the East*

I am a sixteen-year-old Native-American/African-American female. I go to a predominately white (Caucasian) school and live in a majority European-American environment. I have faced a lot of struggles. It has been very hard for me to grow up in an area where I am looked upon as an interracial female, different from the majority. I have faced racism, prejudice, and stereotypes throughout my life, and I always will.

When I was fourteen, I first realized that racism and stereotypes were being used against me. When I was younger I knew all of this negative stuff existed, but I never imagined it happening to me. At least, I never expected prejudice to come from the people I grew up with, people in my school.

My freshman year in high school, I started seeing a white

boy. Race and culture did not even faze us. We were too proud to even think of such thoughts. As our relationship progressed, we started becoming really affectionate in public. That's when our problems began. People started staring at us. Everywhere we went people whispered and blurted out rude comments. It was bad enough to hear it from strangers, but worse when I heard it from schoolmates. One of my so-called friends said if we had children, they'd be part monkey. She let me know she did not believe in interracial couples.

I was devastated. I was torn apart by the thought of my own friend betraying me. I started thinking, If my friend isn't on my side, the whole world must be against me. How could I deal with this problem? I was willing to stay with my boyfriend, but he could not deal with all the pressures. So, he ended our relationship. For the first time ever, I felt helpless. I experienced a loss because of my ethnic identity.

Not only is it hard being a female in today's society, it is very hard being a minority and especially an interracial minority.

In my heart I know that I am a good person, with a good heart. I will not allow someone else's ignorance affect who I am and how I feel. But sometimes, I wish I were little again. I did not have to face a lot of racism. If I did, maybe I didn't catch on. I didn't understand it, because it is too cruel to comprehend.

# THE ONLY ONE
*By Anonymous, 16, from a city in the Northeast*

> We but half express ourselves, and are ashamed of that divine
> idea which each of us represents.
> —*Ralph Waldo Emerson*

"Hey, there's a black girl on the team."
"What's up, baby?"
I keep walking.
"Why aren't you talking to me?"

Now they're right beside me.

"Do you think you're too good for us, or something? . . . Sell out."

I turn and glance at them. They're smiling at me, as if something funny had been said. I say nothing, though I want to say so much to them. They're nameless, but I will always remember their faces.

They looked a little older than me, probably eighteen. Both were wearing Tommy Hilfiger jackets even though it was close to 70 degrees outside. Only one was wearing a hat. *Nike* it said on the front. Walking advertisements. They looked cruel, but happy they had gotten my attention.

At that moment, while I walked back to the team bus, I reflected on what they had said. Did I really think that I was too good for them? What made me better than anyone else? Why didn't I stop to talk to them? Was I a "sell out"? It's true I go to a private school where the majority is white. I don't dress in Tommy Hilfiger or Nautica. I'm not into hip-hop or rap. So where was I? Did I have to choose between being black in a white world or being "black"?

I didn't speak on the bus ride to school. The world seemed to function without me. Everyone on the team was talking about the game tomorrow against our number-one rival. Things irrelevant to my train of thought. I was still playing the one-sided conversation over in my head.

My best friend was sitting next to me. When she asked what was wrong, I said nothing. Would she understand? I mean, she's white. In my years at a private school I have learned to ignore the color of people's skin and other outward appearances. But have I become colorblind to the extent that I have ignored the problems that occur most everyday with minorities? Minorities. People like me. I'm the minority.

All through middle school I had yearned to be like everyone else. I wanted to shop at the Gap, just so I could dress like everyone else. I remember constantly imagining how I would look if I were white: had a cute small nose, perfect teeth, and lighter eyes.

I wanted to be like them. I wanted to be them. I got my hair straightened. I started reading all the fashion magazines, just like my white friends. But I wasn't happy. It got to a point where I became more isolated than ever before. I was losing my identity. Not just my racial identity. I was losing what I valued most of all, uniqueness and difference. I was losing myself.

My freshman year in high school was different. I became depressed, insecure, unsure, and withdrawn as I started to reveal my true self. But at the end of the year, I realized that the way I look is a gift. It is what makes me me. From my features stem feelings and emotions no one else has. My looks hold my opinions. Everything I feel is there. I am who I am. I can't, I won't, change for anyone. If people think I'm a "sell-out" for not being "black," well, that's their opinion and their problem. Everyone is entitled to their opinion. I'm just not always interested in hearing it.

Sometimes I still think of those two guys by the field. I picture them in five years still trying to pick up women and still trying to be people they aren't. I know in five years I'll be truly happy with myself. I'll think, Yeah, I am too good for you.

# Questions of Faith

≈

My parents raised me in a fuzzy place between religion and spirituality. In the end I just called it "family tradition." We celebrated Hanukah and Christmas, Passover and Easter. We said grace with my grandparents and held hands and *Om*ed three times with my neighbors. I went to church once with my grandparents, but didn't know any of the songs they sang. I went to synagogue for the first time the day after my guinea pig died. We got there late and I felt like everyone was looking at us.

Then, in eighth grade Judaism unexpectedly became my life. That's not to say that I had a sudden religious epiphany. No. The motivation was purely social. A disproportionate number of the "cool" kids were Jewish. The older boys were terribly enticing. BBYO (B'nai B'rith Youth Organization) was the thing to do in my junior high. It didn't take long, though, for the crowds to dissipate. A year later the boys weren't as exciting and BBYO wasn't as cool. But I remained a devout member.

My interests broadened. I questioned the role of religion in my life. My parents hadn't decided it for me. I took the opportunity to figure out my faith for myself. In a hopeful quest, I learned more about Judaism. I found my own beliefs and morals reverberating in the words of Jewish writers.

Still, I struggled with what made me Jewish. Everyone told me, "It's your beliefs, your traditions, your values that make you Jewish." But, I shared these things in common with my Protestant-raised mother, too. After toiling over my Jewish identity, a Reconstructionist Rabbi gave me an answer that made me finally feel Jewish. He told me, "Judaism teaches us to doubt and to question. To me, that makes you Jewish." His affirmation of my religious identity led me to question more.

BBYO continued to dominate my time, but never dictated my thoughts. In eleventh grade I kept a journal; I wrote almost exclusively about religion and spirituality. I no longer felt awkward or alone at the high holiday services I attended without my family. By that time, I had become regional president of the B'nai B'rith Girls. But, as a young Jewish leader, I attempted to incite change with my feminist ideals more than my loyalty to Israel. So for now, I have landed where my parents raised me—most comfortably situated someplace between religion and spirituality, at a crossroads where tradition, tolerance, and universality intersect.

The contributors to this chapter have struggled to find their own spiritual grounding. These two writers share how religion has impacted their lives. I used the same criteria choosing selections for this chapter as for every other of *Ophelia Speaks*: I looked for personal experience and honest self-disclosure. But I found, more often than was the case with other subjects, girls sent me opinion pieces. Many seemed to keep their religion at arm's length, talking from their heads or trying to convince others. Others wrote about religion as linked with other subjects such as eating disorders and death, and were placed in *Ophelia Speaks* accordingly. But, in these two contributions girls opened the door directly on religion to find faith or to deny a doctrine.

In *A Silent Wish for Hope*, Shakira Villanueva describes how her uncle's difficult life and death taught her to believe in Allah's mercy. By allowing us to enter her life and meet her family, Shakira opens us to a universal place, where suffering ends in love. In her discovery of genuine faith, Shakira demonstrates admiration for the essence of all religions.

In *Growing Up a Churchless Child* the mood of this chapter changes. Molly M. Gise brings us to an elementary school cafeteria. Juvenile conversations, accusations, and condemnations mobilize her to sort out her own spiritual identity. In the end, she rejects organized religion.

I intended to include a cross-section of contributions from different religions in this chapter. I envisioned a chapter representing Christianity, Judaism, Islam, perhaps Buddhism and atheism. But, the contributions themselves changed my purpose. I realized that for adolescent girls questions of faith are more personal than institutional. In these contributions, the authors' messages push at the border of being confined to any one religion; the basic sentiments expressed are true of many faiths. Speaking personally, I found their touch universal.

## A Silent Wish for Hope
*by Shakira Nesha Villanueva, 17, from a city in the East*

I remember when Allah erased all doubt from my mind. As in any religion, maintaining faith is highly important. My discipline of Islam believes once a follower's loyalty is challenged, Allah answers. The legacy of my uncle's death has transformed me into a devout Muslim.

Zaneib, my uncle, was always an outcast in the family. During dinner gatherings he would sit by himself in the kitchen and eat alone. I still remember gazing into his innocent eyes, wondering what he constantly sat thinking about. Zaneib talked on occasion. When he did, no one ever understood him. He would discuss reasons for his own strange behavior. I remember one day he tried to explain why he would always start to walk with his left foot, why he ate only fish, and why he never removed his hat from his head. Zaneib claimed he performed these acts as a follower of Ayatollah Khomeini. My uncle said a quiet voice came to him in his sleep, and directed him to make these daily changes. At times when he tried to explain the meaning of his actions to the family, it was quite funny. We all nodded our heads like we understood his purpose, but no one ever did. Zaneib was mentally disabled. Knowing his disability made his ways difficult for even me to comprehend. As I think back on his ways, my uncle's character remained a mystery to me.

Zaneib always dressed in cut-up jeans and he wore strange, colorful shirts. To me, his features and complexion were quite handsome. His very toned brown color highlighted like gold whenever he stood in the sun's shadow. Zaneib's eyes were extremely unique. Somehow I believe they were mirrors to his inner thoughts. Sometimes his eyes looked radiant and full of energy. But most of the time, they remained in a state of either depression or pain. Zaneib was a very intriguing person. But for those who did not know him, his appearance was a horrid scare.

Zaneib's countenance was always covered by his facial hair. He had a thick, black, long beard, which would hang under his neck. The hair on his head was always disheveled and grew into stiff knotted dreadlocks. I remember, when I was a young child, looking at his hair. I imagined thin, brown snakes dancing to his muffled, wild thoughts. His dreads were scary at first. But I guess after years of seeing them grow longer and longer, I started to like them. They represented the individuality of my uncle.

After many years, I began to understand that Zaneib's helping hands, harmless voice, and dreadlocks were all symbols of the purity of his heart. They showed that he lived as he was, and that he would not change for anyone. To me, my uncle seemed to have a conscience and be different by choice. But mine was just an outside view. Inside, Zaneib never had a definite choice to be who he was. As awful as it may sound, this was true—my uncle, from his very first day in this world, was a victim.

Victims have no right to decide the outcome of an action or event, which most times will affect them in a negative manner. Zaneib was a victim, who was faced with all the horrors this dark world offered him. He did not choose his mental disability; it just happened.

Nor did my uncle want to be assaulted and injected with a heroin overdose. No, once again, it just happened. After his experience with heroin, he was suddenly addicted to it. Soon this first addiction lead to use of other drugs. I still remember watching my uncle smoking crack from a kitchen stove, inhaling the poisons of cocaine which rested on a dining room table, and even one day, watching him lie in a pool of blood because of an over-dose of some sort. But my sad memories do not end there. After years of drug abuse, my uncle had become a victim of the HIV virus, which eventually led to his death.

The memory of the final days of his life still remains vivid to me. At the time, I was fifteen years of age. My grandma, mother, and I were the only ones present. Most of my family members were on vacation, when the sudden deterioration of his health unexpectedly occurred. The decline started during the end of July. The humidity was high and the temperature remained hot, without a single breeze. The air had no movement, creating a period of stillness. As I looked at my uncle, I felt my insides wanting to explode in tears. I still remember myself saying, "It's not fair."

During the last days of his life, Zaneib, who was five feet, six inches, weighed only about 70 pounds. His bones were notice-able; they protruded against his flesh, leaving me the horrid thought that I would soon see them pierce through his skin. At times like this, I still remember looking at my uncle's body think-ing if I looked hard enough, I would see the virus slowly eating away at his precious nutrients, cells, and other organs. During these moments my stomach turned in disgust. I began to scorn my uncle, because of his appearance. Though I hated myself for feeling this way, controlling these thoughts seemed nearly impos-sible. As I looked at my uncle from afar, it was strange. A man who had lived thirty-two years as an outcast of the family, a man with no real friends, was now awaiting his death surrounded by three ladies who loved him so dearly.

As I viewed the virus continuing to eat away at my uncle's senses, an intense anger grew within me. I was mad at my Lord. I felt he had not only taken part in my uncle's suffering, but he was responsible for making my grandmother, mother, and me cry with hurtful tears of distress. I felt that Allah was simply glaring at us from a distance, watching our hearts shatter, like fragile glass broken by a sudden hit. Believing Allah did not care, I silently hoped my innocent uncle would soon experience eternal happiness. I guess at times, when I could not bear to witness my uncle dying with that nasty virus, I wished him dead. I believed dying was the only way he would be completely free of his pain and anguish.

For a whole two days, Zaneib laid on my Grandma's bed like a child in a crib. Whenever he needed anything, he cried aloud in his humble, shaking voice, "Ma, Ma." Sometimes he wanted water, other times a blanket, or some ice. Zaneib's cries were like a newborn baby begging for milk. My grandma answered her baby, never seeming the least bit annoyed or stressed. She always ran to him, bringing him anything he asked for with a painful smile, and a gentle kiss on his sweaty forehead. As my grandma showed her loving acts of maternal love, I knew she was suffering. She had not eaten a full meal in two days, and her face began to look quite pale. Zaneib was her second son, out of her five children, to die from this disease, this severe epidemic.

My mother was accustomed to this epidemic, because she was a nurse. She was a woman who daily watched people die, but I soon learned these experiences did not make her "immune" to feelings. Though at times she would try to hold her tears back, she finally learned that by releasing her inner sorrows with sobbing, she made herself stronger. In that apartment, my mother was the only one who understood the reality. My uncle's death was soon to come, but she never let on. No. That day she did not listen to her years of knowledge and wisdom. Instead, she took off her robe as a nurse, and with tearful eyes she made a silent wish for hope. She wished for her older brother's recovery, for his severe sickness to end. For once, my mother assumed the role that little sisters tend to take during a family crisis. Like a naive little child, I wondered, "Why?" As she prayed in a corner, why did my mother still have the least bit of faith within her?

During those final hours I knew I needed Allah's help. If there was, in fact, anything Allah could do, if his help was true, a reality, I figured, he would now show me "miracles." If there was ever the time to show them, it was now. Having doubt Allah would help me, I crossed my warm trembling fingers. Though my hope had started to fade, during these hours I began to wish somewhere deep within me, for extreme help. I knew this last hour would be the most critical stage of Zaneib's life and that I needed Allah's comfort.

In a matter of minutes, Zaneib began to lose his voice and sight. His dreadlocks, which many times seemed to give him strength, were slowly becoming disheveled. (Many people say one's power comes from their hair. After witnessing Zaneib's strength slip away as his dreads began to shed, I became one of those people.) He no longer could speak. When I looked at him, I knew it was time.

My mother told me to take a quick shower and to put on a long outfit, to cover my entire body. So I did. With some reluctance, I then opened the Koran. As I sat beside Zaneib's bed, I read aloud a prayer over and over again, and my Grandma soon joined me.

My uncle inhaled about once every thirteen seconds, evidence that his last breath was near. My grandma and I watched beads of sweat run slowly down Zaneib's face. I quickly put on plastic gloves and placed a cube of ice on his tongue, but he was unable to swallow. My elderly grandma, at that moment, started crying hysterically. She screamed, "Zaneib go! Leave me, I'll be okay. . . . Pa is waiting for you. . . . Go baby. I love you . . ." She started kissing his fragile, skinny body. The body that I started to scorn, she kissed. I sat beside him reading a prayer, hoping it would help cure his pain. I could not stand the fact that my innocent Zaneib was about to die of full-blown AIDS.

Suddenly, my tears began to flow, one after the other forming a river of sorrow on my breasts. I began to recite, "*Oh Allah, please don't make him suffer. Oh Allah, please don't make him suffer.*"

As I raised my head, I saw three tears slide slowly away from Zaneib's eyes. My Grandma then yelled, "Oh Lord! Don't make my *behti* (Hindi for "baby") cry." It was at that moment Zaneib exhaled his last breath.

My mother quickly entered the room and saw her older brother still and dead. From a distance, I thought I heard her heart stop and crumble. She started to cry so loudly that just listening to her, both my grandma and I started to weep. My mother closed the eyes of Zaneib while my grandma and I tied his feet together with white cotton cloth—a ritual done by Muslims when someone dies. It is believed when the dead meet Allah, the cotton, which represents purity, will be used to unwrap the soul.

As I looked at my mother and Grandma I could not believe our suffering had finally lessened. Three women who at one time believed the intense hurt would never end, had overcome the most sorrowful pressure. We had survived Zaneib's death.

Since the day of my uncle's death, I have never forgotten the way Allah answered my voice and prayers. My experience was one that only I could truly understand. It was I who was listened to that day. I know because of his guidance I will never again give up on Allah. That day He never gave up on me.

## Growing Up a Churchless Child
*By Molly M. Gise, 17, from a city in the Southwest*

When I was in third grade, a girl walked over to the lunch table where my friends and I sat. She boasted proudly that she could tell whether a person was Protestant or Catholic. She went around the table, correctly guessing most of my friends' religious affiliation (which couldn't have been that amazingly difficult considering most went to the same church). Then my friend Laura cried, "Do Molly!" I blushed, wishing she would just take her "gift" to another lunch table. The girl looked at me, tilting her head. "You're Catholic," she decided. I shook my head, and my friends laughed.

"You're Christian?" she asked.

I shook my head again.

"Well, what *are* you?"

I gave my usual response: "I'm nothing."

I grew up without religion. My mother was raised Catholic,

while my father was raised Jewish. As a result, my brothers and I were brought up with no particular ideas about God or religion of any kind, including Christianity. I grew up with morals—I knew the difference between right and wrong—I just didn't have the Ten Commandments to dictate what was what. My mother taught me to share, to help others, to be responsible for myself—basically to be a good person, because it was the right thing to do, not so God would let me into Heaven.

As a young child, I didn't know the difference between myself and other kids. A churchless life was all I had ever known. I considered my life to be normal

It wasn't until the last three years of elementary school that I realized most other kids in my school went to church on Sunday, were in youth groups, and prayed to some guy named Jesus. I still didn't think that my way of life was any big deal, but some of my classmates felt differently. Some were nice about it, politely inviting me to their churches. However, others were a bit more brutal, insisting that if I didn't go to church, I couldn't be "saved."

"And if you're not saved," they sneered, "you'll go to *hell*."

The threats were intimidating. I found them hard to ignore, especially since I was one of those horribly shy kids who was always afraid of doing something wrong and getting in trouble. Equally as painful as the taunts was the isolation I felt as a churchless child. Almost all of the girls in my Camp Fire group belonged to the same Methodist church. I remember coming back from a visit to a museum and all of the girls, save myself, were singing their church choir songs. They weren't purposely excluding me—I just didn't fit in.

I felt so left out I actually tried to understand and believe the Christian faith. I recited prayers at night, went to mass with my grandmother, and even wore a small gold cross around my neck. I tried everything: the Catholic Church, various Christian churches, plus a week long stay at a Mormon church camp. Despite my efforts, I felt more awkward with Christianity than I did without it.

I was uncomfortable with churches and Christianity. I just

simply didn't believe it. I tried to become involved because I felt left out. I was afraid I was somehow wrong for not going to church, like everyone else around me. After my experience, I decided desire for acceptance and fear are two of the worst reasons to be a part of a religious faith. I often wonder how many others who go to church do so for those very reasons.

Because of my church-free upbringing, I have pretty much missed out on the whole religious experience. As a result, I've been subject to criticism, isolation, and annoying zealots who make it their goal to convert me. On the other hand, I have gained a valuable asset—a religiously unbiased mind. I can think for myself about what I truly believe, as opposed to being spoon-fed my beliefs by a priest or minister. The more I think through organized religion, the happier I am not to be a part of it. I see too much hate, rivalry, and arrogance in and among different religions. I may be "nothing" officially as religions go, but at least I know and am honest about what I believe.

# Feminist Pride

≋

Ryan was nonconformist, wore his shorts down to his ankles, covered his feet with Converse All-Stars, finger-combed his long curly brown hair, and put together a students' rights 'zine every few months. We took a class together one summer, and shared the same circle of friends.

The air was heavy the afternoon we exited our class and walked toward Thayer Street. I needed to pick up a few things at the drugstore, and had successfully coaxed Ryan into coming with me. The brisk air-conditioning welcomed us inside. I went through the aisles picking up necessities: face wash, deodorant, variety flavor Mentos. I found Ryan in the magazine section flipping through *Rolling Stone*. I picked up *Vogue*.

"Ryan, I'm ready when you are."

"Please, God, tell me you're not buying *that*," he said, finger extended, pointing at my *Vogue* magazine. Ryan, who was also an actor, had a way of being a little dramatic.

"Um, yeah. Is there a problem?"

He exhaled heavily, obviously disgusted. "And you call yourself a feminist."

In the ensuing conversation, Ryan graciously explained to me that I was supporting an industry devoted to making me feel inadequate, and making other girls anorexic. According to him I was the women's movement's worst nightmare. I explained to him that he had no right to pass judgment on my actions. I reminded him that he had only known me for a few weeks. I let him know I didn't appreciate his self-righteous speech on the media and fashion industries' representation and oppression of females. *I was the female.* We argued mostly about what right *he* had to tell *me* that I was an irresponsible feminist. I became convinced in a matter of moments that he didn't know me at all.

But, his evangelistic critique wasn't the real reason I cried when I got back to the privacy of my dorm room. I cried because he was, in part, right. Not in his judgmental behavior, but in his argument, which caused me to question my actions.

It hadn't been the first time a boy had accused me of being a traitor to the feminist movement. An eccentric kid named Jonah who sat in front of me in Algebra II had passed me a note with the names various cosmetic products crossed out. In capital letters underneath the drawing it read, "Stop oppressing yourself." I laughed it off at the time. I mean, I was one of the most vocal feminists in our left-of-center high school. I believe in women's strength and independence, and rights, and voices, and. . . . And, well, so what if I wear makeup and like fashion magazines. I don't wear makeup for anyone else's benefit—I feel better when I do. I don't buy fashion magazines to find out the latest fad diet or compare my body to barely clad, airbrushed models. I just really like clothes. So I could justify my actions to myself. Usually. But then there were moments of self-analysis, more frequent as time went on, when I wondered if my motivations were always as enlightened as I wanted them to be.

That afternoon at the drugstore I told Ryan about how, when I was little, I never really played with my Barbies, I just made clothes for them. I told him about sitting in front of CNN for hours waiting for the fashion runway report hosted by the woman with a British accent. I told him about how much I still loved clothes. I made my fashion addiction sound as simple as an appreciation for neat lines and materials cut on the bias. In reality, I realize the way the clothes hang on the tall, slender figures is almost as fascinating as the clothes themselves.

It has taken me a year to admit that to myself and not cringe, not think I am some sort of feminist failure. I am human. It is always easier to believe in something "right," to regurgitate what

I am so well trained to know is responsible and fair, than to examine my actions—the actions that keep me neat and pretty and smart and warm—that keep me the girl who can always be brought home to Mom and Dad. Which is not to say I preach one thing and practice another. No, no, that would be too simple.

I expect most people would prefer to read my reflections on feminism and have an analysis all laid out into neat categories—what we adolescent girls do and what we think; where our thoughts and actions overlap, and where they don't. I can't even figure out all that about myself, let alone sum it up neatly for all of us. But what I can say with some amount of certainty is that we are terribly complicated creatures. Take me as one representative young feminist. But remember this too: I wear makeup and buy fashion magazines, and sometimes wear short skirts and tall clunky shoes. Once in a while, I feel guilty about the way I look. More often I just wish all of the feminists could be on the same team. I wish Ryan and others hadn't perpetrated some politically correct judgment, relegating me to an unproductive role in socially aware society, all because of my shaven legs and artificially lengthened lashes.

The contributors to this section have written about feminism. Taken separately they represent three very individual conceptions of female self-respect. Taken together, they represent the range of the young feminist movement with its the intrinsic complexities.

In the first contribution, *Fight Girl Power*, Emily Carmichael mobilizes her irrepressible personality in a call to resist America's greatest minds, the money-mongering geniuses of fashion and entertainment. Rather than buying into "Girl Power," she recommends a new movement aligned with the old feminism—"The Big Movement of Women Not Buying Shit."

Next, Emma Christine Black brings her feminist concerns home. In *Saving Sarah*, Emma takes a concerned look at how she's influencing her little sister. Recollecting her own childhood, she talks about her own faltering fight to prove her feminist power. When she sees her sister posed in front of a mirror, imitating her mannerisms, she wonders if two generations have sunk to the lowest level of social expectation.

Finally, in the last contribution to *Ophelia Speaks*, Sara Bright recalls the moment of her feminist epiphany—her transformation into a female force. With a self-affirming flourish, she declares herself a winner. As a model of young feminism, she walks on with confidence, showing us how to *Score One for the Revolution.*

And, as for Ryan, he still doesn't understand why I got so angry.

## FIGHT GIRL POWER
*By Emily Carmichael, 15, from a city in the Northeast*

Wanna know the dumbest thing I've ever heard of? Girl Power. If you haven't heard, it's this attempt to wrest feminism from muscly gay girls who don't shave and to give it to cute models who have everything. Here's actually an explanatory quote from the analytical text *Girl Power,* coauthored by Posh, Scary, Sporty, Baby, and Ginger Spices: "Feminism means skipping a date and going out with your friends instead." Ah, I thought feminism was saying "I'm not asking you to find me desirable, because I'm smarter than you and could bench press your house, which coincidentally, is the size of my sauna." I thought feminism was Marie Curie, exposing her self to free-radicals and all other kinds of dehydrating skin conditions to perfect the cure only she could find. I thought feminism meant we are not playing the game of physical appeal, we have worth beyond our looks.

But no, no no no no. That's not the story anymore. Feminism, as in *We crush all barriers* died, some other time when I was a baby. What happened then? Everyone got scared to be a feminist. Feminists were angry and unattractive. They liked girls and didn't shave, or else they wore only plant fibers and spelled "woman" with a *y.* Men were scared and repulsed by the lesbians and found the earth muffins deeply amusing. (How many feminists does it take to screw in a light bulb? That's not funny!) It's such a confusing thing. People are scared of black panthers and white supremacists, but factionalist feminists are objects only of derision. So no one wants to be a fighting feminist anymore. We want to work for equality in a nonoppositional, fine-by-me kind of way. We want to sort of blend in and play along.

America's greatest minds work where they can earn the greatest profit, so before long the magazine-makers caught wind of this phenomenon. Some woman or other, who's the editor of *Jane*, talked about it, and, I can't find the article, but she said something like, "We need to remodel feminism into an attractive, marketable concept so we can start making money off it, eat at Boule and send our children to Spence." So they did, and they called it Girl Power. So far, they've made bundles. I have a really good grasp on what girl power means. So far I have a file on it *this* thick.

*Jane* is just like any other woman's magazines except its how-to articles are entitled "How to Get What You Want" instead of "How to Give Great Head." ("Do unto him what you want done unto you.") It also has Drew Barrymore giving her "quirky" and "individual" opinion on how to lead a great life. ("Beauty is a good thing.") Then some more articles ("Make Your Hair Something It's Not," "Kickboxing for Perfect Thighs," "What Do Cellulite Creams Really Do?"). And of course, ads. Pages of hot girls in cute clothes drinking Slurpees, while perched on vintage vehicles. Prado. Express. Allure.

Then there was this Sprite ad on TV a while ago. Here's a case where "girl power" means instead of beautiful women running on beaches wearing French cologne with pec-laden studs, they have beautiful athletic women inspiring devotion in attitude-laden studs by jumping out of planes. Message: Girl power means six-packs instead of famine victims. Of course, what progress! If you're going to have a completely unrealistic goal for your body, it might as well be an unrealistically healthy one! This is truly a movement about empowerment, as expressed by the choice of intellectually prominent women to wear engine red instead of pink. Take the Spice Girls' debut novel—the author-protagonists are buoyed by their incredible "girl power" to venture daring feats such as wearing short skirts or kicking at the camera lens. The simple explanation for this farce is the profit motive. "Girl power" is a product, like for instance peanut butter, not a movement, like for instance suffrage. The Girl power icon is made to inspire envy in female consumers, not to make them feel more powerful themselves! If they felt more powerful, maybe they'd decide to stop reading magazines and buying clothes and go find a cure for cancer.

And, I'm sorry, but why do we buy this shit? What is it about girls that everyone is writing books like *Resuscitating Ophelia* about how we have no selves, and my friends think they're fat, and aren't eating lunch, and boys are saying "Yeah she's hot, but did you hear about her and those two juniors and she's really messed up and don't fuck her, you'd feel bad if you messed her up more," and everyone is deeply, deeply concerned, except people trying to take our money and even they try to pretend? Just what is up with girls, anyway?

It's something about being beautiful. That's what it is. We want to be happy, to be surrounded by boys who lend us sweaters and girls who share their Slurpees, always with a party to go to, always with someone to call and another exciting adventure to create. And the way to do that is to be beautiful, right? That's what everyone's telling us. We want to achieve and excel, but we're not sure if the way to succeed isn't to have longer eyelashes and if perfect thighs aren't the ultimate signs of achievement. Girls today care about winning respect and admiration, not just affection, but, so often it seems like looks are the way to both.

And I'm not saying boys are any better, they just have better luck. Guys can be crazy, offbeat dreamers and everyone will like them more for it. They're supposed to be stubborn and rebellious. It's sexy when boys tell the world to go fuck itself. (Example: Sid Vicious—a dirty, skinny bass-totter who made a career out of being offensive and bleeding on people. He's the twelfth most requested dead guy on the Internet.)

But that kind of behavior is just not profitable for a girl. I should know! I've tried! I cut my hair short and started weight training, I call-out in class and wear only Wranglers and Wifebeaters, and frankly, everyone liked me better before. Maybe the guys I know enjoy an occasional slap, but it's not like crowds of skaters are staring slack-jawed. Do you understand? I'm bold. I'm smart. I can bench 150. I'm a powerful girl, but I don't have that thing, girl power.

I mean, girl power, right, what is it? Perfect legs, so you can wear short skirts. Perfect skin, so you look good in red vinyl. A firm little ass, so boys will love you when you turn your back on them. Girl power is being pretty enough so people call it "spunk" when you act like a baby. Girl power is jumping out of planes, hitting life feet first in knee-high boots, a crop top, and a glistening micro-mini. Girl power is the world as a playground full of friends, hot guys, extreme sports, and sparkly purple lipstick. I fell for it. Did you? I leafed through the magazines, searching for dynamite and pride, looking for someone to tell me, *We kick ass no matter who wants to fuck us.* But it turns out, the models are still having all the fun.

Did you know that when I was anorexic and looked like a beanpole, I felt more powerful than I do now? Now I can eat cereal without feeling bloated and I no longer have increased risk of heart failure, but I don't feel the same power? Wearing a crop top was definitely better than consuming enough protein to live on. Try eating nothing but apples for a month. It produces an incredible head rush. *That's* girl power.

Look, they want our money, that's what this whole thing is about. Capitalism is the biggest house of mirrors in the world, because everyone's trying to tell us that we *need* something! Especially you, and especially me, 'cause we're dreaming about Slurpees and short skirts and joyful, ecstatic love. Here's some numbers from (irony of ironies) *Seventeen* magazine: Of the $105 million earned by teenagers last year, $103 million were spent last year. That's 98 percent! We're fucking wellsprings. We have some small amount of money, and it's easy as sin to get it out of us. We walk around with big red target signs!

What we need is to perfect the skill of cash warfare. Every political movement—from civil rights to gay rights to environmentalism——has learned this little secret. Don't buy shit. You know what shit is? Anything in print that's kind enough to tell you how to be perfect, and smart enough to show you a picture of just what perfect is. *Seventeen* is shit. *Jane* is shit. The girl power movement is shit. So let's you and me not be targeted. If you don't want to call us feminists, that's fine. We can be the Big Movement of Women Not Buying Shit. There's plenty of other things we can spend our money on. For instance, food. A weimaraner. Soup kitchens. College. Laboratory equipment. A bass guitar. We do and we can kick ass without being pretty, and maybe in the distant future—like when we're seventy and sitting on top of the fortune we amassed in our youth by our inventiveness and roguish business instinct—society will have changed and we can date twenty-year-old models. But until then, things are gonna be ugly.

Hey, we shall overcome, okay?

## SAVING SARAH
*By Emma Christine Black, 16, from a city in the South*

It's frightening to think that you mark your children merely by being yourself. It seems unfair. You can't assume the responsibility for everything you do—or don't do.
—*Simone de Beauvoir*

I recently caught my ten-year-old sister, Sarah, unconsciously mimicking my movements, throwing her long brown hair behind her shoulders and rubbing her legs like I do when they are still smooth from shaving. She glanced up at me timidly, her bright eyes searching for my approval, and I became nauseous. My stomach pulled itself somewhere between my lungs and throat as I tried to avoid her glance. The thought that I could be influencing her, that I could be pulling her into whatever is considered proper, petrified me.

I believe I am a feminist. My ears perk up every time I hear the words *chick* or *bitch*. I stand proud and loud to defend my ovaries, my right to equal pay, to equal education, to hairy legs. I'm proud to be female.

So it scared me beyond belief to realize my younger sister watches me from the bathroom mirror as I tweeze my eyebrows and paint my face. It scares me that the little girl I have been pro- tecting for so long, the little girl I have been tutoring—"Let him cook his own meals, you go fix the car"—the little girl who still wears cut-up blue jeans that fall below her knees and still sings to our mixed-breed terrier and still believes in science and in Jesus, will eventually have to grow up and serve two gods.

One god will remind her to let the man pay, giggle at his jokes, and allow him to open the door and carry the boxes. This god will lecture her, "Sometimes it takes a man to do the job," and tell her he likes his ladies pretty. But she will also be obliged to bend to the second god, one who tells her to fight against old standards, to stand up for herself and be independent.

As I saw her mimicking me, I grew more sickened than afraid—sickened by the fact that I had presented her with both of these gods. I had introduced her to the hypocrisy that I face as a young female, the hypocrisy she will now enter.

When I was in elementary school my mother took pictures every Easter beneath the small dogwood tree in my neighbor's front yard. She posed me in the frilly Sunday dress I had been squeezed into despite tears and temper tantrums. When I had finally calmed down and stopped pulling at the collar of my dress, she positioned me in front of the dogwood tree, whose petite blooms seemed wilted, and my face contorted into a staged smile. The pictures never turned out right.

My mother also forced me into those Easter dresses at least once a month during the school year, just to make sure they were not wasted. My friends picked at me playfully when they saw I was not wearing my usual T-shirts and off-brand blue jeans. My hair was brushed against my back, instead of pulled into a neat ponytail. On these dress-up days I was always given orders not to get the pink ruffles and blue bows dirty. My mother wanted them preserved, to function as hand-me-downs for my younger sister. This never happened; I never stayed clean. Once a month I arrived home with a mud-soaked dress full of holes and leaves.

As a child I played football, arm wrestled, and provoked fist-fights with boys who were twice my size. I, the shortest, frailest girl in second grade, was the elementary school's bully. If there was a problem, it was addressed to me. On tiptoes and with squared shoulders, I was invincible.

Once, riding home, I told my mother about the boy who had picked on me before class, and how I had punched him in the stomach and stopped him for good. She pulled the car over to the side of the road and grabbed both my hands, yelling about boys being stronger than girls, and if I didn't stop, I would get injured. She asked if I understood, then glanced with hurt eyes over my tear-stained face and deflated smile. I don't remember backing down, though. Now, I'm too old to be in fistfights, too mature to draw blood. I never had a very good swing, anyway. That doesn't mean I don't still stand up for myself, still fight.

I still battle with teachers who ask only for guys to move tables or answer questions. I complain when the heroine of a modern movie or book falls helplessly into the arms of her supporting actor, the camera angle focused on her cleavage, her tucked stomach. I cringe when my friends ask why they can't look like that, and I watch them stop eating, start buying diet pills only to vomit them up. I fight with church leaders who don't think I'm fit to serve Eucharist and a government that does not think I'm fit to serve in combat. I argue when a friend falls powerlessly into the grasp of any guy who will hold her, then whimpers that he never asks her permission anymore and she can't get out of it. I fight to convince her that vulnerability is not a female requirement, but my best friend cuts designs into her arms with a razor blade because she finds herself unattractive. I watch my friends fall to sex, drugs, alcohol, their parents' wishes, their friends' wishes, suicide. I battle those who tell me, "You can't because you're a woman," and their only explanation is, "It's a hard world, that's just the way it is."

I'm still fighting to prove I can do anything, and not sink into society. I try to tell this to my sister, to show her that we are not wrong. But I think sometimes that I'm losing. When I caught Sarah unconsciously mimicking my movements, and I thought, The female race has lost two more generations.

## Score One for the Revolution
*By Sara Bright, 17, from a small town in the South*

*"Yeah. It's all right to pinch girls in the butt . . ."*

Kids filed out from their congregations in front of Wiley Hall and began making their way back to their dorms for 11:30 sign-in. I was among the herd, drifting quietly away from the social scene. A scene I was boycotting anyway.

And, then, I snapped.

Absolutely and completely flipped out.

Don't ask me why it happened. Why then? Why him? I couldn't really tell you. But, I suppose it all had something to do with the August I spent holed up in my sister's closet, letting the hair on my legs grow out, and pouring over the feminist books, discarded in her room after she had graduated from college with a women's studies degree. That summer was the summer of me— the summer I discovered who I was and what I believed in. Not to sound cliché, but it's true. I left the summer of 1997 ten times more *me* than I ever imagined.

My best friend came home from school for the summer as a pronounced feminist with an eating disorder. And I began to see fault in, well, not everything, but an awful lot. I began to get fired up and contemplated shaving my head . . . but I didn't. I couldn't go that far. I still was semi-unsure of what statement I would be trying to make. So I held my newfound, feminist, body-loving, women-praising, but un–male bashing self within. Until, that is, I returned to boarding school society and almost threw up. Until, that is—I snapped.

*"Yeah. It's all right to pinch girls in the butt. Right Sara?"*

*(Boom!)*

"No. God damn it!" my brain screamed. I wasn't about to agree with that.

"No, I DON'T THINK SO!" Jesus, did I snarl at him. I can't even italicize that phrase because it was *all* stressed by the whole thing.

I guess I didn't think too much of it—the little episode—but I must have been the only one who wasn't a little freaked out. A message light shone from my phone when I reached my room.

"Um, Sara. Uh . . . this is . . . um . . . Jason and I didn't . . . mean to offend you or anything . . ."

Are you kidding me? Did my moment of rage have that much impact on Jason Cabot, jock extraordinaire? That he would call? And apologize? If my voice had that much power I had to make sure I was being heard.

A huge grin came over my face that night as I called Jason back. "Man," I told him, "you just don't say that. You know, I'm sorry I flipped out, but it really bothers me. It's just not a cool thing to say to anyone, even if you're kidding around. Just think about it Jason. I'm not mad at you, just think about it . . . "

I went down the hall and told my friends. They all cheered. Someone sat back in her chair, and smiled. I recognized that smile—it was admiration.

I began attending Women's Forum meetings. I got on the board. I changed my image from that moment onward. No longer was I Sara Bright, hot chick who let Jeff Shepard fuck her. I was Sara Fucking Bright, woman who fucked Jeff Shepard and wore a sly smirk as she floated through campus.

Yeah, I'm standing up in the middle, I'm laughing and talking, and everyone is listening. Score one for the Revolution.

# Final Words

≋

Last September, when I began working on the proposal for *Ophelia Speaks*, I wrote, "Every meal I eat is a conscious choice not to be anorexic." I was barely seventeen then, fresh out of an unhealthy relationship and unsure of my future plans. A lot happened over my senior year in high school. Mostly, I was deeply affected by my work on *Ophelia Speaks*. Through the contributors to this book, I learned a lot about myself. Their honesty demanded reciprocal thoughtfulness. A year and a half later: Meals don't feel like a decision to make, and I can usually eat chocolate without remorse. Things change quickly in adolescence. After all, we are young—a year is a significant fraction of our lives.

But, calling the contributors to this book "young" hardly seems right. Often, we seem far too old. Just a few days ago, the bizarre nature of our old-youth struck me. I received a note from one of the contributors to *Ophelia Speaks*. In perfect adult-cursive, she told me she was moving and gave me her change of address, if I needed to contact her. The long, flowing letters rolled across the small tasteful stationary. I remembered her contribution—mature, insightful, smart. Impressed with her togetherness, I slid the note back into its envelope. But, I noticed something: a small orange sticker in the corner. The shiny pumpkin sticker served as a reminder: The contributors to this book are mature, insightful, self-reflective, but we are still teetering on the edge of our childhood. Our youth compounds the gravity of our words. In adolescence, stickers and dolls mix with sex and depression.

Self-mutilation, drugs, rape, and self-loathing scream from many of the preceding pages. We seem older than we should. But, if you flip through the pages again, perhaps you will see the lighter side of friendship, crushes, sibling relationships, and our burgeoning feminist pride. *Ophelia Speaks* is intended to represent both sides of our adolescence—our often austere reality as well as our self-affirming laughter. Adolescence has robbed us of some of our youthful giggles, but happiness still remains. Despite our struggles, we have faith in our future.

I am hopeful that *Ophelia Speaks* will raise a consciousness of adolescent girls' struggles. I expect our trials will be of great interest to many people. But, there is another message in these pages: We are strong. I am equally hopeful that the strength, the power, and the courage of our voices will be honored.

Compiling this book has made me believe more strongly in our voices than ever before. I am honored to be a part of this project, and grateful to all of the girls who, together, let Ophelia speak.

# APPENDIX A

≋

April 13, 1998

Dear Principal,

I am a seventeen-year-old high school student. In January 1998, I signed a book contract with HarperCollins Publishers. In my book, *Ophelia Speaks,* adolescent girls will write about being young and female. I am currently gathering journal entries, personal essays, and short stories written by girls, ages twelve to eighteen, to be included in *Ophelia Speaks.* I hope you will help the voices of your female students to be heard by giving them a chance to become published writers. Please pass on the word about my project.

Could you ask your English teachers, parent associations, school councils, school psychologist, school counselors, and/or school newspaper to encourage girls to send me contributions? Please feel free to copy the enclosed *Message to Adolescent Girls* and post the enclosed poster.

To assure you that this is a serious endeavor, I have also attached a letter from my editor at HarperCollins Publishers. You will find her letter copied onto the back of the *Message to Adolescent Girls.* You are, of course, welcome to share it as well.

Thank you for your time, consideration, and effort.

Sincerely,
Sara Shandler

# APPENDIX B

≋

## A MESSAGE TO ADOLESCENT GIRLS

Would you like to write for a book? I am seventeen years old and I'm collecting personal stories, journal entries, and essays for my forthcoming book, *Ophelia Speaks*. This book will be published by HarperCollins Publishers, a major New York publisher.

Last year, when I was sixteen, I read *Reviving Ophelia*. The author, Mary Pipher, a psychologist, wrote about adolescent girls. Horror stories of eating disorders, self-mutilation, abusive relationships floated across the pages. Pipher equated our contemporary adolescent experiences to Shakespeare's ill-fated Ophelia. As I read, I identified with the underlying emotional experiences of these girls. However, I did not feel simply spoken to, I felt spoken for. Pipher had awakened in me a desire to respond. We are capable of speaking to our experiences with an accuracy and an intimacy inaccessible to those outside of our generation. If Ophelia is to be revived, it should be by our own words and our own actions. In January 1998, I signed a book contract with HarperCollins Publishers for *Ophelia Speaks: Adolescent Girls Write About Their Search for Self.*

I am collecting personal writing from girls, ages twelve to eighteen, about our experiences being young and female. *Ophelia Speaks* will be a compilation of these contributions. You are invited to contribute. Your contributions may focus on different aspects of your pre-adult existence. Possible subjects include:

- body image or eating disorders

- romantic relationships

- friendships

- drug experimentation or abuse

- relationships with parents and siblings

- death

- depression

- sexual preference

- sexual abuse

- religious faith

- socioeconomic, cultural, and racial issues

- why are you proud to be female

However, I know our teenage years cannot be placed neatly into categories. So, if you have an important or defining experience that does not fit perfectly into any one of these sample sections, please do not feel discouraged. The bottom line: I am looking for personal writing by adolescent girls. Contributions to *Ophelia Speaks* may be from one page to ten pages long. Each contribution may be published with your name, or completely anonymously, if you wish. All contributions in *Ophelia Speaks* will say where you are from in general terms, such as: "Northeastern city." It is important that *Ophelia Speaks* represent the diverse backgrounds of adolescent girls. If you choose, your contribution will give your racial, ethnic, and religious identity.

I would like to receive contributions as soon as possible, but no later than June 1. Special consideration will be given to submissions received before the June 1 deadline. Unfortunately, I will not be able to include all submissions in *Ophelia Speaks*. I am looking for honesty. Self-disclosure and specific experiences will be the primary criteria for inclusion in the book. I will gladly edit personally powerful contributions for clarity and grammatical correctness.

I am eager to read about your experiences. Please send personal stories, essays, and journal entries and include: Name, return address, and, if you wish, your racial, ethnic, and religious identity.